Poetry of the Heart Collection

Framed inspirational poetry (11" x 14" or 8" x 10") to focus your thoughts and uplift your heart in times of indecision; to encourage and inspire your soul in times of upheaval; to calm and heal your emotions in times of reconciliation, and to generate peace in times of restoration:

Choose
Days of Night
Dayspring
Destiny's Faith
Heart Song
Mentor I
Reasoning
Snowflake
Sunflower
Sustained
The Artist
The Past
Trust

To book the author for a speaking engagement; go to: www.healthylivingusa.com; click **Speakers** on the navigation bar and follow the prompts or email author@healthylivingusa.com

To place an order for a framed title from the Poetry of the Heart Collection, go to: www. healthylivingusa.com; click **Poetry** on the navigation bar and follow the prompts.

To order additional copies of The 2008 Presidential Election Handbook and Commentary: The Connection to Hope, go to: www. healthylivingusa.com; click **Books** on the navigation bar and follow the prompts.

To register for a Politics of Life Seminar, go to: www. healthylivingusa.com; click **Seminars** on the navigation bar and follow the prompts.

To register for a Personalized Training and Fitness Boot Camp, go to: www. healthylivingusa.com; click **Fitness Boot Camp** on the navigation bar and follow the prompts.

Personalized Training and Fitness Boot Camp

*"If you are a good athlete,
we can help you to become a great one."*

Healthy Living USA Personalized Training and Fitness Boot Camp provides strength training, cardiovascular exercise, and flexibility training. The exercise programs are personalized to meet your needs. Special training is offered to athletes at the high school, college, and professional levels to enhance performance through natural techniques. All programs are administered by Emery Schexnayder, Certified Personal Trainer.

To register for a Personalized Training and Fitness Boot Camp, go to: www. healthylivingusa.com; click *Fitness Boot Camp* on the navigation bar and follow the prompts.

The 2008 Presidential Election
Handbook and Commentary

The Connection

to Hope

Linda E. Schexnayder

Healthy Living USA
Publishing Division Nevada

This publication is designed to provide competent and reliable information regarding the subject matter covered. However, it is sold with the understanding that the author and publisher are not engaged in rendering professional advice. Laws and practices often vary from state to state and if expert assistance is required, the services of a professional should be sought. The author and publisher specifically disclaim any liability that is incurred from the use or application of the contents of this book.

Published by Healthy Living USA Publishing Division Nevada

Visit our web site at www.healthylivingusa.com

Healthy Living USA Publishing Division Nevada
Healthy Living USA, *Healthy Living In All Five Areas of Life*
1230 New London Place
Riverside, CA 92506

Printed in the United States of America

First Edition: June 2008
Second Edition: September 2009

Library of Congress Cataloging-in-Publication Data

Schexnayder, Linda E.
    The 2008 Presidential Election Handbook and Commentary:
    The Connection to Hope / Linda E. Schexnayder / 1st ed.   2nd ed.
        p. cm.
        ISBN 978-0-615-21483-2
        1. Political Process I. Title. 2. Electoral College, Political Process and Law   3. Voter Registration, Political Process, Law and History

The 2008 Presidential Election Handbook and Commentary

The Connection to Hope

Be a well-informed, active participant in the national agenda. Understand how the politics of life affects your economic future. Use the congressional directory to stay in touch with your elected representatives. Enjoy the commentaries on the 2008 Presidential Election mandate, the new and former administrations, and the responsibility of citizenship. Glean wisdom from presidential quotes of history which are relevant today. Study the United States Constitution and the Bill of Rights. Learn strategies for effective community organization and economic development. Brush up on your social, dress, and dining etiquette should you be invited to the White House. Comfort your heart with patriotic songs and poetry of America. Learn military theme songs and sing them with your soldier. Experience the solace of inspirational poetry from the *Poetry of the Heart Collection*. Display the American flag according to federal flag code. Adopt the cause of paying off the U. S. National Debt by 2040.

Linda E. Schexnayder

**Healthy Living, USA
Publishing Division Nevada**
Las Vegas, NV
http://www.healthylivingusa.com

Acknowledgements

I would like to thank my family, friends, and colleagues for their extraordinary effort to get this book to you. When I thought I could not write another sentence, encouragement met me like the first light of day to renew and invigorate my soul. Sometimes, after being shut in for days to complete this task, just a glimpse of my beloved family was all I needed to continue. Thoughts of my children and my grandchildren and the kind of America they would inherit were ever-present in my mind. I want to make this country better for them and future generations.

After studying the political interaction of elected officials and citizens of this country during the last decade, I am convinced that you, the grassroots of this country to whom this book is dedicated, can succeed throughout your lifetime only if you are well-informed about the politics of life and your role in it. To that end, I give you this book of hope that you may glean from it at any moment of the day—before leaving for work each morning, after dropping the kids off at school, on a work break, during lunchtime, before dinner in the evening, or at bedtime. It is yours to cherish throughout this new season of change and thereafter. The Directory of the 111th Congress is provided to help you stay connected with Washington long after the excitement of a campaign is over.

To my son, Emery, an exemplary son, husband and father; and to my grandson, Emery II, a young man of principles and honor—a gifted football player of enormous talent, who is characterized by some as having the physical ability to play Division I football as a junior in high school— thank you for your deeds of love. You give life to my being.

To my daughter, LaTura, a loving daughter, wife and mother; and to my granddaughters, Imarri Jeré, the lifeline; Sidni Lorin, the connoisseur of knowledge; and Jordyn Taelor, the female version of Rodin's, The Thinker; your seeds of joy grow in my heart with the dawning of each day.

To my great granddaughter, Lyric Imarri, the baby genius; I have been waiting for you. I loved you even before I saw your face. God has sent you to bless the world. And they will be blessed.

To my fellow members of the Nevada State Democratic Party, I thank you for guiding me through the process of being an effective district, county and state delegate. It is an unforgettable experience; difficult and protracted work at times, but exhilarating. I am thankful for every phone call and email at all times of the day and night.

Silent Praz Mime Team

"There are no words to express our praz."

For booking information on the 2010 Tour:

Contact LaTura Schexnayder, Producer

951/801-1411

To view Silent Praz Mime Team, go to: www.youtube.com/silentpraz

Contents

Introduction   From Heart to Heart xi

Chapter 1   A Connection to Hope 1

Chapter 2   Winds of Change 9

Chapter 3   Citizenship, the Highest Calling 21

Chapter 4   Politics of Life 35

Chapter 5   Our Companion in Democracy 47

Chapter 6   Who Controls America?............................ 67

Chapter 7   The Eight-Year Power Grab 81

Chapter 8   The Party of Kennedy 91

Chapter 9   The 2008 Presidential Campaign 105

Chapter 10   Mr. Perfect President? 113

Chapter 11   Race Identification in America 123

Chapter 12   Poetry of America 131

Chapter 13   Songs of America 139

Chapter 14   Old Glory Etiquette and Display 153

Chapter 15   Restoration and the Future 161

Chapter 16   Yes, Mr. President, It Would Be My Pleasure! 169

Appendix A   Procedural Guide to the Electoral College 189

Appendix B   Constitution of the United States of America 217

Appendix C   Directory of the 111th Congress 243

INTRODUCTION

From Heart to Heart

"This great Nation will endure as it has endured, will revive and will prosper. So, first of all, let me assert my firm belief that the only thing we have to fear is fear itself — nameless, unreasoning, unjustified terror which paralyzes needed efforts to convert retreat into advance. In every dark hour of our national life a leadership of frankness and vigor has met with that understanding and support of the people themselves which is essential to victory." President Franklin D. Roosevelt, 1933

Political Representation

It began in 2001; twelve months after the 2000 Presidential Election. There was a change in the political landscape of this country that I had not seen or felt before.

Unlike elections of the past when citizens chose sides, communicated their beliefs on what was best for us all, cajoled, debated, supported to the last of the liquid assets, worked tirelessly, gave their best for the country, then reconciled—becoming one nation again united with the newly elected leader, who always led us through the process of healing and reconciliation until we were whole and ready to do the work of the republic again.

That healing process did not take place after the 2000 election nor did it take place after the 2004 election. Consequently, for over eight years, we were a divided nation; a nation in permanent campaign mode.

Like many of you, I didn't feel represented politically at the national level during those years. Oh, I knew I still lived in a republic—a government of the people, by the people, and for the people—in which elected representatives did my bidding. But where was my representation? Where was *our* representation in government?

For eight years we, the people, were marginalized, ostracized from policymaking, shackled at debates, silenced at the bargaining table, considered a relic, painted with a broad brush and minimized by elected officials who put their self-interest above God, country, and constituency. We didn't remind ourselves nor did we behave as though we were one nation; party affiliation was preeminent. Our speech was no longer free; it cost us friendships, jobs, finances, and peace in our local communities. Our national government had drawn a daring line in the sand from north to south and east to west. If your speech did not agree with theirs, you were labeled un-American and unimportant. You were deemed unfit for the rights and privileges guaranteed a citizen of our country by the Constitution.

I marveled at how quickly millions of supposedly intelligent Americans got into lockstep because they were fearful or sought benefit. All open debates ceased. Public viewpoints we established; talking points were issued. First Amendment rights were circumvented. I wondered then if I could rely on a report by a national news network of an alleged threat by a family member of an administrator against someone whose words he considered contrary. Were millions of Americans considered public enemies for having an opinion? It appeared to be censorship.

Political ridicule, mean-spiritedness, and misrepresentation for the sake of power and money ran rampant. The powers that sought to divide us were emboldened by their success. Their decades-long plan rooted during the Nixon administration had finally paved the way to the ultimate prize of unfettered power and financial dominance. The man that symbolized power, according to our vote, didn't appear to be in power at all. Those who subscribed to the agenda were in a position to do as they pleased. So they did.

We were a divided nation destined to reap the fruit of that division— a financial system in crisis, a deepening recession, and a dismantling of the middle-class through higher taxes, lower wages, and joblessness. Main Street was blighted and relegated to the unseen side streets — leaving the American dream in question.

We have witnessed considerable change in America during the first decade of the twenty-first century — both positively and negatively. The positive change seeks the betterment of all mankind; the negative change is self-serving to the detriment of all mankind. It's a battle between good and evil. Americans of active biblical conscience will determine the outcome from this day forth.

Walking in Destiny

The United States of America was founded as a country of destiny, indeed a light to the world. The position of leadership that we have held in the world for decades is not by happenstance. Evidence displayed in our nation's capital verifies that we are a God-ordained nation, which we have chosen to honor by majority.

If you were to study our history, songs, poetry, and humanity, you would find that we have always been an extraordinary people that fought for the rights of others. In spite of our shortcomings and missteps, we are a pliable and compassionate fabric of enduring truth. When in aberration, we chose to torture other human beings; we were not operating within our established principles.

Biblical history tells us that God destroyed evil men by the numbers sometimes, as He did with Sodom and Gomorrah. But their destruction was swift and sure. If leaders wanted information then, they didn't torture men, they sent for an ordained prophet of God, who still exists in the land today wearing jeans, sweat suits, dresses, and Italian suits. They are God's go-to people for information and wisdom — more reliable than the CIA.

During this season of American history, many Christians in our land are seeking God's mercy and favor to counteract the dehumanization that brothers are heaping upon brothers, and to abolish the constitutional breaches at our national level of governance that are now oozing through every facet of

American life; defacing and dislodging core principles that have been in place since the founding of our nation. For the causes of freedom and justice, they are being conscientious in their efforts to right these wrongs.

Our actions during the 2008 election signaled four things: First, we will not allow the thread that holds the fabric of our republic together to be severed at the will of a few for personal gain; second, we will not allow the attacks on our constitutional rights by our government to continue; we will call upon Congress to begin the arduous task of plugging up the holes through which our liberties have been seeping out; third, we will seek polices and regulations that ensure the economic security of all Americans; finally, we will summon Americans to engage the politics of life at the national level to do the work of the republic whether there is a Democrat or a Republican in the White House. We will take the local community to Washington, and bring Washington to the local community.

Our selection of Barack Obama in 2008 as the forty-fourth President of the United States gave us an essential element in undertaking our tasks — a President that is a visionary; one who sees the end at the beginning and focuses like a laser to that end.

Obama is endowed with the gifts necessary to lead us to a more perfect union in this period of our history. He will measure his steps over an extended period to mend constitutional breaches and restore economic security in an atmosphere of peace. Then he will move forward aggressively to prepare the next generation for the task of maintaining the union. You will not see the work of a clever man, though he could be described as such; you will see the work of a visionary — unaware of special endowments that are very obvious to us. For should he ever perceive them as we do, the shroud of humility which protects him will cease.

Seeds of Hope

Hope is the visionary part of our soul that gives us inner strength to believe and to do what is necessary to achieve what seems to be impossible. It keeps our head connected to our heart, thereby making us courageous in times of difficulty and uncertainty. It propels us to walk in high places of achievement for the good of mankind. Hope can drive an individual, it can drive a group, and it can drive a nation.

Decent men and women across this country of all ages and races have decided that they will be unwaveringly proactive in the governance of our nation as a way of life. They believe it is an obligation of citizenship and necessary to maintaining our democracy, to honoring Christian values which we hold dear, and to restoring our leadership role in the world. Hope will sustain their effort—without hope, people perish; without hope, people shrink and die. Hope is a connector, an anchor, and a lifeline [to the American dream]. It is the glue that holds things together while the work is being done. And if these coalitions stay active, strong, and agreeable, the United States of America will not implode under the weight of gross mismanagement, debt, greed, malice, corruption, and fear.

The ruling thought in our country today is that terrorism is the greatest threat to our freedom. But it takes a back seat to economic and moral decline. Terrorism has capitalized on these domestic factors by injecting massive doses of fear into our society to paralyze hope—the two are diametrically opposite concepts. The video messages of proclamation that are submitted to the news media by terrorist organizations are designed to enhance that process and to shift the spotlight from internal threats and abuses to external ones. But our greatest threats are within, though they are present on the world stage. For instance, we've heard it said that "war is business." But the question to be asked is, "Who's benefiting from the business?"

During the Great Depression era, the rich got richer on the backs of the working-class, which is happening again. The economic strain on the middle-class is now measurable. And just as the people turned to government for survival during the Great Depression; they have again turned to government for survival now. But this time, government is a part of the problem. Our elected officials give *billions* of dollars to other countries annually, even to our enemies, who squander it, in some cases, on lavish living. But they refuse to provide assistance in full measure to the working-class of this country.

What prevents them from eliminating wasteful spending and using those funds to provide a hand-up to the working-class through comprehensive healthcare, mortgage relief, education and training, and increased tax credits? What prevents them from appropriating adequate funding for crumbling, outdated, and dangerous infrastructure that's been declared unsafe by inspectors for years? What prevents them from helping those who pay the greatest portion of the bills of this country even though international trade agreements have thrown them into an economic compactor?

We Americans have sown seeds of hope, through our votes for the current administration, to correct the many injustices that have been perpetuated upon us. We expect positive results. And with the understanding that words of hope spoken to others are as seeds planted in their hearts which will produce after their kind in due season; we are planting words of hope in the hearts of our family, friends, neighbors, and colleagues to germinate through a series of events and crescendo into power and momentum that can't be stopped. Any farmer will tell you to keep the weeds out and to nurture your crop with water and sunlight for an abundant harvest. So we'll keep out the weeds of judgment, criticism, doubt, fear, and foolish chatter and apply the water of faith and the sunlight of love in expectation of a great harvest of socioeconomic security.

Pursuit of Happiness

Working two or three jobs at $10.00 or less per hour is not true prosperity. Rearing children without parenting is not prosperity. Living from paycheck to paycheck is not prosperity. Living on borrowed money is not prosperity. Living in a large lovely home that you are unable to heat or cool is not prosperity. Having no health insurance is not prosperity. Having no retirement fund or adequate life insurance is not prosperity.

Minimum wage and a forty-hour work week should always yield income that is above the poverty index—any American, who works forty hours a week, should earn wages that are above the poverty line. To have them earn less is a shameful indictment against the richest country in the world. And it brings the moral conscience of our government officials into question. What prevents them from legislating a living wage for all working Americans?

Too often our elected officials give the appearance of goodwill, but they seem unwilling to allocate funds to the extent needed to propel tens of millions of its citizens into sustainable prosperity, which could stimulate economic growth to a level we have not seen before. Contrarily, they continue to extend a string, a short one at that, when a long sturdy rope is needed; never understanding that a problem solved lightens the load. We should declare another "War on Poverty" as President Kennedy did to bring all the stray and wounded sheep into the fold again. We can't allow millions upon millions of Americans to slide deeper into poverty. Just as a rising tide raises all ships; a lowering tide lowers all ships:

"We hold these Truths to be self-evident, that all Men are created equal, that they are endowed, by their Creator, with certain unalienable Rights, that among these are Life, Liberty, and the Pursuit of Happiness.—That to secure these Rights, Governments are instituted among Men, deriving their just Powers from the Consent of the Governed, that whenever any Form of Government becomes destructive of these Ends, it is the Right of the People to alter or to abolish it, and to institute new Government, laying its Foundation on such Principles, and organizing its Powers in such Form, as to them shall seem most likely to effect their Safety and Happiness."— **Declaration of Independence.**

Of course, we have some responsible and well-meaning elected officials who have tried to remedy our problems. But they have encountered gridlock year in and year out to the point of discouragement. Repeatedly, they have modeled to their colleagues in Congress to the best of their ability to *"love your neighbor as you love yourself."* And if you are a member of Congress who's asking, "Who is my neighbor?" Just gaze at your constituents and the people of this country and you will find your neighbor.

The ballot box of 2008 was our new beginning and it will continue into 2010 and 2012, as we choose honorable people from communities across the country who are willing to *serve* in Washington for four to twelve years — raise your hand before a mirror now if you are one of those who will go. Then vet your heart and begin today by studying the Federalist Papers, building viable relationships, and browsing the daily Federal Register online. "Experience" will no doubt come up. But knowledge and fortitude can rival experience if they are brought to the forefront of the debate. You and I can serve our country as effectively as anyone who has been in Congress for a long while. Cabinet members, representatives, senators, congressional aides, faithful government employees and in-service training are all available to assist newcomers. Experience will come in due course as wisdom is sought. Then you can mentor the next newcomer; thus the process goes on. So, if you feel called to service and this is part of your destiny; get to it!

How will you know if you should serve? You have thought of it all of your life, and its now a foggy dream of a time gone by stamped *"IMPOSSIBLE."* Even if you are homeless or jobless; accept no excuses — this is the United States of America. *"IN GOD WE TRUST"* is our motto; it is *possible!*

Domestic Tranquility

"We the People of the United States, in Order to form a more perfect Union, establish Justice, insure domestic Tranquility, provide for the common defence, promote the general Welfare, and secure the Blessings of Liberty to ourselves and our Posterity, do ordain and establish this Constitution for the United States of America."— **Preamble to the Constitution of the United States of America**

Here in America, most of us can't imagine life without freedom and prosperity. Such a thought is unspeakable; it would reduce our sense of domestic tranquility which we thrive on. Yet history tells us that many nations much older than ours prospered and flourished for hundreds and hundreds of years, then either suddenly or gradually slipped into non-existence. We can only engage them in the annals of history. So as usual, I asked myself a question — "Can socioeconomic decline brought about by moral decline ripple through the core of a nation and tear it apart?" Is that what happened to the Great Roman Empire? Why was Pompeii covered by heaps of ash during the eruption of Mount Vesuvius in 70 A.D.; never to be seen again until its recent excavation? Why does the strength of Jericho only live through a song and scripture? Where is the U.S.S.R. today? How can one tsunami kill almost one quarter of a million people in a day? How can a thriving American city be totally underwater in a matter of hours? How can many of its survivors subsequently starve and die in a public arena and on portions of its freeway system for days in the heat of summer with their deceased family members abiding with them or floating in the flood waters unattended and without the dignity of burial? — as the nation watched and waited for the Calvary to arrive at the eleventh hour as it always does. But it didn't. Some shocked and dismayed American citizens and Christian organizations rallied to help immediately; but they were forbidden by our government.

"How did we come to this?"

We didn't allow such a catastrophe to occur after World War II when the Soviets cut off the transport of all food and supplies to West Berlin—there were four occupying powers in Berlin at that time: U.S.A., Great Britain, U.S.S.R., France. We began dropping tons of food, coal, and other supplies from airplanes almost immediately and continued daily drops for fifteen months to keep two million plus people alive. In their zeal, the military even dropped candy for the children.

Several arms of our government are designed as stabilizers; equipped to intervene at any moment of crisis, to stabilize conditions, then to retract itself. We have declared ourselves the guardian of peace and calm in our nation; we insure our own tranquility. What a huge responsibility we have placed upon ourselves? Yet we have done it successfully for generations; putting down with the heavy hand of the vote sometimes, every uprising that sought to rob us of the privilege.

Since history repeats; we should analyze it, learn from it, and respond accordingly. Such a process could reveal the need for change in moral, economic, political, social and environmental conditions which are seen as threats to our domestic tranquility. If change is deemed necessary, we must refuse to fear and refuse to apply the "survival of the fittest" plan of action. We must come together as one people, as one voice, united in the cause of reconciliation and restoration for the good of all Americans. We cannot allow ourselves to be divided and conquered as in the recent past. We can be assured that any internal or external force which attempts to destabilize our democracy and to threaten our domestic tranquility will not come from a low place; it will come from a high place which wields power. And its weapon of choice will be ignorance.

I believe President Abraham Lincoln had such an epiphany when he began his crusade to abolish slavery in this country in the 1800s. He understood that the moral deprivation of slavery would inevitably destroy the republic. He began as a lone dissenting voice of government in an atmosphere of fear of economic ruin if a long-standing vice of this country was forsaken for righteousness and justice.

President Franklin Delano Roosevelt, "The New Deal," elected for four terms, understood that an economic safety net for all citizens would create a thriving economy and promote domestic tranquility. He gave himself in service to that vision and to the people of this great land, so much so that even after the nineteen thirty-two election, people were still singing across the land, *"Happy Days Are Here Again!"* Executing a plan of recovery from the Great Depression is cause enough to make one sing a happy song.

President John Fitzgerald Kennedy, "The New Frontier," understood the urgency to negotiate an agreement between the superpowers to suspend and ban testing of nuclear weapons to prevent a nuclear holocaust. As short as his presidency was, he still fulfilled his destiny through the Cuban Missile crisis, the subsequent Limited Nuclear Test Ban Treaty—the Soviet Premier had nuclear weapons pointed at the United States (see more in the chapter entitled, *The Party of Kennedy*), the Peace Corps, a comprehensive housing bill, and much more. He enhanced the socioeconomic safety net for Americans that President Franklin Roosevelt began.

Economic Enslavement

Economic enslavement in the twenty-first century is just as despicable as it was at other times in our history. Today, however, it has become more inclusive and multiracial. Everyone is being affected equally: black, brown, red, white, yellow. Many of the enslaved nowadays don't even recognize that they are enslaved. The American people are constrained daily by big oil companies who have pulled in record profits despite a lagging economy. The American people are constrained daily by big healthcare companies who deny their family members life by denying them medical care that they deem too costly—the very thing they contracted to do, they refuse to do.

Do integrity and decency apply to business as they apply to our personal lives? "All is fair in business," "it's not personal"— of course it is, "above all, get the money," and "collateral damage is acceptable" are all bad chapters in the corporate playbook. They have caused economic enslavement to become pervasive in the United States of America.

But "Corporate World's" behavior isn't new, is it? Most corporations throughout our history have operated that way. Why? Is it because they are engulfed with greed and applauded by their shareholders as profits come on the backs of laborers? Look at their pattern—companies merge; jobs are cut; the quality of their products diminish; the profit margin is enhanced; the stock price goes up; "Corporate World" executives and shareholders are ecstatic.

President Kennedy said, "power narrows the areas of man's concern," Would you say that's still true today?

President Franklin Roosevelt faced this same dilemma in 1932. He felt that the American working-class needed a hedge against such practices to insure domestic tranquility and to secure the blessings of liberty. His speech at the Democratic National Convention in Philadelphia, Pennsylvania on June 27, 1936, expressed his concerns:

The Connection to Hope

"It was natural and perhaps human that the privileged princes of these new economic dynasties, thirsting for power, reached out for control over government itself. They created a new despotism and wrapped it in the robes of legal sanction. In its service new mercenaries sought to regiment the people, their labor, and their property. And as a result the average man once more confronts the problem that faced the Minute Man.

"The hours men and women worked, the wages they received, the conditions of their labor — these had passed beyond the control of the people, and were imposed by this new industrial dictatorship. The savings of the average family, the capital of the small-businessmen, the investments set aside for old age — other people's money [OPM] — these were tools which the new economic royalty used to dig itself in. Those who tilled the soil no longer reaped the rewards which were their right. The small measure of their gains was decreed by men in distant cities. Throughout the nation, opportunity was limited by monopoly. Individual initiative was crushed in the cogs of a great machine. The field open for free business was more and more restricted. Private enterprise, indeed, became too private. It became privileged enterprise, not free enterprise.

"For too many of us the political equality we once had won was meaningless in the face of economic inequality. A small group had concentrated into their own hands an almost complete control over other people's property, other people's money, other people's labor — other people's lives. For too many of us life was no longer free; liberty no longer real; men could no longer follow the pursuit of happiness.

"Against economic tyranny such as this, the American citizen could appeal only to the organized power of government.. The collapse of 1929 showed up the

despotism for what it was. The election of 1932 was the people's mandate to end it. Under that mandate it is being ended.

"These economic royalists complain that we seek to overthrow the institutions of America. What they really complain of is that we seek to take away their power. Our allegiance to American institutions requires the overthrow of this kind of power. In vain they seek to hide behind the flag and the Constitution. In their blindness they forget what the flag and the Constitution stand for. Now, as always, they stand for democracy, not tyranny; for freedom, not subjection; and against a dictatorship by mob rule and the over-privileged alike.

"The brave and clear platform adopted by this convention, to which I heartily subscribe, sets forth that government in a modern civilization has certain inescapable obligations to its citizens, among which are protection of the family and the home, the establishment of a democracy of opportunity, and aid to those overtaken by disaster.

"We do not see faith, hope, and charity as unattainable ideals, but we use them as stout supports of a nation fighting the fight for freedom in a modern civilization.

> **Faith** — *in the soundness of democracy in the midst of dictatorships.*
> **Hope** — *renewed because we know so well the progress we have made.*
> **Charity** — *in the true spirit of that grand old word. For charity literally translated from the original means love, the love that understands, that does not merely share the wealth of the giver, but in true sympathy and wisdom helps men to help themselves.*

"Governments can err, presidents do make mistakes— better the occasional faults of a government that lives

in a spirit of charity [love] than the consistent omissions of government frozen in the ice of its own indifference.

"There is a mysterious cycle in human events. To some generations much is given. Of other generations much is expected.. This generation of Americans has a rendezvous with destiny."

Our newly elected President will face the same dilemma that President Roosevelt faced in 1932, when he went on to build a hedge of protection for American families with the outcries of opposition before him. Roosevelt's words tell me that he was an extraordinary man of courage, who made personal decisions to follow his heart.

Did he know fully the importance of his actions to this country? Probably. Did he know that America was at the threshold of success or failure? Probably. Visionaries sense urgency of time, while others sense due course of time.

The United States of America was in the midst of an economic meltdown brought about by corporate greed when FDR came into office. Such problems don't happen apart from the deeds of men; they happen because of the deeds of men. Because we are a nation founded on hope and prayer, God always bestows a gift of wisdom in the heart of a man or woman to dig us out of the rubble. President Roosevelt rallied the people and achieved great redemption through the inner strength of hope. One doesn't know where we would be today if he had not passed the safety nets of the Emergency Conservation Work Act, Social Security Act, Glass-Steagall Act, Federal Deposit Insurance Reform Act, Tennessee Valley Authority Act, Securities Exchange Act, Fair Labor Standards Act, and the National Labor Relations Act. He repaired the breach of economic inhumanity that had consumed this country and hardened her core of decency. He stimulated job growth to 18.31 million during his first term with an average annual increase of 5.3% throughout his administration. *At his urging, Congress also gave the Federal Trade Commission broad new regulatory powers to provide mortgage relief to millions of farmers and homeowners.* His "New Deal" programs are now described as three-fold: relief, recovery, and reform, which were achieved very rapidly and effectively. *"It is common sense to take a method and try it: If it fails, admit it frankly and try another. But above all, try something..."* he said at a commencement address in 1932.

History Repeats

A generation and a half is all it took for us to once again allow corporate greed and big business to overcome workers to the point that the middle-class of this country has shrunk dramatically. We forgot that the prosperity in which we had basked since the Great Depression was achieved at a great price. We took it as an absolute sustaining condition, so we slept. We awoke two years ago to find that it had vanished. We were marginally better than we were in 1929 because of the "New Deal" programs. But we were back in economic decline and had been for about 20 years.

The cost of goods and services has skyrocketed as wages have decreased. Fathers and mothers are working two or three low-paying jobs — leaving the children to develop their own moral standards through peer pressure, causing a disintegration of the family unit, and demoting the general welfare of the people.

Just as companies said in the past, they say now — "there isn't enough money to pay workers a living wage in America and still maintain our desired profit margin" — to which President Roosevelt said, *"No business which depends for existence on paying less than living wages to its workers has any right to continue in this country."* Many of the socioeconomic gains made during the "New Deal" have been eroded through the courts, as companies echo to their workers, "we can't afford to pay you a living wage, healthcare, and a retirement pension and still maintain our *desired* profit margin; therefore, your loss of quality of life, and that of your children and your grandchildren are acceptable collateral damages to us." They can't see now, as they couldn't see then – nor do they care to see – that they are eating away at the economic fabric of this country, their country, while their personal rewards are measured in billions.

Do you find it amazing that President Roosevelt took us from a great depression to prosperity; from a world war to the steps of peace; from two terms as president to four — not even asking for the nomination for the third and fourth terms; while confined to a wheelchair? And who, on occasion, shunned his wheelchair to stand in demonstration of his resolve. Some of us would shudder today at the thought of a President of the United States staying in office for more than two terms; the law forbids it now. No doubt there was a cause at that time. But who can withstand the pressures of the office of the President of the United States for so long a time and through such dire circumstances?—only a man of hope, only a man of destiny.

A Call to Action

So, once again workers have to defend against the cruel reality of actions by their employers who say, "I am not your keeper; I will break my word to you at will, even if I must use the judicial system to do it. I am not thankful for your dedication in representing and building this company as your own for most of your life. You and your family are not important to me."

How can the United States of America maintain its number one status in the world if sixty percent of its jobs are low-wage? Can it be economically strong without a thriving middle-class?

Big corporations have seemingly forgotten or have chosen to ignore America's formula for success, which signals the need for change. History has proven that immorality and inhumanity do not contribute to a strong and lasting union, and wealth gained by minimizing human life will at some point bring about the destruction of the whole. To destroy the family unit and its socioeconomic base is to destroy America as we know it. So I ask you. Would you support tax breaks, subsidies, or bailouts for such companies? Would you continue to support these companies with your business?

We must begin again.

You may be asking yourself at this moment—how shall we begin again? The same way we began before — new business start-ups by the thousands that will vow to keep living-wage jobs in America. Those of you who receive severance pay from your company, when it gives you the boot, should pool your resources immediately rather than going your separate ways. If you can say as a team, "together we have the knowledge and expertise to do for ourselves, what we did for others; we will be their competition; we will do it better." You'll have a plan of hope that can be realized, if you dare to dream big and act accordingly. The dreaded lay-off could become the sling that propels you to your destiny—the world awaits companies which regard the tenets of our Constitution and honors the service of those who make it great. Providentially, years of professional marination will have produced seasoned leaders who are wiser and better able to rally the American people to support and to invest in a company that is morally, and environmentally sound — Americans only need opportunity.

In enduring hope, I would say that the United States of America is still leader of the free world in moral excellence and human rights, in spite of our recent aberrations. And though we are inundated nowadays with new arrivals to our shores who are not interested in becoming Americans, but only in amassing wealth; there are some yet that come with the spirit of those who came through Ellis Island for the sole purpose of becoming American citizens and contributing to her greatness. Those were fortified with hope upon their arrival by the Statue of Liberty and the inscribed words of Emma Lazarus which they read or had read to them:

"The New Colossus"

Not like the brazen giant of Greek fame,
With conquering limbs astride from land to land;
Here at our sea-washed, sunset gates shall stand
A mighty woman with a torch, whose flame
Is the imprisoned lightning, and her name Mother of Exiles
From her beacon-hand
Glows world-wide welcome; her mild eyes command
The air-bridged harbor that twin cities frame.
"Keep, ancient lands, your storied pomp!" cries she
With silent lips. "Give me your tired, your poor,
Your huddled masses yearning to breathe free,
The wretched refuse of your teeming shore.
Send these, the homeless, tempest-tost to me;
I lift my lamp beside the golden door!"

This was the initial "American Experience" which captured their souls. And as I ponder those moments of history, I can't imagine not having, even now, the *Sound of Music,* which depicts the great music and lyrics of Rogers and Hammerstein, to watch and listen to in my leisure. Though gone from the earth for many years, they are still contributing, as are many.

Finally, *evil thrives when good men and women do nothing.* I'm sure you've heard the proverb many times through the years. Evil thrives when citizens ignore their heart's cry to engage change when their system of government has gone awry.

The heart's cry is always now, never later. The beginning is always in the moment of revelation. We travel the road of "NOW" into the future. Sometimes we don't recognize defining moments in our lives until history records them. But we can follow our heart. We can follow a visionary leader. We can connect our hope to his; he can connect his hope to ours. And in doing so, we can work together as cogs of a wheel to achieve our high and lofty goals of reconciliation, restoration, and increase in all areas of human existence.

The Connection

to Hope

CHAPTER 1

A CONNECTION
TO HOPE

"Few will have the greatness to bend history; but each of us can work to change a small portion of events, and in the total of all those acts will be written the history of this generation ... It is from numberless diverse acts of courage and belief that human history is shaped. Each time a man stands up for an ideal, or acts to improve the lot of others, or strikes out against injustice, he sends forth a tiny ripple of hope, and crossing each other from a million different centers of energy and daring, those ripples build a current that can sweep down the mightiest walls of oppression and resistance."

Robert (Bobby) Francis Kennedy, University of Cape Town, South Africa, "Day of Affirmation" Speech, June 6, 1966

Americans are people of hope. It's not a confidence we've aspired to in a presidential election year, but a part of the natural fabric of our country; galvanized by the Constitution and the Bill of Rights. We've spoken words of hope more during the 2008 Presidential Election season, than at any other time in our generation, as a testament to our resolve to reverse the moral and economic deterioration we are facing in our nation today.

The heightened sense of patriotism we have experienced in the first decade of the twenty-first century allows us, in small measure, to understand the intensity of the passion, strength, power, and force that our forefathers garnered to stand against a mighty empire—a dynasty who claimed them as its own from distant shores—to establish a government in which every man could rule himself according to the principles of God. They sought a model to ensure God's humanity to all people throughout all generations. It is evident through history, that they came to know, as we do today, that such a nation is a work ever in progress. And our greatest challenge is choosing leaders who believe in the tenets of our Constitution and Bill of Rights, who understand and are willing to undertake the process of perfecting the union, and who honor God and serve the people.

Tens of millions of us enjoy the ceremonial splendor of the Fourth of July, our nation's birthday, because it revitalizes and fortifies the American spirit and connects us to our hope of peace, security, prosperity, and freedom in this generation. It's the time when we are reminded that some of America's songs are prayers; communion with God on behalf of our nation. These prayers have been voiced daily in our country for generations — contributing to the high blessings and favor we have received from above.

But what would happen if we, as a nation, no longer sought God and his ways of doing things? What would happen if we began to pervert the Constitution and the Bill of Rights which is evidently rooted in scripture?

On a Saturday morning back in 2004, I made my weekly trip to the public library as usual. I browsed for an extended time, chose items, then joined the checkout line. When I arrived at the counter the clerk informed me that my library card had been cancelled. "It's a mistake," I assured him, "just swipe my card again." But it wasn't a mistake. The library had indeed cancelled my card within the seven-day period of my last visit. I was told I had to provide more information for reinstatement. And as patron after patron complied, I resisted. I sought an answer, but none was given. Not even the administrators could tell me, or would not tell me, the reason for the sudden change. After years of checking out books, suddenly, I had been stripped of the privilege. Consequently, I refused to provide additional information and they refused checkout. I returned the ten or twelve items I had checked out previously and left. As I walked out I felt the loss of a personal experience and liberty that I had enjoyed most of my life. Who or what was responsible for this? Orwell's 1984 came to mind—*is big brother h-e-r-e?* Never mind being tracked by satellite twenty-four hours a day or being monitored by camera moments after I exit my home; this was different. It was cloaked. The intensification of my patriotism was actualized at that moment.

Peace and security in my homeland had been a constant state of being to that day. The Constitution—unchangeable except by great contemplation and extended consideration—somehow had been circumvented to intrude on my privacy and freedom. But how? That single act by the county library represented a fundamental shift in the structure of our democracy. It seemed unreal. Yet, it was.

As I went about my daily activities after that day, America's songs began to pop into my head more and more. And without conscious thought, I began to sing them aloud.

Months turned into years as I pricked my ears for the outcries against the constitutional violations that were assaulting American citizens. But there was only deafening silence. There was no revolt; not even an inkling of one. It was as though everyone was in total denial—the "what do you have to hide" psychology had worked. An affront to our civil liberties was met with submission. Was it the beginning of a "clear and present danger?"

My mom and my mentor were such strong activists in the political process that I had a natural inclination to politics at a very young age. Long before I was able to vote I could "talk politics." It was exhilarating to me as a teenager to participate in political debates. Back then there was no personal ridicule associated with the process; political opinions were respected and opposed politely. For many years, however, I had resigned myself to working at a polling place on election day and processing the decennial census. It was my way of contributing as a citizen with relative ease. But the ease is gone.

So, why was I singing America's songs with apparent sorrow in my heart? — The USA PATRIOT Act.

Our government passed a law in 2001 which allows it to legally spy on its citizens. Federal law enforcement agencies can enter your home or business without your permission or the permission of the judicial system., search and seize your personal or business property, and leave you wondering. They can confiscate your phone records from your carrier and your library records from the county without your permission or knowledge. An unscrupulous guy could send his official buddy after you or any member of Congress who doesn't vote as expected, if he so chooses. It doesn't matter that he's no longer in an official capacity in government or that they are violating the Bill of Rights. It smacks of unrestrained power, doesn't it?—a renegade on the loose.

Why would Congress pass such a bill? Were they so paralyzed with fear that they couldn't think clearly? Nevertheless, those who voted for the bill and the subsequent reauthorization of it should give an account to the American people as to why they voted for a bill that is in clear violation of the Fourth Amendment of the Constitution of the United States of America; the right to privacy. (See Chapter 5, "Our Companion in Democracy," for more information on the USA PATRIOT Act). If our Congress makes laws that are contrary to the Constitution, and if our judicial and executive branches of governance trample the rule of law because they feel preeminent; it will set a precedence that will continue until it eventually runs into a wall of citizens' resistance.

I had finally found the source of my anguish—a major constitutional breach in our country had gone unnoticed and unchallenged by most Americans. How could such a major impact on our lives go unnoticed? This act defines the scope of our task of restoration into the next decade.

Here are excerpts of our songs of hope that have been sung every day by someone in this country for over two hundred years. Some date back to the 1700s; making our nation ever-present before God:

God Bless America,

God bless America,
Land that I love,
Stand beside her and guide her
Thru the night with a light from above...

God bless America,
My home, sweet home.
God bless America,
My home, sweet home.

America the Beautiful

America! America! God shed His grace on thee,
And crown thy good with brotherhood
From sea to shining sea!...
America! America! God mend thine ev'ry flaw,
Confirm thy soul in self-control...
Thy liberty in law!
America! America! May God thy gold refine
Till all success be nobleness,
And ev'ry gain divine!,...

Battle Hymn of the Republic

Glory! Glory! Hallelujah!
Glory! Glory! Hallelujah!
Glory! Glory! Hallelujah!
His truth is marching on...

God Bless the USA

…I'm proud to be an American
where at least I know I'm free,
And I won't forget the men who died
who gave that right to me,
And I gladly stand up next to you
and defend her still today,
'Cause there ain't no doubt I love this land
God Bless the U.S.A.

The Stars and Stripes Forever

The emblem of the brave and true
Its folds protect no tyrant crew;
The red and white and starry blue
Is freedom's shield and hope…
Sing out for liberty and light,
Sing out for freedom and the right.
Sing out for Union and its might…

America, My Country, Tis of Thee

Our fathers' God to Thee,
Author of Liberty,
To thee we sing,
Long may our land be bright
With Freedom's holy light,
Protect us by thy might
Great God, our King…

In unity sublime [*of the highest moral or spiritual value*]
To broader heights we climb,
Triumphant over Time,
God speeds our way!…

The hope of all the world,
In peace and light impearled,
God hold secure!

The Star-Spangled Banner

...Blest with victory and peace, may the heav'n rescued land
Praise the Power that hath made and preserved us a nation.
Then conquer we must, when our cause it is just,
And this be our motto: "In God is our trust."
And the star-spangled banner in triumph shall wave
O'er the land of the free and the home of the brave!

These are words of life, without which, we would not be the leader of the free world; we would not be an example to the entire world. We have remedied our aberration, because hope propels a people of high morals to travel the high road of integrity and honor.

Many of you don't sing the songs of hope because you don't know the words. This book has changed that condition. The lyrics are included in a special chapter of this book, entitled "*Songs of America*." Since we have all heard the songs before, you are very likely to remember the tune. Sing them and release the American spirit in your heart — the spirit of brotherhood, the spirit of justice, and the spirit of hope.

HEART SONG

Sing my soul, sing aloud.
Let my heart be glad.
Sing out the words of faith;
Sing out the breath of life.

Hum at first to catch the words
Time has recessed.
Like a geyser come they forth
To heal and to caress.

One verse and then two
Timelessly confessed
To overwhelm, to weed out
To compel my heart to rest,

To love, to cherish, to nurture___
The essence of my best;
To pollinate the souls of life
With warmth from Heaven's chest.

Sing aloud my soul!
Let the crown of life give zest.
Sing aloud my soul!
And free my heart to bless.

Chapter 2

WINDS OF CHANGE

"Allow the President to invade a neighboring nation whenever he shall deem it necessary to repel an invasion, and you allow him to do so whenever he may choose to say he deems it necessary for such purpose, and you allow him to make war at pleasure. Study to see if you can fix any limit to his power in this respect, after having given him so much as you propose. If to-day he should choose to say he thinks it necessary to invade Canada to prevent the British from invading us, how could you stop him? You may say to him, — 'I see no probability of the British invading us;' but he will say to you, 'Be silent: I see it, if you don't.' The provision of the Constitution giving the war making power to Congress was dictated, as I understand it, by the following reasons: Kings had always been involving and impoverishing their people in wars, pretending generally, if not always, that the good of the people was the object. This our convention understood to be the most oppressive of all kingly oppressions, and they resolved to so frame the Constitution that no one man should hold the power of bringing this oppression upon us. But your view destroys the whole matter, and places our President where kings have always stood." President Abraham Lincoln Speech in the House of Representatives, 1848

True Blue American

After 9/11, something profound happened to the American people. Our true nature came forth so vividly that it could be measured in stages. First came bewilderment. "People of the world love us as we love them. What force of hatred would want to harm us? I don't understand!" All three of these comments were typical responses throughout the land.

Bewilderment swiftly transmuted into grief. "How will we overcome losing 10,000 Americans citizens in such an unwarranted attack?" We soon learned that it was closer to 3,000 people and not all of them were Americans. That news, however, did not diminish the deep abiding grief we were feeling. It didn't matter that their names were unknown to us at that moment. It only mattered that they were American citizens and international visitors on American soil.

Grief then shifted to defiance. "We are the United States of America; how dare they come here and violate the sanctity of our homeland. Have they forgotten our resolve after the last unprovoked attack on one of our territories?" Resentment and indignation set in. And when we were informed that the attacks originated from al Qaeda, who was stationed among the Taliban in Afghanistan, everyone was ready to ship out, including the beloved grandmas. We were gonna get those horse-riding, cave-dwelling cowards—just give us a week! We pulled out the camping gear and waited for orders. Obviously we were not thinking straight at that time; we have a very capable military that is combat ready—air, land, and sea. So the orders didn't come as we thought they might. "But I have to do something!" we each thought.

Months went by and nobody stood before the American people to answer for their dreadful deed. Our government had moved on to Iraq. And as America's sons and daughters came home through the door of no return, our defiance converted into fear. Many of us relinquished our constitutional rights and locked our doors until the springtime of 2007. The government which had vowed to protect us was now being scrutinized.

Clearing the Chamber

We entered a long season of congressional assessment in 2007, and made significant changes during the standard 2008 two-year determinations — a time we've set aside to communicate, debate, and reconcile our differences to remain a united nation; a time when we assess and replace, if desired, those who represent us in government.

All seasons of evaluation vary according to current events and perceptions, and this one seemed destined to retract and then to protract in importance. We made major changes in our government because millions of Americans believe that a national course correction is necessary. We are striving to learn from our mistakes of the past and to prevent any decisions in the future which could alter our country's fundamental core values of honesty, fairness, and justice. The 2008 Presidential Election is not a four-year mandate; it's a mandate for the future.

Currently, our new president and Congress are entrenched in a fierce battle on many fronts: primary front—the economy and job creation, secondary front—education and retraining, third front—national healthcare (Reformation of the food production industry in this country is a vital part of the national healthcare equation.), fourth front—the environment and dependence on foreign oil, fifth front—constitutional breaches, sixth front—foreign policy and international affairs, seventh front—the National Debt and deficit spending. It will take a long while to get back on track on all fronts; then to progress, but we have begun.

We will know that we are back on track when the 14,000,000 Americans who lost their jobs are retrained and working for increased wages and benefits; we will know that we are back on track when every American who wants a college education or retraining can receive it; we will know that we are back on track when every person in America has universal healthcare without the government pulling more money out of our paychecks and the food production industry delivers clean nutritious whole food which promotes and maintains good health, and minimizes sickness and disease; we will know that we are back on track when we have cut greenhouse gas emissions by fifty percent; we will know that we are back on track when big oil companies can no longer go to the Reddi and withdraw money from the bank account of every vehicle-owning adult in America in a single transaction without a PIN; we will know that we are back on track when the uneasiness of eroding privacy is gone and the USA PATRIOT Act is repealed; we will know that we are back on track when our domestic arm of the military is no longer fighting on international soil; we will know that we are back on track when we are no longer in two wars and our soldiers are given sufficiency in all things; we will know that we are back on track when our National Debt is zero. *We will know.*

Meanwhile, internal battles seem to be cropping up daily in our national government; lines are still being drawn. Skirmishes are creating new partisan factions on some issues. We have arrived at the proverbial moment when every member of Congress should ask an internal question: "Can sowing discord for the sake of obstruction help resolve the economic issues of our country as we apply vital recovery strategies?" Could it be that the playbook is already open to the 2010 and 2012 campaigns? *When will the work of the Republic be done with the integrity due its people?*

Dreaming Aloud

As the 2008 Presidential Election brought enlightenment in our country, it has also brought enlightenment around the world. For the first time in history, peoples of the world understand that who we elect as President of the United States could affect their well-being. That is different. Previously, the leaders of other nations understood the possible impact on their country, but now, its citizens have come to understand the possible impact on their lives. Citizens of other countries are more informed and more involved in the politics of the United States than ever before.

So, what does it all mean to us? Does it make a difference?

How we are perceived by other countries will determine how warmly we are received in our endeavors to form pacts of cooperation, prosperity, and goodwill with them. But something greater and more consequential has taken hold of the people of the world. They have begun to hope as Americans do. They have begun to believe that the American dream can be their dream, and that liberty is attainable in their homeland and in their lives. So we must teach them the principles of our Constitution and Bill of Rights, and how to apply it as a structural foundation for freedom in their country. The hope rooted in our 2008 Presidential Election has uplifted the world to a new and positive status. The sense of expectancy is of more good and less evil. There seems to be a "new school" worldwide which has connected with the principles of our founding fathers which are derived from the holy scriptures.

Why have we spent millions of dollars and countless hours preserving the original Federalist Papers? Is it not to study them to keep us within the parameters of our constitutional foundation on which we have built our country? Is it not to ensure future generations the same quality of life—freedom and hope of achieving the American dream? People of other nations who aspire to that dream should also have an opportunity to attain it. They cannot, however, be made to aspire to it.

We will be a better nation and a better world if men and women of America are free to prosper in their gifts and to share them with the world.

So who are these people of destiny? And why should they take center stage?

Destiny carries within itself the seed of change—the seed of reconciliation, the seed of restoration., and the seed of increase. That is why you will hear enablers say things repeatedly. They are planting the seed of hope in the hearts of others. Enablers may not even understand it fully themselves, but they are compelled by the vision of their heart. They live it; they breathe it; it's who they are. And as they embark on their journey of destiny, the seed within them begins to grow as they plant it in the hearts of others. If you have been fortunate enough to witness such a process, you have probably noticed that people of destiny seem to persevere and overcome obstacles with relative ease. Things which seem to discourage, anger, confuse, and weaken others have little, if any, affect on them. It is an illuminating experience to watch. If you were to observe those of your own profession; you would begin to appreciate the magnitude of their ability when confronted with seemingly overwhelming odds. You may try to do the same, but it will take you twice as much effort for half the results; their capacity seems to be greater. Their persistence alone assures success; they will not be denied the passion of their heart. And if such an experience causes you to seek your own destiny; the world will be better for it.

A person of destiny succeeds on behalf of others. I can't think of a better story to demonstrate that than the one about Joseph, son of Jacob, as recorded in the biblical book of Genesis. There are others, but this one comes to mind.

Joseph was sold into slavery by his ten brothers when he was seventeen years old. Joseph's mom, whom his dad loved with passion, had passed away many years before while bearing Joseph's brother. Fatherly favoritism toward Joseph caused resentment to brew in the hearts of his brothers over the years, and Joseph's account of a dream of his, in which his family bowed down to him, took them to intolerance. Consequently, at first opportunity they sold him to human traffickers, who in turn sold him to an officer in the service of Pharaoh, King of Egypt.

So Joseph is a slave in Egypt, working in the house of his master, whose wife is enamored of his presence; she wants a close connection with him. But destiny directs him; he made a decision to be prudent; "that would be a mistake," I'm sure he thought. He was still reeling in horror over becoming a slave. Incarceration, should he get caught, must have been unfathomable. After all, he was only a teenager. Do you think he was telling anyone about the vision of his family bowing down to him then? During those days, people only bowed down to noblemen and kings. Joseph's family was not from a "royal line," as it was said. They were shepherds. So I'm sure his destiny was as clear as mud at that time.

Unfortunately, and perhaps not, the wife of the captain of the guard would not take "no" for an answer. And after repeated attempts she decided to take a more aggressive approach by embracing Joseph. Perhaps her confidence as an older woman drove her to believe that she could ignite the passion of an eighteen year old with a warm embrace. But Joseph ran away, leaving his garment in her hand.

Feeling rejected, she sought revenge through her husband and got it. "Joseph was forward," was all her husband had to hear after seeing his garment in her hand. What man would not believe his wife in such a matter? How could she have obtained his garment if he had not been very close to her? Her story seemed plausible, and angered her husband greatly. And because they did not live in the United States of America, Joseph went straight to jail with his integrity intact; he had been honorable and wise. His vision, however, had gotten him into trouble! Now he's in Pharaoh's private prison.

Shortly thereafter, Pharaoh's chief butler and chief baker were imprisoned, and Joseph was given charge over them. "Hi guys, why are you here? I know you work for Pharaoh. Did you lay out wrinkled garments and serve him imperfectly baked bread? What did you do to tick him off?" The men were more than willing to tell their stories.

While sleeping that night, the chief butler and the chief baker each had a dream, which they shared with Joseph the following morning. People during those times considered dreams to be signs of things to come, so they always tried to get an interpretation of them to prepare, if possible, for the impending event.

To their surprise, Joseph says, "this is the interpretation of your dreams"—now we see the traits of a visionary at work! He told the chief butler that Pharaoh would restore him to his position, and he did. He told the chief baker that Pharaoh would hang him, and he did. He also told the butler to put in a good word to Pharaoh for him. But it wasn't until Pharaoh had a couple of dreams of his own two years later which his magicians couldn't interpret that the chief butler remembered Joseph. "Is there anyone in Egypt who can interpret these dreams for me?" Pharaoh asked. "I know somebody Great One," the chief butler replied, "barring bad memories, there is a man in your dungeon who interpreted a dream for me two years ago, and events happened exactly as he said they would! So Pharaoh summoned Joseph.

Joseph showered, shaved, put on new garments, and there he was in the presence of Pharaoh, King of Egypt, interpreting his dreams. Suddenly, his time of destiny had come!

"Great Pharaoh," he probably said—he had learned the culture, "your dreams simply mean there will be seven years of plenty in Egypt followed by seven years of famine. Be of good cheer though; I have a plan. For the next seven years of plenty, store up the excess of your bounty for the following seven years of famine. If you do this, you and your subjects will be fine; you will have enough. Just find a man of Egypt with great wisdom and understanding and have him coordinate and manage the effort for you." Pharaoh thought for a few seconds, then said to Joseph, "Where shall I find such a man? Aren't you the only one in Egypt with the wisdom and the understanding to accomplish such a feat? I choose you! You, Joseph, shall be the top man in Egypt; only Pharaoh will be higher than you in all the land." This guy didn't even have to campaign for the job of Prime Minister of Egypt; it was handed to him. He was appointed immediately because Pharaoh saw his endowments. His gift made room for him at the top of government. How about that?

As head of Egypt, Joseph began to make plans immediately for the storage of the bounty. It had to be stored strategically across the country and kept secure for seven to fifteen years.

Well the bounty came and so did the famine. The food failed as Joseph had said. Everyone in the country sought Pharaoh, who sent them to Joseph. So the people of Egypt and surrounding countries bought food from Joseph. And when their money ran out they bartered for it.

After a few years, Joseph's family showed up at his doorsteps requesting food. Joseph was happy, though not totally surprised to see them. They did not recognize him and he did not reveal himself until their third visit. They had bowed down to him at least three times before they knew he was their brother—confirmation to him that he was, at that very moment, living in his destiny. He was about 39 years old.

When the famine was over Pharaoh was very wealthy and Joseph had saved Egypt and the surrounding countries from death by starvation. He had fulfilled his destiny. The evil that his brothers had perpetrated against him actually set him on his path of destiny.

He moved his family, including his dad and the brother of his mother, to Egypt to provide for them, and arranged for the best land in Egypt to become their home.

So Joseph lived in the country of Egypt until his death at 110 years. His family remained there for another 330 years until God sent Moses to take them back home. What a story of destiny!

And now there is another story of destiny unfolding before our very eyes here in the United States of America. It hasn't happened at our national level in forty-eight years. Consider becoming an active part of this history and recording it for posterity.

The Whirlwind

Americans still trust their government to keep them safe and to enhance their prosperity. But that trust has been violated far to many times recently, as it obviously was in the latter part of 2008 when the former Treasury Secretary asked Congress for $700,000,000,000 to bailout homeowners who were delinquent on their mortgages. His request came as he prepared to walk out of his office for the last time. What a noble departing gesture, we all thought—finally our government will respond to the cry for help of homeowners around the country.

Well, Congress was obliging and he got the money rather quickly. Then immediately he began to disperse the funds to financial institutions—his brethren, the richest industry in this country and the cause of the worst financial downward spiral since the Great Depression. The financial institutions received the money and did nothing for the consumer—it appeared to be the old "bait and switch." This was a classic "in your face" operation. Section 8 of the bailout package said that "whatever the

Secretary of the Treasury does is not reviewable by the courts,"—no future reviews allowed; no agency can establish accountability; no explaining whatsoever; all decisions were his. And it was passed, just as the USA PATRIOT Act and the Declaration of War Against Iraq were passed. I have no doubt that the previous administration must have considered the 110th Congress "sure votes." What else could it have been? — They got away with it! Now as freelancers, some members of the previous team are attempting to use a similar strategy in multiple forums to obstruct legislation. It seems the 111th Congress is more astute as they institute strategies to jumpstart the economy.

The Silver Lining

If you want to understand the complexity of the financial crisis facing us today, which is unlike any other, tune in to NPR's *Planet Money.* The multimedia global economy team of Alex Blumberg and Adam Davidson, contributing editor and producer respectively; are trying to increase financial literacy in this country by placing the financial crisis in narrative form and telling it as a story with non-academic financial language to help people understand the many intricate pieces of the crisis and how they fit together. Be prepare to submit yourself to a very lengthy tutorial. In addition, *This American Life: The Giant Pool of Money* that aired on NPR's *All Things Considered* will also increase your understanding to some degree. Nobel Prize winning economist, Paul Krugan of Princeton University also gives a non-partisan review of the crisis.

In the meantime, I think it is time for Congress to legislate a Business Recovery Fund in the style of unemployment insurance to cover business losses—a safety net of sorts that would help businesses stay solvent. We can no longer take the taxpayers money to bailout private companies. They must prepare for their failures if they insist on being reckless.

How ironic! — we helped the perpetrators of the financial crisis, but ignored the taxpaying-victims who should have been at the top of the rescue list.

During our annual *National Day of Prayer, which is the first Thursday in May,* we should dedicate the block of time from

12:00 Noon to 1:00 P.M. to pray for our political leaders. Having made good choices in representation, we should pray for them as the Bible says, rather than lambasting them at every opportunity. If we are diligent to pray for them daily, we will begin to see the signs of a great moral awakening in our country unlike any this generation has seen before. And as we begin to truly love our neighbors as we love ourselves, we will see that awakening grow. Some of you may be asking now—How do I love my neighbor? Love is a demonstration of caring. Do willingly for them what you would do for yourself; let there be no difference.

And though our economy is built on sand—the suspension of the Gold Standard in 1933 and the establishment of the Keynesian policy of deficit spending — it is not far-fetched to believe that many wealthy Americans who own this country in their heart will eventually give it millions of dollars, if not billions—along with more modest givers, to retire our National Debt. Not all Americans are living in a recession. Some are prosperous beyond measure right now. Some are more wealthy now than they were in 2005.

If we choose 2040 as the target year for final payoff of the National Debt it can be accomplished. How can we do it? — more savings, less debt, and a lot of generosity.

When companies began to ship jobs overseas over twenty years ago, they also began two other strategies: lower wages with less benefits *and* higher consumer prices with increased credit or less for more. By doing so, consumers didn't perceive a loss of consumption. They maintained their sense of prosperity with borrowed money as their wages decreased. Now that they can't borrow money, the truth of their financial standing stares them squarely in the face. Just as our country cannot prosper with protracted debt, nor can its citizens. The bible says that we are to leave an inheritance to our children's children. Can that be done with borrowed money?

The silver lining of this recession may be that Americans will change the way they manage their finances; they may change the way they view debt; they may change their spending patterns to amass real wealth and to reflect true prosperity.

MENTOR I

Observe wisdom; you'll never totter.
Call a friend; you'll never falter.
Change your garb to suit the season.
Pick a flower to stay in reason.

Sing your heart song in domicile.
Walk a mile to make a smile.
Give honor when it is due.
Help others and be their cue.

Listen twice as much as you speak.
Build character from your feet.
Spend time with yourself in stay.
Don't give tomorrow what you can today.

Season your heart with integrity salt.
Render ridicule soup with a halt.
Forge friendships of congeniality.
Plant a tree of life for posterity.

Chapter 3

CITIZENSHIP, THE HIGHEST CALLING

"For of those to whom much is given, much is required. And when at some future date the high court of history sits in judgment on each of us, recording whether in our brief span of service we fulfilled our responsibilities to the state, our success or failure, in whatever office we hold, will be measured by the answers to four questions: First, were we truly men of courage... Second, were we truly men of judgment... Third, were we truly men of integrity... Finally, were we truly men of dedication?" President John F. Kennedy Speech to Massachusetts State Legislature, January 9, 1961

American citizenship is a valuable commodity in the world today. With wars, upheavals and coups happening all over the world, people want to live in a country where they can have peace, respect and prosperity. If we were to place a call to the world today and say "come one, come all of you that would be a citizen of the United States of America," our shores could not contain them; even our enemies, who claim they hate our lifestyle, would come in droves.

Citizens of the United States enjoy the privileges and protections of the Constitution and The Bill of Rights of the

United States of America, which is our rule of law. It is such a profound document that if you are ever challenged on these rights by another citizen; you could seek remedy through the judiciary and be compensated, if appropriate, for any violation of your rights or any wrong done to you. The Constitution keeps our country orderly and peaceful. Every citizen has the same rights regardless of socioeconomic status. The rich man doesn't have more rights than the poor man, unless however, he tries to corrupt the system. And in such cases citizens can rise up and bring forth remedies to correct the infraction. This is where the responsibility of citizenship comes in.

We are still a relatively young nation, two hundred thirty-three years old; very young when compared to other nations like China and Italy. And as each generation of Americans come and go, it's their responsibility to learn about the republic, protect it, and defend it for the next generation. If we don't protect and defend our country within the parameters of the Constitution and The Bill of Rights it can be overthrown and some other form of government established in its place. It happens all the time in other parts of the world as military leaders decide they want to rule the people. They call for a coup d'état and usurp the authority of the citizens, until they are prevented.

Great Britain claimed this country as part of their empire in the 1700s until its inhabitants insisted on "self-rule." And, of course, that did not go over well with the King—his subjects had to be punished for their rebellion. But it was far more than rebellion that had entered the hearts of the people; it was revolution.

Everyone wants to be free to pursuit happiness; everyone wants privacy and respect; everyone wants to be heard verbally and by ballot; yes, we want to govern ourselves. It's our God-given right. Tyranny is and always shall be unacceptable to the American people. We breathe freedom as we breathe air. We need it to live and to function normally. That is why we will fight to the death to keep it. Others fight for the sake of their religion; others for social power. We fight to maintain our freedom, because it is most precious to us both domestically and internationally.

Our domestic struggles are remedied by the application of our Constitution. Our international struggles are remedied with the use of treaties, diplomacy, and military force. We are facing an internal struggle today that's been lurking beneath the socioeconomic radar for decades. We are now seeing the effects of poor judgment, mismanagement, and misuse of power in *our government.*

So we embrace again our inherent responsibility to protect the rights given to us by our Creator and validated by our Constitution and The Bill of Rights, so that our posterity can enjoy the same freedom and prosperity as we do. We must fight for this cause; we must defend our living documents to insure that their enforcement is not gradually suspended. If we don't defend them, they won't be worth the parchments they are written on.

We are in a time when many in our own country are trying to create an uneven socioeconomic playing field; they are trying to control the masses of this country. They are seeking to gain control of the thoughts and actions of many of our elected officials through bribery, influence, and promises of perpetual wealth. While we slept, they gained access to our executive, legislative, and judicial branches of governance to influence and to control the laws, policies, and procedures of this country at the highest level; thereby, embedding themselves into the fiber of this nation.

It is now necessary for the citizenry to uproot these entrenchments and to seek the remedy of change that is vitally needed to stabilize our democracy — which could be a lengthy process. Elected officials who were manipulated to vote for laws, are not likely to repeal them, therefore, they should be voted out of office if it can be proven that they willingly compromised their decisions on matters of law and policy. They cannot be allowed to continue as a representative of the people. New representation should be voted in to repeal these laws. Yes, we have begun the process, but it must be completed.

Meanwhile, it's a race with time. We should prevent those who stand to gain from these misguided laws, in many cases written by them, from reaping their intended benefits of power and wealth—into the billions of dollars. Non-partisan government watch dogs groups have been invaluable in the past by informing us of such irregularities in our government, but they too have become silent in this decade. As we went about our daily lives, they were our eyes and ears; working tirelessly to safeguard the foundation of our democracy. However, that which they have done for us, we must now do for ourselves.

Part of being an American citizen is being well-informed, well-educated, and actively involved in our government. And it all begins with voter registration.

Voter Registration and Updates
One hundred thirty-one million Americans voted in the 2008 presidential election—61.6 percent of eligible voters cast ballots, according to final reports. That is the highest rate since 1968. However, there were signs during a Florida Senate runoff just weeks later that enthusiasm had waned. Many registered voters did not bother to vote in the runoff election.

At this time in our history, every Congressional seat is important, every state seat is important, every county seat is important, and every municipal seat is important. From local government to national government we have to work in unity – in a non-partisan manner to restore our economy, our values, our hope in the American dream, and our leadership in the world. Having said that, I know it isn't an easy task nowadays. To be unified in our endeavors, we must learn to disagree with others without being disagreeable. Many people choose, unfortunately, to vilify those with whom they disagree even to the point of criticizing physical features, which ultimately closes the door to debate and compromise. It happens in my own family, to my dismay, and it may even happen in yours—it's a form of self-exaltation. If we can't agree to disagree respectfully, separation is the only option of peace. Productive resolution seems unreachable. We remain in a never-ending stalemate—reason beacons, but nobody responds.

You may not encounter an active voter registration drive between now and 2010, but remember that the National Voter Registration Act (NVRA) offers a simple way to register to vote and to make changes to your registration by using the National Mail Voter Registration Form. You may use the form to register to vote, report a change of name, report a change of address, and report a change of party affiliation. The national form also contains voter registration rules and regulations for each state and territory. The form may be used to register in any state with the exceptions of North Dakota and Wyoming. New Hampshire town and city clerks will accept the National Form only as a request for their own mail-in absentee voter registration form. As of December 18, 2007, Arizona, Colorado, Delaware, Georgia, New Jersey, and Rhode Island had requested a change to their state instructions. The Commission has not yet approved their requests.

NVRA is trying to make voting accessible to every citizen. Even if you are homebound, in the hospital or stationed overseas, you may print the form from the NVRA website and mail it to the appropriate election office. States that accept the national form will also accept copies of the application printed from the computer image on regular paper stock, signed by the applicant, and mailed in a envelope with first class postage. You may also contact your state election office for more information.

Every two years, the Election Assistance Commission reports to Congress on the impact of NVRA, on the administration of Federal elections, and provides information to states on their responsibilities under the law. If you have moved, changed your name or changed party affiliation; update your registration. *If you have not registered to vote, do so today.* As a result, you too will begin to experience, along with millions of other Americans, the highest calling of American citizenship – the privilege of voting.

Federal Voting Rights Laws
Since history is a teacher, let's use it to fortify our commitment to responsible citizenship and to understand the importance of due diligence in the political arena of life in the United States. Let's go back to the beginning of our country to see what necessitated federal voting rights laws and to see their evolution.

The Voting Rights Act, adopted initially in 1965 and extended in 1970, 1975, and 1982, is generally considered the most successful piece of civil rights legislation ever adopted by the United States Congress that established the highest calling of citizenship. The Act codifies and effectuates the 15th Amendment's permanent guarantee that no person shall be denied the right to vote because of race or color in America. Adopted at a time when African Americans were substantially disfranchised in many Southern states, the Act employed measures to restore their right to vote and intruded in matters previously reserved to the individual states. Special provisions of the Act imposed even more stringent requirements in certain jurisdictions of the country. Some Republicans are currently (2009) preparing a challenge to those special provisions.

Reconstruction and the Civil War Amendments Before the Voting Rights Act

Before the Civil War, the United States Constitution did not provide specific protections for voting. Qualifications for voting were matters which neither the Constitution nor federal laws governed. At that time, although a few northern states permitted a small number of free black men to register and vote; slavery and restrictive state laws and practices led the franchise to be exercised almost exclusively by white males.

Shortly after the end of the Civil War, Congress enacted the Military Reconstruction Act of 1867, which allowed former Confederate States to be readmitted to the Union if they adopted new state constitutions that permitted universal male suffrage. The 14th Amendment, which conferred citizenship to all persons born or naturalized in the United States, was ratified in 1868.

In 1870 the 15th Amendment was ratified, which provided specifically that the right to vote shall not be denied or abridged on the basis of race, color or previous condition of servitude.

This superseded state laws that had directly prohibited black voting. Congress then enacted the Enforcement Act of 1870, which contained criminal penalties for interference with the right to vote, and the Force Act of 1871, which provided for federal election oversight.

As a result, new black citizens—former slaves who in some cases were the majority of the eligible voting population in a former Confederate State—registered to vote. The number of new voters is believed to have been in the hundreds of thousands. Black candidates began for the first time to be elected to federal, state, and local offices and to play a meaningful role in their government.

Disenfranchisement Prior to the Voting Rights Act
The extension of the franchise to black citizens was strongly resisted. Some terrorist organizations, through violence and intimidation, attempted to prevent the 15th Amendment from being enforced. Two Supreme Court decisions in 1876, which narrowed the scope of enforcement under the Enforcement Act and the Force Act, and the end of Reconstruction marked by the removal of federal troops after the Hayes-Tilden Compromise of 1877, resulted in a climate of violence and fraud that was used to suppress black voter turnout and change the results of lawfully cast votes.

Once whites regained control of the state legislatures using these tactics—a process known as "Redemption," they then used gerrymandering of election districts to further reduce black voting strength and to minimize the number of black elected officials. In the 1890s, these states began to amend their constitutions and to enact a series of laws intended to re-establish and entrench white political supremacy.

Such disenfranchising laws included poll taxes, literacy tests, vouchers of "good character," and disqualification for "crimes of moral turpitude." These laws were "color-blind" on their face, but were designed to exclude black citizens disproportionately by allowing white election officials to apply the procedures selectively. Other laws and practices, such as the "white primary," attempted to evade the 15th Amendment by allowing "private" political parties to conduct elections and establish qualifications for their members.

As a result of these efforts in the former Confederate states, nearly all black citizens were disenfranchised and removed from voter registration rolls by 1910. The process of restoring the rights taken by these tactics took many decades.

Attacks on Disenfranchisement Before the Voting Rights Act

In *Guinn* v. *United States*, 238 U.S. 347 (1915), the Supreme Court held that voter registration requirements containing "grandfather clauses," which made voter registration in part dependent upon whether the applicant was descended from men enfranchised before enactment of the 15th Amendment violated that amendment. The Supreme Court found that an Oklahoma law was adopted in order to give whites, who might otherwise have been disenfranchised by the state's literacy test, a way of qualifying to vote that was not available to blacks. In 1944, the Supreme Court held that the Texas "white primary" violated the 15th Amendment; *Smith* v. *Allwright*, 321 U.S. 649 (1944). The Southern states experimented with numerous additional restrictions to limit black participation in politics, many of which were struck down by federal courts over the next decade.

Congress passed legislation in 1957, 1960, and 1964 that contained voting-related provisions. The 1957 Act created the Civil Rights Division within the Department of Justice and the Commission on Civil Rights. The Attorney General was given authority to intervene in and institute lawsuits seeking injunctive relief against violations of the 15th Amendment. The 1960 Act permitted federal courts to appoint voting referees to conduct voter registration following a judicial finding of voting discrimination. The 1964 Act also contained several relatively minor voting-related provisions. Although court decisions and laws made it more difficult, at least in theory, for states to keep all of their black citizens disfranchised, the strategy of litigation on a case-by-case basis proved to have limited success in the jurisdictions that were sued, and did not prompt voluntary compliance among jurisdictions that had not been sued. As soon as one discriminatory practice or procedure was proven to be unconstitutional and enjoined, a new one would be substituted in its place and litigation would have to commence anew. Literacy tests, poll taxes, and other formal and informal practices combined to keep black registration rates minimal in Alabama, Louisiana, and Mississippi, and well below white registration rates in the other southern states.

Faced with the prospect that black voter registration could not be suppressed forever, some states began to change political boundaries and election structures to minimize the impact of black enfranchisement. In 1960, the Supreme Court struck down one such effort, in which the state legislature had gerrymandered the city boundaries of Tuskegee, Alabama to remove all but a handful of the city's black registered voters. The Supreme Court ruled that by doing so Alabama had violated the 15th Amendment; *Gomillion* v. *Lightfoot*, 364 U.S. 339 (1960).

The "Reapportionment Revolution"
In the early 1960's, the Supreme Court overcame its reluctance to apply the Constitution to unfair redistricting practices. Prior to 1962, the United States Supreme Court had declined to decide constitutional challenges to legislative apportionment schemes, on the grounds that such "political questions" were not within the federal courts' jurisdiction. In *Baker* v. *Carr*, 369 U.S. 186 (1962), however, the Supreme Court recognized that grossly malapportioned state legislative districts could seriously undervalue or dilute the voting strength of the residents of overpopulated districts and overvalue the voting strength of residents of underpopulated districts. The Supreme Court found that such malapportionment could be challenged in federal court under the Equal Protection Clause of the 14th Amendment.

In later cases including *Wesberry* v. *Sanders*, 376 U.S. 1 (1964) and *Reynolds* v. *Sims*, 377 U.S. 533 (1964), the Supreme Court established the one-person, one-vote principle. In many states malapportioned legislative districts had resulted in sparsely populated rural counties having a much greater share of their state's political power, though they had less of their state's population. Correcting this imbalance led to dramatic realignments of political power in several states. In *Fortson* v. *Dorsey*, 379 U.S. 433 (1965), the Supreme Court suggested, but did not hold, that certain types of apportionment might unconstitutionally dilute the voting strength of racial minorities.

The Enactment of the Voting Rights Act of 1965
By 1965, concerted efforts to break the grip of state disenfranchisement had been under way for some time, but had achieved only modest success overall and in some areas had proved

almost entirely ineffectual. The murder of voting-rights activists in Philadelphia and Mississippi gained national attention, along with numerous other acts of violence and terrorism. Finally, the unprovoked attack on March 7, 1965, by state troopers on peaceful marchers crossing the Edmund Pettus Bridge in Selma, Alabama, in route to the state capitol in Montgomery, persuaded the President and Congress to overcome Southern legislators' resistance to effective voting rights legislation. President Johnson issued a call for a strong voting rights law at the urging of Dr. Martin Luther King Jr., and hearings began shortly thereafter.

Congress determined that the existing federal anti-discrimination laws were not sufficient to overcome the resistance of state officials to enforce the 15th Amendment. The legislative hearings showed that the Department of Justice's efforts to eliminate discriminatory election practices by litigation on a case-by-case basis had been unsuccessful in opening up the registration process to black citizens. President Johnson signed the resulting legislation, the Voting Rights Act of 1965, into law on August 6, 1965, five months after Selma. Dr. King was present at its signing.

Special enforcement provisions of the Act targeted areas of the country where Congress believed the potential for discrimination to be the greatest. Congress considered such a far-reaching statute only in response to compelling evidence of continuing interference with attempts by black American citizens to exercise their right to vote. When the Act was first adopted, only one-third of all black Americans of voting age were on the registration rolls in the specially covered states, while two-thirds of eligible white Americans were registered. Now black voter registration rates are approaching parity with those of white voters in many areas, and Hispanic voters in jurisdictions added to the list of those specially covered by the Act in 1975 are not far behind. Enforcement of the Act has also increased the opportunity of black and Latino voters to elect representatives of their choice by providing a vehicle for challenging discriminatory election methods such as at-large elections, racially gerrymandered districting plans, or runoff requirements that may dilute minority voting strength. Virtually excluded from all public offices in the South in 1965, black and Latino voters are now substantially represented in the state legislatures and local governing bodies throughout the region.

Section 2 of the Act, which closely followed the language of the 15th amendment, applied a nationwide prohibition against the denial or abridgment of the right to vote on the basis of literacy tests.

Section 4 ended the use of literacy requirements for voting in six Southern states (Alabama, Georgia, Louisiana, Mississippi, South Carolina, and Virginia) and in many counties of North Carolina, where voter registration or turnout in the 1964 presidential election was less than 50 percent of the voting-age population.

Under the terms of Section 5 of the Act, jurisdictions covered by special provisions could not implement any change affecting voting until the Attorney General or the United States District Court for the District of Columbia determined that the change did not have a discriminatory purpose and would not have a discriminatory effect. In addition, the Attorney General could appoint a *federal examiner* to a county covered by these special provisions to review the qualifications of persons who wanted to register to vote, and assign *federal observers* to monitor activities within the county's polling places.

The Voting Rights Act did not have a provision prohibiting poll taxes, however, it directed the Attorney General to challenge its use. In *Harper* v. *Virginia State Board of Elections*, 383 U.S. 663 (1966), the Supreme Court held Virginia's poll tax to be unconstitutional under the 14th Amendment. Between 1965 and 1969 the Supreme Court also issued several key decisions upholding the constitutionality of Section 5 and affirming the broad range of voting practices that required Section 5 review. The Supreme Court issued the following opinion in its 1966 decision to uphold the constitutionality of the Act:

Congress had found that case-by-case litigation was inadequate to combat wide-spread and persistent discrimination in voting, because of the inordinate amount of time and energy required to overcome the obstructionist tactics invariably encountered in these lawsuits. After enduring nearly a century of systematic resistance to the Fifteenth Amendment, Congress might well decide to shift the advantage of time and inertia from the perpetrators of the evil to it's victims. South Carolina v. *Katzenbach*, 383 U.S. 301, 327-28 (1966).

The 1970 and 1975 Amendments

Congress extended Section 5 for five years in 1970 and for seven years in 1975. With these extensions Congress validated the Supreme Court's broad interpretation of the scope of Section 5. During the hearings on these extensions Congress heard extensive testimony concerning the ways in which voting electorates were manipulated through gerrymandering, annexations, adoption of at-large elections, and other structural changes to prevent newly-registered black voters from effectively using the ballot. Congress also heard extensive testimony about voting discrimination that had been suffered by Latino, Asian and Native American citizens. As a result, the 1975 amendment added protections from voting discrimination for language minority citizens.

In 1973, the Supreme Court held certain legislative multi-member districts unconstitutional under the 14th Amendment, on the grounds that they systematically diluted the voting strength of minority citizens in Bexar County, Texas. This decision in *White* v. *Regester*, 412 U.S. 755 (1973), strongly shaped litigation through the 1970's against at-large systems and gerrymandered redistricting plans. Later, in *Mobile* v. *Bolden*, 446 U.S. 55 (1980), the Supreme Court required that any constitutional claim of minority vote dilution must include proof of a racially discriminatory purpose, a requirement that was widely seen as making such claims far more difficult to prove.

The 1982 Amendment

Congress renewed the special provisions of the Act in 1982 for twenty-five years, triggered by coverage under Section 4. Congress also adopted a new standard, which went into effect in 1985, providing how jurisdictions could terminate (or "bail out" from) coverage under the *provisions of Section 4*. Furthermore, after extensive hearings, Congress amended Section 2 to allow a Plaintiff to establish a violation of the Section without having to prove discriminatory purpose.

The 2006 Reauthorization and Amendments

On July 27, 2006, President George W. Bush signed the Voting Rights Act Reauthorization and Amendments Act of 2006: "The Voting Rights Act that broke the segregationist lock on the ballot box rose from the courage shown on a Selma bridge one Sunday afternoon in March of 1965. On that day, African Americans, including a member of the United States Congress, John Lewis, marched across the Edmund Pettus Bridge in a protest intended to highlight the unfair practices that kept them off the voter rolls... Today, we renew a bill that helped bring a community on the margins into the life of American democracy. My administration will vigorously enforce the provisions of this law, and we will defend it in court. This legislation is named in honor of three heroes of American history who devoted their lives to the struggle of civil rights: Fannie Lou Hamer, Rosa Parks, and Coretta Scott King. And in honor of their memory and their contributions to the cause of freedom, I am proud to sign the Voting Rights Act Reauthorization and Amendments Act of 2006."

The Effect of the Voting Rights Act

Soon after passage of the Voting Rights Act, federal examiners were conducting voter registration, and black voter registration began to increase sharply — the cumulative effect of the Supreme Court's decisions and Congress' enactment of voting rights legislation. The ongoing efforts of concerned private citizens and the Department of Justice have been to restore the right to vote guaranteed by the 14th and 15th Amendments.

The following table compares black voter registration rates with white voter registration rates in seven Southern States in 1965 and 1988:

The Connection to Hope

Voter Registration Rates (1965 vs. 1988)

	March 1965			November 1988		
	Black	White	Gap	Black	White	Gap
AL	19.3	69.2	49.9	68.4	75.0	6.6
GA	27.4	62.6	35.2	56.8	63.9	7.1
LA	31.6	80.5	48.9	77.1	75.1	2.0
MS	6.7	69.9	63.2	74.2	80.5	6.3
NC	46.8	96.8	50.0	58.2	65.6	7.4
SC	37.3	75.7	38.4	56.7	61.8	5.1
VA	38.3	61.1	22.8	63.8	68.5	4.7

Adapted from Bernard Grofman, Lisa Handley and Richard G. Niemi. 1992.
Minority Representation and the Quest for Voting Equality. New York: Cambridge Press.

Overseas Citizens and Military Voters

The Uniform and Overseas Citizens Absentee Voting Act (UOCAVA) of 1986 protects the voting rights of members of the Uniformed Services (on active duty), members of the Merchant Marine and their eligible dependents, Commissioner Corps of the Public Health Service, Commissioned Corps of the National Oceanic and Atmospheric Administration, and U.S. citizens residing outside the U.S. UOCAVA requires states and territories to allow these citizens to register and vote in elections for federal office using absentee procedures.

Source: United States Department of Justice, Civil Rights Division, Voting Section

Chapter 4

POLITICS OF LIFE

"We the people of the United States, in order to form a more perfect union, establish justice, insure domestic tranquility, provide for the common defense, promote the general welfare, and secure the blessings of liberty to ourselves and our posterity, do ordain and establish this Constitution for the United States of America."
Preamble to the Constitution of the United States of America

Promoting the General Welfare

Politics is activity associated with government, political life, power relationships in a specific field, and calculated advancement. It's the theory and practice of government, especially the activities associated with governing, with obtaining legislative or executive power, or with forming and running organizations connected with government. It's political activity as a profession and the interrelationships between the people, groups, or organizations in a particular area of life especially insofar as they involve power and influence or conflict. And, of course, it's the use of tactics and strategy to gain power in a group or organization; it's political science.

Politics is about how well we live and how prosperous we are in our everyday lives — fulfilling our dreams and passing our net worth on to our posterity, thereby creating wealth in the family line.

Do you see politics as fundamental to your way of life? Do politically active individuals fare better in life than those who are not? Does involvement in politics enhance a citizen's economic and social prosperity? Does politics come to bear when we buy stock, buy a home, buy a car, shop for clothing, shop for groceries, go to college, look for a job, see a doctor, or retire. Does politics matter at all?

I have come to the conclusion that our lives can be affected positively or negatively by our political choices as a whole. Our lives are impacted daily by legislation that our lawmakers and Presidents have passed. Laws that were passed many years ago are now beginning to impact our lives, even though some of their proponents have left office and have even left the earth. Today we live with the effects of their decisions. To some degree they control what we earn, what we save, what we invest, where we live, what we spent, where we go to school, where we vacation, what we eat, where we eat, what we wear, our children's upbringing, our marriage, and our assistance to our aging parents. And the list goes on and on because these are all issues of money. If you don't see an immediate impact of laws passed by Congress and signed by the President, give it a little time — chances are you will, either directly or indirectly. The effects of laws eventually trickle down to each citizen.

Some people, however, tend to think in terms of how laws affect others. But you must begin to think of how a law will affect you, your family, your community and your state.

Providing for the Common Defense

Who knew upon entering the voting booth in 2000 that their vote would be contributing to the loss of American sons and daughters who were loyal and patriotic? Who knew that the domestic branch of our military would be sent for one, two, and even three tours of duty in an international conflict? Who knew that our soldiers would be expected to fight a vicious enemy without essential equipment? Who knew that our wounded of two wars would come home to suffer in silence?

Recently, the 110th Congress faced Republican opposition to a new G.I. Bill. The existing bill at that time had not been updated for twenty-seven years. Lawmakers who opposed the bill believed that we, the people, might be giving our veterans too much..." How much is too much? How much is a soldier's life worth? How much is his/her physical sacrifice worth? How much is his/her mental sacrifice worth? How much is his/her financial sacrifice worth? How much is his/her social sacrifice worth? Can his/her sacrifice even be measure in dollars? And these same lawmakers are proponents of the Iraq War—"poppycock." In light of the overall budget of the two wars and the immeasurable contribution of our military, could it have been anything other than nonsensical behavior on display?

The nonpartisan Congressional Budget Office (CBO) has done projections on the cost of the wars in Afghanistan and Iraq. The 2008 budget was 155% more than the 2004 budget, with Iraq accounting for approximately three-quarters of the costs. The cumulative cost through 2017 will be $1.2 to $1.7 trillion, by CBO projections, which does not factor in interest on the borrowed money or lifetime healthcare for the wounded and disabled. Auditors of the Government Accountability Office predict that the cost will be huge, "requiring decision makers to consider difficult trade-offs as the nation faces an increasing long-range fiscal challenge," according to a January 2008 report to Congress.

All of these circumstances reflect the power of our vote and the extent to which it can affect our personal lives and the lives of others.

Truth and Consequence

The World Trade Center was bombed on February 26, 1993, with al Qaeda's support. And before the attack on 9/11, al Qaeda had bombed our embassies in Nairobi, Kenya and Dar es Salaam, Tanzania in August 1998. They bombed the USS Cole in October 2000, as well as other facilities of our allies in Europe and Africa, and gave financial support to others. Many attacks were averted. And after each of those attacks, we managed to rally wisdom and restraint through diplomatic channels, established alliances, and reliable intelligence to target our response for the greatest effect. After all, al Qaeda is not a nation; they are a pack of renegades that are not even welcomed in their own country. Their leaders, who seem to be feuding with some of our citizens, hide in caves to escape capture. They have grown in notoriety only because we elevated their status by supplanting the word "retaliation" with the word "war" through a national campaign of indoctrination to describe our response to them. An act of "war" gives extreme powers to the leader of a great nation. 9/11 was foreshadowed in intelligence reports, without a single response. But the actual attack has been answered by the toppling of two regimes, the death of over 4000 Americans, and injuries to over 30,000 more, with no end in sight as we approach the ninth year of conflict. And after all this time, do we see Bin Laden before a high court for crimes against the United States of America. Where is he? Who among you believe that the Special Forces of the United States of America are incapable of catching Osama Bin Laden after almost eight years in pursuit? We call strikes at will from our central command centers in Florida and Nevada and get results. Are we to believe that we can't catch this man? We could have rearranged the landscape and finished him off years ago — DNA evidence is sufficient. But to have caught him, however, would have brought forth a call for withdrawal of our military from Afghanistan and Iraq. Have you ever considered these things?

Furthermore, did you ever consider the sudden appearance of an Osama Bin Laden taped confession to the 9/11 bombings just days before the Presidential Election of 2004 to be odd? Did it make you fearful? Did it change your vote?

Have you wondered why the chief economic indicators of the past four years never seemed to coincide with what you, your family, your neighbors, and the people of your community were experiencing?

Did you consider the new jobs counted in the national employment figures to be jobs at or near minimum wage? How does one go from earning $50,000 – $100,000 a year to $15,000 – $25,000 a year and still be considered gainfully employment?

Has anyone other than the parents of college age children noticed that funding for college tuition has decreased while costs have increased? Nevertheless, financial institutions are generating huge profits from student loan programs — unwilling even to negotiate new terms with graduates who have lost their jobs or have been forced to take lesser jobs for survival. We have subsidized other countries to the amounts of billions of dollars. Can't we subsidize the college education of our citizens with a little more monetary vigor?

PBS NOW aired a program entitled "Downward Mobility" in which it overviewed the plight of wage-earners in our country. According to a U.S. Census Bureau Report of October 2003, three stark changes have affected the economic security of millions of American households:

★ Median household incomes are falling
★ The number of Americans without health insurance rose by 5.7 percent to 43.6 million individuals
★ The number of people living below the poverty line ($18,392 for a family of four) climbed to 12.1 percent — 34.6 million people.

"Wages make up the majority of income for most American families," the report went on to say, "American workers are still facing corporate efforts to cut pay and benefits, which could lead to more American families struggling to stay out of poverty." The PBS report added, "the precarious position of those at the bottom of the wage scale is due to a number of factors. Americans are working more — more women are working for wages and all are working more hours. On average, a middle income married couple with children had added an average of 20 weeks of work per year since 1970. Still, it's increasingly hard for families to make ends meet. According to October 2003 formulations of the Economic Policy Institute, drawn from Bureau of Labor Statistics figures, the purchasing power of the minimum wage has declined." And might I add, substantially.

"One measure of how families at the lower end of the wage scale struggle is the federal figures on food insecurity. According to the USDA, *food insecurity is: "limited or uncertain availability of nutritionally adequate and safe foods or limited or uncertain ability to acquire acceptable foods in socially acceptable ways."* In 2002 the national rate for food insecurity was 10.7 percent. Of those who are food insecure, only 36.5 percent live officially below the poverty line. The Economic Policy Institute offers regional calculators to illustrate just how much income different types of families need to make ends meet."

Dawning of Middle-Class Insecurity

At the beginning of the current economic downturn in our country, four thousand five hundred and fifty jobs were loss unexpectedly in one week, as three airlines—Airbus of Ohio, Aloha Air of Hawaii, and ATA home-based in Indiana, called it quits. This was in addition to thousands more loss the previous week through the collapse of Bear Sterns. In eight days, almost 20,000 Americans loss their jobs due to company failures induced by high fuel costs, skyrocketing operating costs, and the collapse of the housing market; hitting the economy when the nation's unemployment rate was already at its worst level in three years. We were shocked by those numbers. Since then we have seen the jobless numbers increase to over 500,000 a month for several consecutive months—that horrified many. And that number does not include the many self-employed people who called it quits due to high operating costs. According to economist, Brian Wesbury, as reported by NBC news correspondent, Mike Taibbi; "weak employment will lead to weaker retail sales and weaker retail sales will lead to weaker production which will cause more job losses."

It seems that we've got to get the "politics of life" right, and we must begin now. It is not politics as usual anymore. We are facing a new beast, which we have not encountered before. Everyone compares our current recession with the Great Depression, because there is nothing else to compare it with. But if the truth be told, it is worse. Even though the unemployment rate has not reached twenty-five percent, the variables are much harder to manage because we are in an international recession. We need quick fixes along with long-term policy changes to alter our economic course. We want to avoid the slippery slope altogether, which could wear out our welcome in Japan and China. Besides, foreign entities are already heavily invested in America at this very moment. Shall we hock the whole country?

Reality Sets In

Today's reality proves that we as Americans have, more times than not, voted against our own interest in choosing our representatives? And if that is true, what has contributed to those decisions? The number one cause could be the "power of persuasion." The number two cause could be a lack of knowledge.

What would convince you, a wage-earner, to put your hopes in a millionaire who has not walked a mile or two in your shoes; who has not given directly to the poor; who has not offered a struggling small business a day of counsel or a grant of consolidation; who has used our military as a possible sacrifice for power and greed; and who convinces you that "your" cause is a noble one in service to your country. And daily, in the privacy of your home, you struggle to maintain that mental alignment with your sacrifice, your need, and your pain before you walk out of your door yet again to face the world with a semblance of confidence in your government leaders.

Further observation has revealed that we have even allowed our government leaders to formulate our questions to them; accepting their predetermined responses, and somehow we are pleased. Should we wonder why some politicians speak to us today as though we are void of reasoning and subject to remote brainwashing at their will? How long shall we allow this cycle of ineptitude to continue? As I said in chapter three, *"Citizenship, the Highest Calling,"* part of being an American citizen is being well-informed and well-educated about our style of government. Political ignorance can cost you both time and money. Time spent in political activism is time spent in quality of life. Americans should spend at least ten percent of their week in study and review of the tenets of our republic and their role in it. Additionally, every citizen should keep a watchful eye on legislation being introduced by Congress, rulings by the Superior Court, and new regulations being adopted by the executive branch. Keeping up with all three branches of government: legislative, executive, and judicial may require a community effort facilitated by town hall meetings which would make the task easier and serve to galvanize the village.

Preparing for the Life

Historic diligence in our efforts to self-teach and to tutor our children in the tenets of democracy will produce a cohesive community that has a better chance of socioeconomic survival and prosperity than a group of individuals operating with personal agendas. If we allocate the watchdog tasks among community members and hold monthly briefings to discuss and to archive our research, we will begin to invoke the change sought during the 2008 Presidential Campaign by thousands upon thousands of new registrants who entered the political arena, not really knowing the political process, but understanding one thing—they had to vote; which was sufficient to get them through.

Now it's time to commit to learning the process of political activism. And even after studying for a few years, it's important to maintain your knowledge level with periodic mental tune-ups, preferably when we are not in the heat of a campaign.

The road of the "politics of life" may be long and winding at times, but it is easy to navigate if you are familiar with it. The 2008 Presidential Election was unusually long and tedious. It not only wearied the candidates and their staff, but their supporters too. The result is we have elected a President who wants to change our country for the good of all. And Americans are ready to work in partnership with him on every level of governance because they now understand it's a necessary part of living the American dream.

So let's begin with in-service training. Our goal is to turn a lion into a lamb – the Electoral College.

What is the Electoral College?

The Electoral College is administered by the National Archives and Records Administration (NARA). It is not a place as some have suggested, but it is a process that is instituted every four years to elect a president and then dissolved. The process began as part of the original design of our Constitution. The Electoral College was established by the founding fathers as a compromise between election of the president by Congress and election by popular vote.

Presidential Electors

When Americans vote for a President and Vice President, which is held on *Tuesday after the first Monday in November*, they are actually voting for presidential electors, known collectively as the Electoral College. It is these electors, chosen by the people, who elect the chief executive. The Constitution assigns each state a number of electors equal to the combined total of the state's Senate and House of Representatives delegations; at present, the number of electors per state ranges from 3 to 54, for a total of 538. Aside from Members of Congress, and persons holding offices of "Trust or Profit" under the Constitution, anyone may serve as an elector. In order to forestall partisan intrigue and manipulation, the electors assemble in their respective states and cast their ballots as state units, rather than meet at a central location.

In each presidential election year, a group of candidates for elector is nominated by political parties and other groupings in each state, usually at a state party convention, or by the party state committee. In most states, voters cast a single vote for the slate of electors pledged to the party's presidential and vice presidential candidates of their choice. The slate winning the most popular votes is elected; this is known as the "*winner-take-all*," or general ticket system.

Electors assemble in their respective states on *Monday after the second Wednesday in December*. They are pledged and expected, but not required, to vote for the candidates they represent. Separate ballots are cast for President and Vice President after which the Electoral College ceases to exist for another four years. At least one of the candidates for whom the electors vote must be an inhabitant of another state (a presidential candidate and a vice-presidential candidate cannot reside in the same state). The electoral vote results are counted and certified by a joint session of Congress, held on *January 6* of the year succeeding the election. A majority of electoral votes (currently 270 of 538) is required to win. If no candidate receives a majority, then the President is elected by the House of Representatives, and the Vice President is elected by the Senate, a process known as *contingent election*.

Changes to the Original System

The Constitutional Convention of 1787 considered several methods of electing the President, including selection by Congress, by the governors of the states, by the state legislatures, by a special group of Members of Congress chosen by lot, and by direct popular election. Late in the convention, the matter was referred to the Committee of Eleven on Postponed Matters, which devised the Electoral College system in its original form. This plan, which met with widespread approval by the delegates, was incorporated into the final document with only minor changes. It sought to reconcile differing state and federal interests, provide a degree of popular participation in the election, give the less populous states some additional leverage in the process by providing "senatorial" electors, preserve the presidency as independent of Congress, and generally insulate the election process from political manipulation. The original method of electing the President and Vice President, however, proved unworkable, and was replaced by the 12th Amendment, ratified in 1804. Under the original system, each elector cast two votes for President (for different candidates), and no vote for Vice President. The votes were counted; the candidate receiving the most, provided it was a majority of the number of electors, was elected President, and the runner-up became Vice President. The 12th Amendment replaced this system with separate ballots for President and Vice President, with electors casting a single vote for each office. As with so many constitutional provisions, the Electoral College system has never functioned as intended. The document prescribed only the basic elements of the system, leaving room for the process of perfecting. As the republic evolved, so did the Electoral College system. By the late nineteen century the following contemporary system was in place:

★ *Allocation of Electors and Electoral Votes*
★ *Popular Election of Electors*
★ *The Electors: Ratifying the Voters' Choice*
★ *Nominating Elector-Candidates: Diverse State Procedures*
★ *Joint Tickets: One Vote for President and Vice President*
★ *General Election Day, The Electors Convene, Congress Counts and Certifies the Vote*

(See "Appendix A – The Electoral College" for more information on the 12th Amendment, state electoral allocations, the U.S. Code, and to follow your candidate's success on an election night.)

Sources: PBS NOW (The Bureau of Labor Statistics; Economic Research Service, U.S. Department of Agriculture; "The State of Working American 2002-03," The Economic Policy Institute; The World Bank; THE ECONOMIST), the U.S. General Accountability Office, Congressional Budget Office, U.S. National Archives and Records Administration

THE ARTIST

Winds dance across the heavens
In perfect rhythm like feathers
That whirl, swirl, curtsey and bow
On the canvas of the sky.

The brushstroke of the special head
Paints the sky of blue with red;
Engraves the life of chosen solemn
And seals the soul with eternal power.

Every glance of hope draws near
With opened eyes to peer
The One who fills the mind with treasure
In a sanctuary of peace unmeasured.

Ever present to reveal
To the heart that makes appeal
To the Artist who ever frames
The canvas of the sky.

Chapter 5

OUR COMPANION IN DEMOCRACY

"The very word "secrecy" is repugnant in a free and open society; and we are as a people inherently and historically opposed to secret societies, to secret oaths and to secret proceedings. We decided long ago that the dangers of excessive and unwarranted concealment of pertinent facts far outweighed the dangers which are cited to justify it. Even today, there is little value in opposing the threat of a closed society by imitating its arbitrary restrictions. Even today, there is little value in ensuring the survival of our nation if our traditions do not survive with it. And there is a very grave danger that an announced need for increased security will be seized upon by those anxious to expand its meaning to the very limits of official censorship and concealment. That I do not intend to permit to the extent that it is in my control."
President John F. Kennedy – Address before the American Newspaper Publishers Association, April 27, 1961

Our Companion in Democracy

When most of us hear the word, "companion," we think of someone who is with us at all times, if not physically, certainly mentally. Our Constitution (see Appendix B) has been the protective canopy and constant companion of all American citizens since the beginning of our republic, a form of government in which people freely and equally participate in a majority-rule decision-making process to elect representatives to exercise power for them both at home and abroad. The first seven articles of the Constitution outline our form of government and the role of the legislative, executive, and judicial branches of power. Amendments 1 thru 10, called the Bill of Rights insures our liberty and freedom of choice. Amendments 11 thru 27 reflect changes made to the Constitution from February 7, 1795 to May 7, 1992.

In two hundred thirty-three years, we've only made 16 changes to our Constitution. One was to abolish slavery, another to give women the right to vote, and still another to limit the term of President of the United States.

The Spirit of Liberty

Like most of you, our family has this adorable canine whose name is Teddy. I can see the conceptual evidence of liberty in him — once free, always free. We brought him home a few days after his birth, so he only knows one way of life — being home with his family, unconstrained, with full authority over his dwelling — he thinks he runs the place. He attempts to tell us who can visit, when he wants to eat, when he wants to cruise the neighborhood, when he wants to go for a ride and return home — which is hardly ever, unless he's very tired—as though we don't have a clue as to how to meet his needs or choose our friends. This pooch and I have had many battles of the wits, because he doesn't understand who's in charge. He thinks he is; I know that I am. If I try to measure that in any way, he doesn't accept it. He rebels as a teenager on restriction. And when he thinks everything is back to normal, he celebrates by running around the house from room to room in a circular pattern — I, of course, must be stationed somewhere along the path. There he celebrates, running as fast as he can until he's exhausted.

Then he stops, sits in front of me, looks up with "I love you" eyes and the most serene of faces to be had in all of doggie-world, and he goes back to the standard behavior of liberty. If such freedom prevails in animals, how much more does it prevail in human beings?

Loss of liberty is not accepted by anyone who has lived in freedom. Throughout the generations, citizens of our great land have sacrificed, given earthly possessions, fought, and died that we as a people might remain free — we accept nothing less in the face of all odds, it's in the American DNA. "Give me liberty or give me death"—a quote attributed to Patrick Henry as he spoke to the Virginia House of Burgess on March 23, 1775, in an effort to convince them to pass a resolution to deliver troops to the Revolutionary War, as Thomas Jefferson and George Washington looked on—is truly the American way, no doubt.

As twenty-first century Americans, most of us have not even thought about life without liberty in this country. We hold it in the essence of our being unconsciously. It makes us who we are — free in mind and spirit. Regardless of external pressures, our hearts forbid us from succumbing to life without liberty — we are unable to grasp the concept, though we hear reports of it daily from around the world. It's a false reality to us; our spirit automatically rejects the thought. We forget that the parchment on which our Constitution is printed began with a clean slate and grew word by word. We forget sometimes that the freedom we enjoy in this country came at the great price of human sacrifice. Consequently, in honor of our heritage, each successive generation becomes the guardian of the evidentiary truths *"...that all Men are created equal, that they are endowed, by their Creator, with certain unalienable Rights, that among these are Life, Liberty, and the Pursuit of Happiness. — That to secure these Rights, Governments are instituted among Men, deriving their just Powers from the Consent of the Governed, that whenever any Form of Government becomes destructive of these Ends, it is the Right of the People to alter or to abolish it, and to institute new Government, laying its Foundation on such Principles, and organizing its Powers in such Form, as to them shall seem most likely to effect their Safety and Happiness. Prudence indeed, will dictate that Governments long established, should not be changed for light and transient Causes; and accordingly all Experience hath shown, that Mankind [is] more disposed to suffer, while Evils are sufferable, than to right themselves by abolishing the Forms to which they are accustomed. But when a long Train of Abuses and Usurpations, pursuing invariably the same Object, evinces a Design to reduce them under absolute Despotism, it is their Right, it is their Duty, to throw off such Government, and to provide new Guards for their future Security."* Each successive generation is charged with the responsibility of safeguarding the Republic with the Constitutional sword, to maintain liberty and prosperity for our children, our grandchildren, and their children.

The Future American

But if one doesn't know that his liberties are being taken away, there will be no response; no resistance at all. He will continue to live in blissful ignorance. Democracy is not for the ignorant, nor is it for the faint-hearted. If we, as citizens, cease to be active in our democratic governance, our democracy will exist in name only. I heard a phrase back in the 1980s that I didn't give credence to — "the dumbing down of America." When I first heard it, I immediately thought about adults citizens. How does one extract knowledge from adults after they have internalized it. Yet I am beginning to see the evidence of that very thing in the children.

I have heard quite a few comments about our public school system's inability to "control" children. But it has not been given parental control, nor does it seek it. What an educator desires more than anything is a parental partnership. Parents are their children's first teacher. Therefore, I would suggest that parents judge themselves introspectively before judging the system. Here's a basic test for your child before entering the public or private school system: *What's the name of our country? What's the name of our state?* Every child should know these answers before crossing the threshold of any formal classroom; and certainly by third grade. It's hopeful to think that they might know the name of the continent on which they live. Some of you might be saying, "surely you jest." But I could take you to fourth and fifth grade classrooms today and demonstrate to you that ninety-five percent of the students cannot answer these questions correctly; two percent might guess correctly, but are unsure of their answers. Yet, the rudimentary statistic of the illiteracy of our children seems to be overlooked in assessing the strength of our democracy. These children won't possess the basic skills to enter a junior college, nor will they be able to pass the National High School Proficiency Exam. Illiteracy has become an ever-present threat to our national security.

Illiterate children will become illiterate adults; subject to more emotional decisions and political brainwashing than any American with a basic education. They will not have the opportunity of attending university later on in life should maturity offer an epiphany. And illiteracy among people who thirst for liberty and prosperity creates an explosive social dilemma; it is difficult to reason with ignorance. It can't link education to democracy. Consequently, our democracy could become unsustainable.

I face the daily challenge of how to get kids to learn, as they deny the value of math, language arts, and science on a basic level. Some will even tell you that it is irrelevant to their lives and they choose not to participate; they attend school only because they are made to do so. Some of these kids would not hesitate to curse you, me or the Pope, if they didn't like what we said and thought they could get away with it. And they would be perfectly willing to throw in a good measure of personal criticism to boot, to demonstrate – according to their understanding – how free they really are. They equate freedom of speech with ultimate liberty and power. But remember, they have had high-ranking members of our government model such behavior for them. Of course we know that a human being is ever learning and adapting to his environment, so learning has to be channeled to socioeconomic prosperity.

Constitutional Change Since 2001–The USA PATRIOT Act

In the dead of night on October 23, 2001, as most of us slept in preparation of the dawning of a new day, Congress passed the USA PATRIOT Act – Public Law 107-56 (Uniting and Strengthening America by Providing Appropriate Tools Required to Intercept and Obstruct Terrorism Act of 2001) which assaults the fourth amendment of the Constitution. With little knowledge of its content and/or not having read the bill at all, the 107th Congress of the United States of America voted for a bill that changed eleven existing U.S. Statutes and virtually nullified our Fourth Amendment rights in a matter of minutes with little debate or forethought; thereby shifting and minimizing the principles of our democracy which is the anchor of our peace.

The "PATRIOT" Act, as it is commonly known, was signed into law on October 26, 2001 by the forty-third President of the United States of America despite his oath to the American people on January 20, 2001, in accordance with Article II, Section I of the Constitution: *"I do solemnly swear that I will **faithfully** execute the office of President of the United States, and will to the best of my ability, **preserve, protect and defend the Constitution** of the United States, so help me God."*

The Act expanded the authority of US law enforcement agencies for the stated purpose of fighting terrorism in the United States and abroad. Among its provisions, the Act increased the ability of law enforcement agencies to search telephone logs, e-mail communications, medical, financial and other records; eased restrictions on foreign intelligence gathering within the United States; *expanded the Secretary of the Treasury's authority to regulate financial transactions [see Chapter 2, Winds of Change, The Whirlwind]*, particularly those involving foreign individuals and entities; and enhanced the discretion of law enforcement and immigration authorities in detaining and deporting immigrants suspected of terrorism-related acts. The Act also expanded the definition of terrorism to include "domestic terrorism," thus enlarging the number of activities to which the PATRIOT Act's expanded law enforcement powers could be applied.

Although the Act was passed by wide margins in both houses of Congress, it has been criticized from its inception for weakening protections of civil liberties. In particular, opponents of the law have criticized its authorization of indefinite detentions of immigrants; sneak-and-peek searches through which law enforcement officers search a home or business without the owner's or the occupant's permission or knowledge; the expanded use of "National Security Letters," which allow the FBI to search telephone, email and financial records without a court order; and the expanded access of law enforcement agencies to business records, including library and financial records. Since its passage, several legal challenges have been brought against the Act, and *Federal courts have ruled that a number of provisions are unconstitutional.* Many of the Act's provisions were to sunset beginning December 31, 2005, approximately four years after its passage. In the months preceding the sunset date, supporters of the Act pushed to make its sunsetting provisions permanent, while critics sought to revise various sections to enhance civil liberty protections. In July 2005, the U.S. Senate passed a reauthorization bill with substantial changes to several sections of the Act, while the House reauthorization bill kept most of the Act's original language. The two bills were then reconciled in a conference committee that was criticized by Senators from both parties for ignoring civil liberty concerns. The bill, which removed most of the changes from the Senate version, passed Congress on March 2, 2006 and was signed into law by the President on March 9, 2006.

Acts Amended by the USA PATRIOT Act Public Law 107-56
Electronic Communications Privacy Act (ECPA)
Computer Fraud and Abuse Act
Foreign Intelligence Surveillance Act (FISA)
Family Educational Rights and Privacy Act
Money Laundering Control Act
Bank Secrecy Act (BSA)
Right to Financial Privacy Act
Fair Credit Reporting Act
Immigration and Nationality Act
Victims of Crime Act
Telemarketing and Consumer Fraud and Abuse Prevention Act

The sweeping changes made by our government as to how foreign and domestic intelligence information is gathered and used, how domestic investigations are conducted, and how virtually every activity of government is cloaked in national security, has caused its citizens to pause, question, and ultimately to make a change in leadership — a change in direction. The obvious disconnect between the leadership of this country and its citizens brought about a call for accountability.

USA PATRIOT Act Titles
Title I – Miscellaneous Provisions
Title II – Surveillance Procedures
Title III – Anti-Money Laundering to Prevent Terrorism
Title IV – Border Security
Title V – Terrorism Investigation
Title VI – Victims and Families of Victims of Terrorism
Title VII – Information Sharing for Infrastructure Protection
Title VIII – Terrorism Criminal Law
Title IX – Improved Intelligence
Title X – Miscellaneous Provisions

The First Legislative Challenge to the USA PATRIOT Act

The first challenge to the USA PATRIOT Act came a year and nine month later in the form of an amendment to an appropriations bill. I cite it because it was the beginning of the long road back to reclaiming our liberties under the Bill of Rights. It gave rise to other challenges of rectification. Almost eight years later, we still have much work to do, though we have scores of Acts designed to reinstate our rights under the Constitution. So far, Congress has not tried the direct approach of repealing the Act. Prior to the

USA PATRIOT Act, we had sufficient laws on the books to fight terrorism. The Act had little to do with terrorism and much to do with Executive Power. The power grab was so extensive that it conjured up the waning days of the Nixon Administration when the prevailing belief was that the President of the United States should have supreme authority—kingly authority. But remember two things: first, terrorism is not new, we've faced it for decades; second, the President of the United States swears or affirms that he will faithfully preserve, protect and defend the Constitution of the United States of America—not nullify it in pursuit of an executive power grab. Perhaps we should consider asking a question of every President-elect before swearing him in — Do you believe in the Constitution and the Bill of Rights?

History once again has shown us how easy it is to make a mistake; yet how difficult it is and how long it takes to rectify it. It does appear that Congress is now thinking in more personal terms however. They are no longer looking outward; they are looking inward to themselves and their families. They consider the USA PATRIOT Act to be a personal affront and violation of their civil liberties — they are citizens too.

Now, perhaps, we will all ask ourselves the question — How is it possible to write and pass such sweeping legislation in 45 days with such a clear target of power transference? For that answer, we would have to look to the Justice Department, the reported author of the bill. It does appear that the bill had been drafted prior to the events of 9/11 and only awaited a moment of injection. That time came when Congress and the country were paralyzed with fear and confusion after the events of 9/11. The administration supplanted the bill drafted by the House and Senate with the bill we now know as the USA PATRIOT Act. The Act that was passed in the dead of night was not a 45-day planning document; it was a document that was years in the making to subjugate the Legislative and Judicial branches of government to the Executive branch, thereby tilting the balance of power, and taking us back to what Richard Nixon said, "when the President does it, that means that it's not illegal." If anyone believes that statement, I dare say that they do not believe in the Constitution. They choose to make it up as they go.

As you read the following excerpts, notice how "hoodwinked" these members of Congress felt. Their sentiments echoed the feelings of a large percentage of Congressional members.

It is time for the citizens of this country to step forth in a responsible and knowledgeable manner to manage and to protect our democracy from enemies within. It is possible for the USA PATRIOT Act to pale in light of future legislation and power grabs. Once a bill becomes law, we can do nothing but abide by it until we repeal it or modify it, which could take years. Once a law has been passed, its supporters are not concerned with your afterthoughts and feelings. Even if you were 100-million strong in your dissent, it would not matter. It would be considered only as your opinion. The law is on their side — as we commonly say — until you change it, which is not an easy task. Opposition will meet you at every turn.

I commend those members of Congress who did not roll over for this vote or the vote for aggression against Iraq.

Consider for a moment — what better way is there to control a person in opposition to you than to remind him that you have ultimate power to know everything about him at will, including power to enter his home or office secretly at will. It would be difficult for anyone to represent their constituency or to do what they know in their heart is right, when they are in fear of their family being violated or ruined. A majority of the Congress of the United States of America has lived in such fear.

The Congressional record of July 22, 2003 (House pages H7284-H7311) records an amendment offered by the Idaho Congressman as they debated the Departments [of] Commerce, Justice, And State, The Judiciary and Related Agencies Appropriations Act (correct wording and spelling) for fiscal year 2004 bill, which was the first real legislative challenge to the USA PATRIOT Act since it was passed. It was an attempt to stop the flow of money for sneak-and-peek operations.

The approach was very unexpected and unassuming, so much so that the vote was taken by question. The Chairman pro tempore announced that the "noes" had it, after some representatives said the appropriations bill was not the place to debate the USA PATRIOT Act — Debate! There had never been a debate on the bill. Only when the Congressman from

Idaho demanded a recorded vote did the Chairman pro tempore state, "Pursuant to clause 6 of rule XVIII, further proceedings on the amendment offered by the gentleman from Idaho will be postponed. Upon resumption, five minutes were allotted for the recorded vote by electronic device. The results were: ayes 309, noes 118, not voting 7 (Roll No. 408). So the amendment was agreed to and the result of the vote was announced and recorded.

Here's how the gentleman from Idaho began:

"Mr. Chairman, over 200 years ago when the formulation of this great republic was being put together, John Stuart Mill sat down and probably put the essence of this Government in writing better than anyone could. 'A people,' he said, 'may prefer a free government, but if from indolence or carelessness, or cowardice, or want of public spirit, they are unequal to the exertions necessary for preserving it; if they will not fight for it when it is directly attacked; if by momentary discouragement or temporary panic, they can be deluded by the artifices used to cheat them out of it; or if in a fit of enthusiasm for an individual, they can be induced to lay their liberties at the feet of even a great man, in all these cases, they are more or less unfit for liberty. And though it may have been to their good to have had it for a short time, they are unlikely long to enjoy it.'

"The United States PATRIOT Act was well intentioned, Mr. Chairman, especially during a time of uncertainty and panic. However, now we have had a chance to step back and examine it objectively. The legislation deserves serious reevaluation. While I agree with some of the new powers granted to the Federal law enforcement authorities that may be, and I stress "may be," necessary, many more are unjustified and are dangerously undermining our civil liberties.

"We have the opportunity to revisit these sections of the USA PATRIOT Act and to correct these mistakes from those first frenzied weeks after September 11, 2001. One provision, section 213, allows delayed notification of the execution of a search warrant. It authorizes no-knock searches of private

residences, our homes, either physically or electronically. By putting off notice of the execution of a warrant, even delaying it indefinitely, section 213 of the USA PATRIOT Act prevents people, or even their attorneys, from reviewing the warrant for correctness in legalities. These "sneak-and-peek" searches give the government the power to repeatedly search a private residence without informing the residents that he or she is the target of an investigation. Not only does this provision allow the seizure of personal property and business records without notification, but it also opens the door to nationwide search warrants and allows the CIA and the NSA to operate domestically.

"American citizens, whom the government has pledged to protect from terrorist activities, now find themselves the victims of the very weapon designed to uproot their enemies.

"It is in defense of these freedoms that I offer this amendment today to the Departments of Commerce, Justice, And State, The Judiciary, and Related Agencies Appropriations Act for fiscal year 2004 bill. This amendment would prohibit any funds from being used to carry out section 213 of the USA PATRIOT Act as signed into law on October 26, 2001.

"Through the passage of this amendment, Americans would have reinstated a different kind of security, one giving them renewed confidence in their government in tirelessly protecting their individual freedom from unjustified and unnecessary intrusion.

"Being secure at the expense of our freedom is no real security. Like many Idahoans who have come to me with their concerns about the USA PATRIOT Act and in passionate defense of their freedoms, we must continue to examine our actions to correct our mistakes to guard against the apathy or the indifference to safeguarding our liberties.

"To these Federal agencies, it is a house, it is a building, it is a business; but to us, Mr. Chairman, it is our homes, and there is nothing more sacred than homes in America because it is the foundation on which we build our families. It is the arsenal in which the virtue and hope of every generation resides, and it is the fundamental primer of any free people.

"We can, with the adoption of this first alteration to the PATRIOT Act, begin the reclamation of our title of a Nation as a people fit for liberty."

This gets more interesting as the Congressman from Ohio speaks followed by the Congressman from Texas who mentions USA PATRIOT Act 2.

The Congressman from Ohio:
"Mr. Chairman, I rise in support of the amendment of the gentleman from Idaho and am proud to join with him and the gentleman from Texas in cosponsoring it.

"It has been said that Members may not know the impact of this amendment. This amendment seeks to deny funds which would be used to carry out section 213 of the PATRIOT Act, which allows for so-called sneak-and-peek searches. It has been said that Members may not know the impact of this amendment.

"Let it be stated here that when this House passed the PATRIOT Act, most Members, as diligent as they are, nevertheless did not have access to see the very bill they were voting on, that, in fact, we were not voting on at 6 o'clock in the afternoon, we were voting on in the dead of night. In an atmosphere of apprehension and confusion and chaos, the Congress passed the PATRIOT Act, which has led to a destructive undermining of numerous provisions of the Bill of Rights. The amendment of the gentleman from Idaho is the first opportunity that we have had in this House to correct something that has been a grievous assault on our Constitution.

"We are offering this amendment to restore integrity to the fourth amendment by denying funds from being used to carry out section 213 of the PATRIOT Act, that section which allows for the sneak-and-peek searches. Common law has always required that the government cannot enter your property without you and must, therefore, give you notice before it executes a search. That knock-and-announce principle has long been recognized as having been codified in the fourth amendment to the United States Constitution.

"The PATRIOT Act, however, unconstitutionally amended the Federal Rules of Criminal Procedure to allow the government to conduct searches without notifying the subjects, at least until long after the search has been executed. Let me tell you what this means. This means that under this law, this law which was passed by the Congress, the government can enter your house, your apartment, your office, with a search warrant, when the occupants are away, search through your property, take photographs , and, in some cases, even seize property and not tell you until later. This effectively guts the fourth amendment protections.

"In response to questioning by the Committee on the Judiciary, the Department of Justice makes it clear that the fourth amendment is already in peril as a result of section 213. Listen to this box score of their activity: the Department of Justice reports that sneak-and-peek searches have been used on 47 separate occasions and that the period of delay for notification has been sought almost 250 times. I would suggest to you just once constitutes a threat to our Bill of Rights.

"These secret warrants have been used in Federal criminal investigations not necessarily related to terrorist investigations.

"Notice with a warrant is a crucial check on the government's power. It forces authorities to operate in the open. It allows citizens to protect their constitutional rights. For example, it allows subjects to point out problems with a warrant, for instance, if the police are at the wrong address or if the scope of the warrant is obviously being exceeded.

"If, for example, authorities in search of a stolen car go into someone's apartment and rifle through a dresser drawer, search warrants rightly contain limits on what may be searched. But when the searching authorities have utter control and discretion over a search, American citizens are unable to defend their constitutional rights.

*"This assault on the fourth amendment is wrong, it is unconstitutional, it is un-American; and it must stop. I would ask my colleagues to recall the oft-invoked words of a great American, Benjamin Franklin, who once said: '**Those who***

would give up essential liberty to purchase a little temporary safety, deserve neither liberty nor safety.'

"I say today that section 213 of the PATRIOT Act destroys an essential liberty. The Otter amendment restores it."

The Congressman from Texas:

"Mr. Chairman, I rise in support of this amendment. I want to compliment the gentleman from Idaho for bringing this to the floor.

"When the PATRIOT Act was passed, it was in the passions following 9/11, and that bill should have never been passed. It was brought up carelessly, casually, in a rapid manner. The bill that had been discussed in the Committee on the Judiciary was removed during the night before we voted. The full text of this bill was very difficult to find. I am convinced that very few Members were able to review this bill before voting. That bill should have never passed. We certainly should continue to maintain the sunset provisions. But that is a long way off, and we should be starting to reform and improve this particular piece of legislation. This is our first chance to do so.

"I have had many Members in the Congress come to me and on the quiet admit to me that voting for the PATRIOT Act was the worst bill and the worst vote they have ever cast; and this will give them an opportunity to change it, although this is very narrow. It is too bad we could not have made this more broad, and it is too bad we are not going to get to vote on the amendment of the gentleman from Vermont to make sure that without the proper search warrant that the Federal Government would not have access to the library records.

"But there is no need ever to sacrifice liberty in order to maintain security. I feel more secure when I have more liberty; and that is why I am a defender of liberty, because my main concern is security, both in the physical sense as well as the financial sense. I think the freer the country is, the more prosperous we are; and the freer the country is, the more secure we are.

"Yet it was in the atmosphere of post-9/11 that so many were anxious to respond to what they perceived as demands .

by the people to do something. But just to do something, if you are doing the wrong thing, what good is it? You are doing more harm.

"But my main argument is that there is never a need to sacrifice liberty in order to protect liberty, and that is why we would like to at least remove this clause that allows sneak-and-peek search warrants.

"It took hundreds, if not thousands, of years to develop this concept that governments do not have the right to break in without the proper procedures and without probable cause. And yet we threw that out the window in this post-9/11 atmosphere, and we gave away a lot.

"Yes, we talked about numbers of dozens of examples of times when our government has used this and abused it. But that is only the beginning. It is the principle. If they had only done it once, if they had not done it, this should still be taken care of, because as time goes on, and if we adapt to this process, it will be used more and more, and that is throwing away a big and important chunk of our Constitution, the fourth amendment.

"Not only should we do whatever we can to reform that legislation, but we already know that there is a **PATRIOT Act No. 2**. *It has not been given to us, the Congress; but the administration has it for the future. It is available, but we have only gotten to see it from the Internet.*

"In that bill there is a proposal that **the government can strip us of our citizenship**, *and then anybody then stripped of their citizenship could be put into the situation that many foreigners find themselves in at Guantanamo before the military tribunals.*

"I see this as a very, very important issue, if anybody cares about liberty, if anybody cares about personal freedom and the rule of law and the need for probable cause before our government comes barging into our houses. It has been **under the guise of drug laws** *that have in the past instituted many of these abuses, but this is much worse. This has been put into an explicit piece of legislation, and* **the American**

people and this Congress ought to become very alert to this and realize how serious the PATRIOT Act is.

"I hope that the Congress and our colleagues here will support this amendment. It is very necessary, and it will be voting for the Constitution; and it will be voting for liberty if we support this Amendment."

Provisions in the USA PATRIOT Act Are Illegal

In September of 2007, a federal judge in Oregon ruled that parts of the USA PATRIOT Act were unconstitutional, which came as no surprise to anyone who had ever read it. The judge cited federal surveillance and searches of American citizens without demonstrating probable cause. The judge was quoted, "For over 200 years, this nation has adhered to the rule of law — with unparalleled success." The Judge's opinion said, "in finding violations of the Fourth Amendment prohibitions against unreasonable search and seizure — 'A shift to a nation based on extra constitutional authority is prohibited, as well as ill advised.'"

The ruling by Judge Anne L. Aiken of Federal District Court in Portland was in the case of Brandon Mayfield, a lawyer in Portland who was arrested and jailed after the FBI mistakenly linked him to the Madrid train bombings in March 2004.

Reauthorizations of the USA PATRIOT Act

Many bills have been introduced in both houses of Congress to correct the unconstitutionality of the USA PATRIOT Act since the appropriations bill in 2003. Most of them have failed. A bill that virtually nullified the Writ of Habeas Corpus, however, was passed (see the next section of this chapter).

The PATRIOT Act has already been reauthorized by two bills. The first, the *USA PATRIOT and Terrorism Prevention Reauthorization Act of 2005*, was passed by both houses of Congress in July 2005. The second, the *USA PATRIOT Act Additional Reauthorizing Amendments Act of 2006*, amended the first and was passed in February 2006. Still, the battle to repeal the act goes on.

Writ of Habeas Corpus Suspended on U.S. Soil

Habeas Corpus is another broad protective umbrella of democracy that hovers over citizens and non-citizens of this nation. It is a fundamental right provided to us by our Constitution. A Writ of Habeas Corpus orders a detained person into court to determine if their detention is lawful. It is a protection against unwarranted detention on American soil for any length of time. The Military Commissions Act of 2006, however, suspended that right to non-citizens, even though the Constitution is explicit in Article 1, Section 9, Clause 2, where it states: "The privilege of the Writ of Habeas Corpus shall not be suspended, unless when in Cases of Rebellion or Invasion the public Safety may require it." Neither of these circumstances exist today.

Supreme Court decisions have made it clear that habeas corpus is available to citizens and non-citizens alike in the United States and its territories. There are millions of legal residents in this country who would not receive the privilege of Habeas Corpus under the Military Commissions Act. And don't forget the provision of the USA PATRIOT Act 2 that would allow the government to strip American citizens of their citizenship—if stripped of your citizenship, you too could be held indefinitely without due process of law. Hasn't one American citizen already been held by our government without due process? One is too many; one signifies a beginning.

The Habeas Corpus Restoration Act was introduced in the 109th and the 110th Congress in an attempt to restore constitutional order. But why did Congress pass the bill in 2006? Our legislative branch of government seems to have developed a pattern of passing bills that are unconstitutional; then introducing a number of bills later to correct the problem, which never gets corrected fully. This kind of behavior is irrational.

Has Congress failed in its responsibility to check the Executive branch as provided by the Constitution? Can we maintain a healthy democracy if our legislative branch of government surrenders its power to the executive branch?

The Congressional Record of January 4, 2007 (Senate Pages S179-S181) records the comments of Democratic Senator Patrick

Leahy, a co-sponsor of the Habeas Corpus Restoration Act of 2007, as he makes his case once again for restoration of Habeas Corpus.

"We have eliminated basic legal and human rights for the 12 million lawful permanent residents who live and work among us... and pay taxes in America... This new law [Military Commissions Act of 2006] means that any of these people can be detained, forever, without any ability to challenge their detention [in] Federal court—or anywhere else—simply on the Government's say-so, ... to say nothing of the millions of other legal immigrants and visitors who we welcome to our shores each year. We have removed a vital check that our legal system provides against the government arbitrarily detaining people for life without charge. We may well have also made many of our remaining limits against torture and cruel and inhuman treatment obsolete because they are unenforceable. We have removed the mechanism the Constitution provides to check government overreaching and lawlessness. This is wrong. It is unconstitutional. It is un-American... Giving Government such raw, unfettered power as this law does should concern every American... Some Senators uneasy about the Military Commissions Act's disastrous habeas provision took solace in the thought that it would be struck down by the courts. Instead, the first court to consider that provision, a federal court in the District of Columbia, upheld the provision. We should not outsource our moral, legal and constitutional responsibility to the courts. Congress must be accountable for its actions and we should act to right this wrong... It is from strength that America should defend our values and our Constitution. It takes commitment to those values to demand accountability from the Government. In standing up for American values and security, I will keep working on this issue until we restore the checks and balances that are fundamental to preserving the liberties that define us as a nation. We can ensure our security without giving up our liberty."

The bill, *S185*, passed the United States Senate Judiciary Committee on Thursday, June 7, 2007, on a vote of 11 to 8, without debate. A version of the bill has been introduced in the House of Representatives. The Act was attached, as an amendment, to a Defense bill. Debate began on the bill on September 17, 2007.

On June 29, 2007, the Supreme Court agreed to hear outstanding habeas corpus, opening up the possibility that they might overturn some or all of the Military Commissions Act.

Chapter 6

WHO CONTROLS AMERICA?

"These capitalists generally act harmoniously and in concert to fleece the people, and now that they have got into a quarrel with themselves, we are called upon to appropriate the people's money to settle the quarrel." President Abraham Lincoln - Speech to Illinois Legislature, January 1837

America's Economic Shift

Bill Moyers, in his ***PBS Now: America and Jobs*** highlighted the Department of Labor's estimate of jobs to be shipped overseas through 2015. The major focus thus far has been manufacturing jobs which are now minuscule in the United States; we have lost over millions to date. In order of progression, there is now a shift to white collar jobs in our economy. Here's an excerpt from the show's transcript of May 7, 2004: "The numbers are startling: 3.3 million jobs in less than 15 years. That's the number of U.S. jobs expected to be lost overseas by 2015 according to a recent report by Forrester Research. [That's in addition to downsizing caused by the economic recession in our country today — over 14.5 million jobs lost in 2008 and 2009 so far. Corporations are now using the recession as a covering to ship even more jobs overseas than estimated by the Department of Labor.] But the sheer size of the exodus isn't what's worrying analysts the most — it's the type of jobs. Some critics are worried that this time it's the corporate main office [that] is getting ready to shut down and head out of the country, packing up cubicles and all. As reported on NOW, a new wave of jobs are leaving U.S. shores: software development, customer service, accounting, back-office support, product development and other white collar endeavors. And it's not just technology jobs that have ended up in India. According to Deloitte Consulting, 2 million jobs will move from the United States and Europe to cheaper locations in the financial services business alone. The exodus of service jobs across all industries could be as high as 4 million. It forecasts that *three-quarters* of leading financial institutions and investment banks will allocate tasks to Third World countries in the next five years and that India will be at the top of the list. Charles Schwab recently moved part of its information technology division to a contractor in Bangalore, India. AOL already has a large presence in India. American Express and British Airways have ramped up their employment in the country during the past year as well. ***FRONTLINE WORLD*** reported last year that over *half of Fortune 500 companies* have moved jobs offshore, including famous names from many fields: Oracle, Dell, HSBC, Delta Air Lines, Novartis, J.P. Morgan Chase, Hewlett-Packard, American Express, and British Airways. More are expected to follow. According to the U.S. Bureau of Labor Statistics, job separations due to overseas relocation are at their highest level since 1995."

Projected Number of U.S. Jobs to Move Overseas by 2015	
Classification of Job	**Projected Number**
Management	288,281
Business	348,028
Computer	472,632
Architecture	184,347
Life Sciences	36,770
Legal	76,642
Art Design	29,564
Sales	226,564
Office	1,659,310

Source: Forrester Research, Inc. November, 2002

The transcript went on to cite "the U.S. Bureau of Labor and the International Labour Organization statistics on salary comparisons as reported by the International Labour Organization and the Paàras Group, 2002."

"U.S. workers are used to seeing manufacturing jobs lost to much lower wages; according to the Bureau of Labor Statistics and the International Labour Organization. U.S. manufacturing average hourly compensation is $21.33, in Mexico: $2.38 and in China less than one dollar an hour. It should be noted that while salaries are much lower in India and other BPO hot spots that does not mean that the companies are providing inadequate compensation — the cost of living is significantly lower in India. However, as both *THE TIMES OF INDIA* and *THE ECONOMIST* have recently noted, some jobs are in turn leaving India for even cheaper locales. And where are those jobs going? Some are heading to China, Russia, Vietnam, the Philippines, Malaysia, and the Czech Republic. In short, they are moving toward cheaper labor costs than those in India."

The Connection to Hope

Job Title	Salary in United States	Salary in India
Software	$66,100	$10,000
Mechanical Engineer	$55,600	$ 5,900
IT Manager	$55,000	$ 8,500
Accountant	$41,000	$ 5,000
Financial Operations	$37,625	$ 5,500

Salary Comparisons: PBS NOW / Source: Paàras Group, 2002 International Labour Organization

American companies tend to lower wages and increase the cost of their products to Americans — the double whammy in the marketplace. One can see clearly that corporations and big business, as a common practice in this country, do not adhere to responsibility, fairness and decency in the workplace. At one desk you may have a worker with healthcare benefits and life insurance, while at the next desk is a worker without healthcare benefits and life insurance — both are doing the same job. David Cay Johnston, a Pulitzer prize winning financial reporter with the New York Times in an interview with David Brancaccio of **_PBS NOW Inequality of Wage Earners in America_** stated a few amazing facts. Firstly he said, "We've been doing very well for a couple of decades now, with only two little blips along the way. The problem is that the benefits of all the economic growth are flowing to the top, and especially to the very top. And here's a telling number about that. If you take the number of taxpayers and then apply how many people live in each household of a tax unit, essentially, the top 300,000 Americans— that's one tenth of one percent—have almost as much income as the bottom 150 million Americans, about 62 million taxpayers. "And that these numbers are just incredible, in terms of how much income there is here, at the very top. The top tenth of one percent have their largest share of income since 1928 and 1929, just before the Great Depression." Secondly he stated, "Well, very recently, there has been wage growth. So that's true. But even the President [Bush 43], in January of this year, said that inequality has been going on for years in this country — about 20 years, I believe he said — and it's a growing and serious concern." He continued, "I saw, not too long ago, that—income for Americans went up twelve and a half percent in the most recent year from which we have statistics. But it turned out, if you factored out the top five percent of rich people in America from those statistics, it only went up 1.5 percent. That's right. And in several recent years—incomes actually fell. That's something we haven't had before. People made less money in 2001 than in 2000, less money in 2002 than in 2001, less in 2003. And during that period, there were people who had gains. But they were entirely at the top. The gains were not going on at the bottom. What have we been doing for the last 25 years or so, in this country? "Let's have less regulation." That is, fewer limits on the things that business wants to do. "Let's lower the taxes on people who are at the very top." And the net effect is, that it's been government policy now, for a good, long time, to make the wealthy in America wealthier." Thirdly he concluded, "But in many cases, what we're seeing is markets that are rigged. For example, you go to negotiate, if you're a worker, for your pay. Well, we've—effectively reduced unions to being insignificant in the private sector, in this country, which has reduced the bargaining power of workers to collectively ask for their pay. On the other hand, if you're a CEO, your pay is set in the market that – that is designed to pay the highest possible wage – not the lowest possible wage – to keep you. And they operate under a set of rules that the government sets, on how we determine pay.

"Well—workers—who are in the wage system, are very effectively taxed by the government. The government has got a very effective system. Your employer tells the government how much you make... So the government very effectively collects that money. And that's a very major portion of it. The tax system for very wealthy people doesn't require them to report all their income. Whereas, you and I, as wage earners, we have to report all our income."

Finally he concluded, "Yeah. And—but it's going to become crucial. When you see that American corporations are moving jobs and assets and intellectual property offshore just as fast as they can, that should be a signal that something is wrong. And that we need to fix it. But the solutions that are being proposed right now, principally, are, 'Well, just let us live tax free.' Or, 'Give us a rule that — we'll work it out. So we live close to tax free.'"

"Well, that doesn't work either. You do have to pay for having civilization. You know, you—somebody's got to provide the roads, the education. You can't have a wealthy society with people who are not well educated. I think enough people, now, are seeing that they've played by the rules. They've worked hard. And things aren't working out the way they heard, that they're beginning to say, 'Wait a minute.' And some people have said to themselves already, 'Well, I've been sold a bill of goods.' I think it's very clear that a growing number of people believe that the rules are not fair. They don't understand what happened. But I think there's a lot of hunger to find out about that."

You may view the entire interview on your public broadcasting station at ***www.pbs.org/now/shows/332/video.html***.

Does Money Still Talk?

Who controls America? According to President Lincoln's quote above, it seems as though we are dealing with the relatives of the idealists of his day. They asked to be bailed-out then, as they have asked and received now—to the sum of $700 billion plus... —without a report of expenditures or a thank-you. They didn't even bother to request the funds formally. The Secretary of the Treasury simply jotted an exorbitant amount on a piece of paper and handed it to a member of Congress, and got every penny requested within a relatively short amount of time. That's a huge measure of control!

You and I must fill out stacks of paperwork to receive the smallest amounts of money from our government, and only if offered. The recipients of the TARP funds are appalled that we would even ask how they spent the money; after all, they are private companies. It hasn't occurred to them that we might wonder, since the money seemingly hasn't been used as intended. To the citizens of this country, the money seems to have vanished without any visible impact on our depressed economy.

So who controls America? The question becomes more valid everyday as we see the way big business is treated versus the way the working-class is treated by members of our government. Homeowners are still begging for adequate help after nearly two years of asking. Most of us have not written huge campaign checks for members of Congress as big business has, so we are not likely to get the same treatment. That's why President Obama's decision to receive the majority of his campaign funds from the grassroots level was necessary to his being a President of all the people—it freed his decision-making. He did not take the oath of office with huge cords around his ankles. It has freed him to do what's right for us all, not just the wealthy.

I heard someone say once that if you are rich and want to become richer; do business with the government. I assumed, at the time, that they were referring solely to government contracts. But I have since learned that its not only contracts, but laws and tax policies that favor big business and the richest of the rich. The only prerequisite to receiving such favor is an Armani-clad representative stationed on K Street in Washington, D.C. with an attaché full of Franklins to dole out with a handshake. These reps are so competent and obliging that they'll minimize an elected official's workload by supplying a draft of the bill to be voted on by Congress.

Money still speaks loudly in our nation's capital. People with the greatest amounts of money control Washington; control our government; control America — oddly enough, they don't pay the bills. Until now, if you could manage to get to that elite status through desire, skill, hard work and a few other unmentionables, you too could obtain a measure of control.

Most people who are elected to public office are average people of average means who walk into the corridors of power lacking one thing – financial independence. And unless they have a strong moral foundation that has been tested by fire they could be facing a destructive path of public life without principles to guide their steps. Every decision could become one of the personal pocketbook with internal justification. A conscience of decency could be severed by corruption. Sound judgment could flee as viable and honorable avenues of financial freedom are ignored.

Who controls America? People with the most money; the least regard for our constitution; and the least moral conscience have ruled this country for many decades. Even when we think they are done for, they regroup within a decade or so and are operating in full force again – they vow to never quit in their pursuit of wealth and power. Should we quit in our pursuit of morality? Nevertheless, let's be objective as we look at other factors.

We have voted for representatives election after election, believing that they would abide by our Constitution in their service to us. Our ever-present thought is that we live in the best country in the world, and so we do — a republic of the people, by the people, and for the people; never to perish because we have the living documents to prove it.

However, have you ever factored in those who consider the federalists papers to be nothing more than words of dead men which are no longer valid to anyone but dreamers filled with ideas, but void of substance and power. It's about power. It has always been about the power. Money gives power — those with great fortunes stick together for the sake of power.

So what is power? Or better yet, what is their power source? I think it's the ability to control, influence, and persuade us to achieve their desired result — no holds barred.

As an American, it is difficult to believe that I'm being controlled in some way. To think that I could be influenced subliminally is unacceptable and deniable. On the other hand, persuasion is considered fair game, unless one uses spin to frame and narrow my scope. So let's look at persuasion a little closer.

The Power of Persuasion

Persuasion is the power that affects us the most because it affects our emotions and our judgment. This kind of power is used by politicians and corporations to get a desired result from us. It is a form of manipulation and indoctrination that is perpetuated on the masses to their detriment. You have heard the word "spin" used on many occasions, haven't you? Well, it's just a synonym for "lie." You have heard us bombarded with negatives for a desired result and then positives to cover the negatives. Sounds confusing; it's designed to be so. It takes diligence to sift through the maze of deception.

Our country is not designed to be ruled by the few, but the majority. When the majority does not participate in government, the few will control eagerly. So we can't blame them for our lack of diligence in governance. Didn't we stand by and allow this country to go to war from which many have gotten wealthy? Didn't we stand by and allow large corporations to lobby Congress for new bankruptcy laws which penalize people for becoming ill? Do we now allow millions of jobs to be shipped overseas with impunity? Have we been divided for the purpose of being conquered?

The power-mongers believe if we allow it to be done to us without objection, we deserve it—that's their code of validation. Meanwhile, by the millions, the working-class citizens are asking in the privacy of their homes, "What can *I* do?" My response is, "what we can't do individually, we can do together." Many of us may not be millionaires, but together, we can pool millions of dollars. In fact, the rich knows this well. As a common business practice, they have used our money to make money – interest free. President Franklin Roosevelt spoke of their use of this practice in 1932 in his speech at the Democratic National Convention in Philadelphia, Pennsylvania on June 27, 1936, which I outlined in my introduction, "Heart to Heart."

But they have become more skillful at their craft—now they often require us to pay them for their use of our money. They flock to and seek to penetrate the greatest pool of American resources – the federal government.

Obviously, nothing has really changed over the years. Some of our words are different – War on Terror – and the faces are different, but everything else seems the same. I can still recall the diligent execution to implant the word "War" in our mouths as part of academic language of conflict. So persistent was the effort that it begged the question – Why? It wasn't until later that I understood it to be about, yes, power and money.

As companies continued to merge, slash jobs, decrease wages, and move jobs overseas, our government continued its robust deregulation policy and marginalization of the economic power of the working-class. Many citizens are now facing the reality that our government has a set of economic rules: one for the rich and the other for the working-class. One increases wealth, the other marginalizes economic growth. Our government, until now, has not offered a hand up as the "New Deal" did during the years of Roosevelt. The previous administration did nothing as mounting foreclosures and rising oil prices sent our economy into a tailspin, to the point that it has affected the world economy as well. They boasted of their "feel good" stimulus package that was designed to help 400,000 homeowners avert foreclosure, while millions of others became homeless. Not even the 400,000 received the help which was promised them. Our government allowed women and children to live on the street.

Who controls America? Is it the richest of the rich, old money, and big business? Could their successes of the past assure their success in the future? Do they actually have power over most Americans to generate a desired response?

It's been proven time and again that their persuasive power rules the masses, influence judgments, and manipulate the emotions of Americans as though they were live puppets. "Believe what we say, not the hardships that you experience in your daily lives," we are told. Have we become "those" people?

They have money and they have power; but together we have more money, and more power. We must unite and maximize our resources relentlessly as they do. If we start a rolling program of economic development in our local communities, we can roll it all the way to Washington, DC.

The Rules of Engagement

Do we want to continue to expand government as we have since the 1940s? Of course, most of the debt incurred from 1940 thru 1973 was wartime debt—World War II, Korean Conflict, Vietnam Conflict. Non-wartime growth began with the Ford administration (1974-1977)—half a trillion dollars. It grew marginally during the Carter Administration (1977-1981)—up one quarter of a trillion dollars. The national debt then skyrocketed during the Reagan administration (1981-1989) from under a trillion dollars to 3.25 trillion. Under the Bush-41 administration (1989-1993) the debt grew to 4.7 trillion dollars—increased by the United Nations Persian Gulf War of 1991, when Saddam Hussein was driven out of Kuwait. It grew another trillion dollars during the Clinton administration (1993-2001) though annual growth began to diminish in 1996. It eventually stopped in 1999. The Clinton administration balanced the budget and left office with a sizable surplus. The growth began again during the Bush-43 administration (2001-2009), wiping out the surplus and increasing the debt by 4.75 trillion dollars. Our national debt now exceeds $13,500,000,000,000 and is increasing as you read this book—on average of about $4,000,000,000 per day. [One organization is reporting a figure as high as $56,400,000,000,000, which includes $36,300,000,000,000 for Medicare costs and $6,600,000,000,000 for Social Security costs]. The deepening recession in our country could cause the debt to double in the next ten years. Therefore, we must continue to pursuit our agenda to drastically reduce and eliminate the debt even as we institute measures to stimulate the economy. We must remember that the borrower is servant to the lender and eventually will become last economically rather than first, according to Proverbs 22:7 of the Holy Bible.

Today we owe Japan about $600,000,000,000 and counting. We owe China approximately $400,000,000,000 and counting. We owe the United Kingdom $340,000,000,000 and counting. And, these numbers will have increased considerably by the time this book is published.

Most of us know and understand the obvious ways that government has expanded since the 1940s. But there are less obvious ways. For generations we have attempted to use money to legislate righteousness, which is an issue of the heart. If you know of a major prejudice or bias in America today that is in the public domain, be assured, it has expanded government. It automatically expands as it intervenes to right a wrong in our society that denies liberties to its citizens as guaranteed by the Constitution. Social conscience applied in our society has a monetary value that can be measured. I am hopeful, however, that this small measure, in the billions of dollars, will be diminished greatly because we, as a people, have crossed a threshold of inclusion that far exceeds the measure of our ancestors.

So how do we pay off the debt we've incurred? The answers are found in every neighborhood, in every state of our union;

waiting to be sought and applied as part of a whole. Two thousand forty could be established as the target-date of final pay-down. If you feel that a debt-reduction czar should be appointed by President Obama, perhaps you can make your request through your congressional representatives [see Appendix C "Directory of the 111th Congress of the United States of America" for contact information] or The Office of Public Liaison & Intergovernmental Affairs (www.whitehouse.gov/administration/eop/opl).

In the meantime, let's look to a brighter future of balanced budgets, zero debt, and balanced trade. And all of the billions we now pay in interest can be spent in vital areas: education, alternative energy, healthcare/preventive care, pensions, retirement investments, global warming, environmental protection, infrastructure, green-jobs training, domestic security, international security, veteran benefits, small business startups, research and development. Now that's the American dream at work!

The National Debt from 1950 – 2010

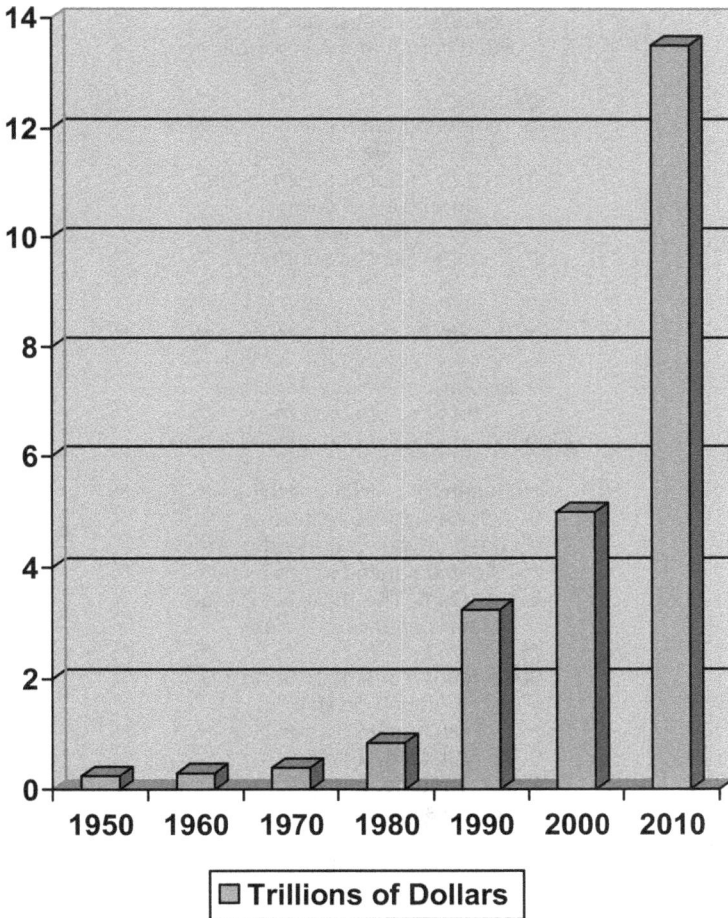

Trillions of Dollars

Sources: For additional information on the national debt, go to:
http://www.publicdebt.treas.gov or
http://en.wikipedia.org/wiki/federal_reserve
The data was gathered from the U.S. Treasury Department's
web site and http://www.brillig.com/debt_clock/faq/html.

REASONING

A plant lives
Within ample space
Beneath the soil to give
Measure and strength above.
Seed inborn and passed on;
In force of the dawn.

How far removed from a plant — do think —
Are we in life's pedigree?
The roots of our souls enshrined
In a heart of design.
Gifts of sight and sound
Through life that surrounds.

"Who are we?" a question in repose
From earth to heaven to compose.
Astronomy, psychology, biology —
Philosophy, sociology, theology —
The past, you and me—
Connected like the branches of a tree.

Independent — folly to think —
Our existence replicates.
My need of you, your need of me;
Perfections balanced in great feats —
Hoover Dam, The Brooklyn Bridge,
Monuments which speak.

In evidence of time I surmised,
Alone I do little;
With many I do much.
A lattice, a trellis —
Aptitude, fortitude, and gratitude wind.
Might one say we are intertwined?

Batons passed to an inner shine.
On and on progressively
I take yours, and then add mine
And give to the successive line,
Seeds of life and of the future —
Could that be our institution?

Chapter 7

The EIGHT-YEAR POWER GRAB

"The President is merely the most important among a large number of public servants. He should be supported or opposed exactly to the degree which is warranted by his good conduct or bad conduct, his efficiency or inefficiency in rendering loyal, able, and disinterested service to the Nation as a whole. Therefore it is absolutely necessary that there should be full liberty to tell the truth about his acts, and this means that it is exactly necessary to blame him when he does wrong as to praise him when he does right. Any other attitude in an American citizen is both base and servile. To announce that there must be no criticism of the President, or that we are to stand by the President, right or wrong, is not only unpatriotic and servile, but is morally treasonable to the American public. Nothing but the truth should be spoken about him or any one else. But it is even more important to tell the truth, pleasant or unpleasant, about him than about any one else." President Theodore Roosevelt, "The Kansas City Star," May 7, 1918

The Last Dance

Though a gallant effort was made on the part of Senator John McCain and his campaign during the 2008 Presidential Election—considered misguided on many occasions by most—the American people voted for change. I was pleased that Senator McCain was the Republican nominee; the party could not have had a better candidate, in my opinion. His leadership ability could be compared to that of one and a half good men, and his efforts on immigration reform, campaign finance reform, and the Patients' Bill of Rights are to be commended. He's a true American hero. I'm sure his counsel will be valued in the Obama administration. Many have said that he's quick-tempered. But that's not an accurate assessment. He's just a little impatient with ineptness and imprudence.

To be perfectly honest with those of you who can bear it; Senator John McCain would have been an excellent President in 2004. But in 2008, we could not allow another Republican administration in the White House until we, the people, had an opportunity to assess the damage, to unlock the secrets, to repeal the laws, to determine which programs were looted and pillaged, and to repair the breaches, relationships, and pacts that were compromised by the Bush administration. We needed someone who was not connected to the establishment to go in and tell us the truth about the internal condition of our government and to offer a plan of action without jeopardizing our security. We needed someone who would be well-received by the nations of the world to counter the ill will toward America. We needed someone who would give the nations hope instead of despair. We needed someone who would broker win/win deals in commerce, global warming, healthcare, education, immigration, nuclear disarmament, and peace. We all needed that—not just Democrats—we all did. Many morally sound Republicans have said it as well.

Who among you will sacrifice your families and your livelihood for a party that's not living up to its creed? — a party that has lost its way; a party that needs internal reflection now. Republicans must step back as a party, gather themselves and serve again inclusively, and abandon the permanent campaign mode of governing that has been utilized for the last sixteen years — yes, Republicans were in campaign mode even while Clinton was in the White House. Campaign mode is another way of saying, "attack or criticize your opponent's words and deeds relentlessly," even if you think he's right.

Many have spoken negatively about the Monica Lewinsky matter on occasion. But no one has spoken about the setup. Was it a setup? If so, was it any less despicable than the resulting deed?

The Republican season will come again without vice, malice, and hatred. It will come again in decency and honor — the true American Spirit.

Where Has All the Money Gone?

The money that circulated in our nation and around the world prior to this recession seems to have vanished. Money doesn't dematerialize! Certainly it is not circulating, but where is it? Even the Fed's infusion of billions of dollars into our economy seems to have disappeared as well. It is not flowing through the working-class communities. One could equate it to strategic financial dams constructed within the United States of America. And since a huge part of the world's prosperity flows from the United States, they are affected as well. Thus the constant phrase, "the recession began in America."

Everyone believes that investment banks and firms are a major part of the equation. But the picture is still blurred for many obvious reasons. Perhaps the answers can be found at the very top of the ladder in a world that is considered to be their own and closed to most of us. But we don't need their permission to enter. Their wealth, without doubt, came from the working-class, who should feel unabashed as they climb the same ladder to retrieve it.

Restoring Unity

Republicans, Democrats and Independents of Congress who put their party and personal interest above their country and their constituents, can expect to be removed from office. When elected representatives of Congress are sent to

Washington to represent the people of their district, that includes all people — Democrats, Republicans, Independents, Moderates, Libertarians, and everyone else. It is equally true that the President must represent all Americans, regardless of party affiliation. That is unlikely if the victorious party is in permanent campaign mode.

Have Republicans forgotten the far-reach of President Reagan across the aisle of compromise? Have they forgotten the Reagan Democrats? Though I was not one of them, I believe he sought compromise with the Democrats. When I think of Reagan, I am reminded that after saying he would not raise taxes, as all Republicans candidates have said in the past — it's part of their platform to get elected; Americans like to hear it — he did exactly that and cloaked it in time. The Alternative Minimum Tax was due to hit the middle-class during the first decade of the twenty-first century. So far, Congress has delayed it rather than repealing it. Nevertheless, Reagan was still seen as a unifier.

America's commander-in-chief, above all others, must exemplify unity. He must protect and preserve the lives of Americans in wartime and peace, and never put them in harm's way for his undisclosed personal cause. He must govern in unison with the people. He should never send our domestic force to a war on foreign soil. Military tradition and order should never be changed without the wise counsel of a multitude of experts who have demonstrated integrity and honor in their professional careers over a protracted period of time. Hasn't that been a lesson of the generation? Hasn't history given us light and taught us truth?

Evil always comes embodied in men and women who seek to subvert that which is good, we can expect it. But we must never be so naïve as to receive it and believe it. Study the cycles of history; there are economic good times, then economic bad times — good times are prompted by the goodness of men; bad times are prompted by the evils of men. And it always takes a revolution to get the good times rolling again.

Do you recall what President Roosevelt said in 1941 in his State of the Union Address to Congress, *"We must especially beware of that small group of selfish men [and women] who would clip the wings of the American eagle in order to feather their own nests."*

These are men and women who stick together in their malice to divide and conquer the masses solely for power and wealth.

President Roosevelt also made a few other statements during that same speech that are relevant today, *"In times like these it is immature — and, incidentally, untrue — for anybody to brag that an unprepared America, single-handed and with one hand tied behind its back, can hold off the whole world."* These words were spoken as this country sought to aid Europe in their fight against world tyranny, before the Japanese had the audacity to bomb a United States territory that housed our Pacific Fleet — a nation that did not pose a threat to the security of their homeland. But over 60 years later, did we not do as they did? Do you recall the proclamations of "shock and awe?" Did we brag of our military superiority on the world stage? Now we wonder why other countries thirst for the power and might of the United States of America. It is far better to be a gentle giant, than a bristling one.

Simultaneously on the domestic front, do you recall being told that we must give up freedom to get more security? Well, those words had also been spoken during the tumultuous times of the FDR administration, to which the President responded, *"Those who would give up essential liberty to purchase a little temporary safety deserve neither liberty nor safety."* He said this, if I may reiterate, in the face of the threat of world tyranny. Many democratic countries of Europe had already been overthrown. But he was moved by hope that the American people would rise up and connect with their internal dream. He was hopeful that they would work together for the common good, develop brotherhood with other nations, defeat tyranny, and establish a foundation of world peace — the United Nations.

His wife, Eleanor, fulfilled his vision as an ambassador of peace and humanity, including his four freedoms in the United Nations Charter which he quoted in the same speech: *"Just as our national policy in internal affairs has been based upon a decent respect for the rights and the dignity of all our fellow men within our gates, so our national policy in foreign affairs has been based on a decent respect for the rights and the dignity of all nations, large and small. And the justice of morality must and will win in the end."*

President Roosevelt further described our national policy as an expression of the public's will without regard to partisanship—an enduring peace that could not be bought at the cost of other people's freedom:

"As men do not live by bread alone, they do not fight by armaments alone...

"The nation takes great satisfaction and much strength from the things which have been done to make its people conscious of their individual stake in the preservation of democratic life in America.

"Certainly this is no time for any of us to stop thinking about the social and economic problems which are the root cause of the social revolution which is today a supreme factor in the world. For there is nothing mysterious about the foundations of a healthy and strong democracy.

"The basic things expected by our people of their political and economic systems are simple. They are:

- ★ *Equality of opportunity for youth and for others.*
- ★ *Jobs for those who can work.*
- ★ *Security for those who need it.*
- ★ *The ending of special privilege for the few.*
- ★ *The preservation of civil liberties for all.*
- ★ *The enjoyment — The enjoyment of the fruits of scientific progress in a wider and constantly rising standard of living.*

"These are the simple, the basic things that must never be lost sight of in the turmoil and unbelievable complexity of our modern world. The inner and abiding strength of our economic and political systems is dependent upon the degree to which they fulfill these expectations. Many subjects connected with our social economy call for immediate improvement. As examples:

- ★ *We should bring more citizens under the coverage of old-age pensions and unemployment insurance.*
- ★ *We should widen the opportunities for adequate medical care.*
- ★ *We should plan a better system by which persons deserving or needing gainful employment may obtain it.*

"No person should try, or be allowed to get rich out of the program, and the principle of tax payments in accordance with

ability to pay should be constantly before our eyes to guide our legislation.

"A good society is able to face schemes of world domination and foreign revolutions alike without fear. Since the beginning of our American history we have been engaged in change, in a perpetual, peaceful revolution, a revolution which goes on steadily, quietly, adjusting itself to changing conditions without the concentration camp or the quicklime in the ditch. The world order which we seek is the cooperation of free countries, working together in a friendly , civilized society.

"This nation has placed its destiny in the hands and heads and hearts of its millions of free men and women, and its faith in freedom under the guidance of God. Freedom means the supremacy of human rights everywhere... Our strength is our unity of purpose. To that high concept there can be no end save victory."

FDR was a man of hope who, along with fellow citizens – with whom he connected through his weekly "fireside chats," – thought it necessary to provide socioeconomic "safety nets" to Americans, which still exist today. Though they have been mismanaged, looted, and defrauded in some cases, they are functioning still for the well-being of American citizens. FDR's intent was to eliminate soup lines in this country forever. Therefore, it behooves us to streamline these programs by improving management, cutting waste, eliminating fraud, and providing adequate funding to sustain his noble cause.

We can learn from the lessons of history. We must learn. When we think of the last eight years, we think of the lives lost, the dreams destroyed, and the hardships suffered. In eight short years the middle-class has been vanquished. I don't think they were targeted; I think they were just neglected. And it could have been for the sole purpose of expanding the power base of the executive branch of government which defied the balance of power as outlined in our Constitution. To know that a few men and women would sacrifice the hopes and dreams of millions of Americans for self-indulgence is unacceptable and will not soon happen again in the United States of America. If history records it accurately and if Americans understand it fully; they will fight it as they fought communism when it tried to suck the essence of freedom from the heart of every citizen of the world. We will have liberty; and we will have security.

History may record that the forty-third President had good intentions which were circumvented by bad judgment — surrounding himself with people of bad judgment and considering them friends. Perhaps they were to him, but certainly not to the millions of citizens of this country. He should have cared for us more. His administration became self-centered — we became "those people" to them. If it sounds personal, that's because it is — personal to every single American that suffered because of his leadership or lack thereof. He took counsel readily from his Judas, who soon formed his agenda.

However, we must forgive in order to move on. A man's misdeeds sometimes can be too much even for him to bear. In such cases, we must lighten his load with earnest prayer; for he too must release to move on. How many of you, after reflection, have wished that you had done better at a task? He will come to that. Self-forgiveness must then take place in order for him to move on to the finer moments of service to mankind.

Judgment is not ours; we can only record the facts as they are revealed. He can certainly move on and eclipse the deeds of his presidency with noble works to mankind as history analyzes and draws its conclusions.

A MOMENT IN THOUGHT

SUNFLOWER

Peace cries aloud at dawning, "Come drink of me, I beseech!"
Fill up the gaping hole left by life's sudden breach.
Lie still while I spill upon your shattered heart,
Warmth aglow with renascent flow to coddle every part.

Days and nights have passed with little comprehension.
When you finally opened your eyes, the months you could not mention
Unsure, barbed, bare—
Once before you flourished, and once more you dare.

Nothing here—your constant thought—I'm all poured out.
It cannot be, I can see passion wrench and spout.
Open your eyes and look inside to life that never ends.
In the birth of time its compassion mends.

Life planted as a seed never goes away.
It only grows to sprout and flower in another way.
So water it and give it light with words of love's power
Until it opens wide inside like a giant Sunflower.

Chapter 8

THE PARTY OF KENNEDY

"The only way a republican government can function, and the only way a people's voice can be expressed to effect a practicable control of government, is through a process in which decisions are made by the majority. This is not a perfect way of controlling government, but the alternatives—decisions made by a minority, or by one person—are even worse and are the source of great evil. To be just, majority decisions must be in the best interest of all the people, not just one faction."
President Thomas Jefferson - Thomas Jefferson on Politics & Government, Majority Rule, http://etext.lib.virginia.edu

The Election for Posterity

The Democratic Party was fortunate this time around to nominate the ultimate leader for this historic time in our country. Before it was the Republican Party, prior to that it was the Democratic Party and so it has been in our history.

I began the 2008 campaign season with an open mind. I prepared myself to listen intently to each candidate as they answered relevant questions from responsible reporters. I hoped that they would state their positions clearly on vital issues of concern to me. It was important in 2008 for the Democrats to nominate the perfect team; two people who would complement one another rather than conflict one another. (See Chapter 11 entitled, *"Mr. Perfect President."*) Every trick in the unpublished political playbook was expected to be used against them — and they were — but they were destined to survive nevertheless.

Senator Barack Obama emerged as the nominee of the Democratic Party; a self-described agent of change. The Senator survived a field of equally capable candidates. Each would have been a formidable candidate against the Republican nominee, Senator John McCain. However, Senator Obama was presumed by the Democrats to be the best choice for President of the United States of America in 2008. He was considered a candidate of destiny as Senator John F. Kennedy was in 1960, therefore, timing was everything. Trekking back to that election, John F. Kennedy -vs.- Richard Nixon; Kennedy alone represented the first in three categories — age, 43; religion, Catholic; and birth, born in the twentieth century. It thrills me to no end that in 2008, we had to choose between a woman, a European/African American, and — on the Republican side — a Super Senior as President for the first time. Each represented a first in their category. But I couldn't make a decision based on external traits; the election was far too important to the socioeconomic status of this country and to me. I had one vote; I had to make it count. History would account for the rest.

Passing the Torch

Many members of the Kennedy family believe that Barack Obama is a president of destiny as Jack Kennedy was. So let's look at some of Kennedy's thoughts, ideas, and accomplishments as an indicator of Obama's fortitude. Let's look at the accomplishments of a man that was President for two years ten months and two days. This was a time after World I, the Great Depression, World War II, the Korean War, and during the Cold War with the Soviet Union which led to the Cuban Missile Crisis during his administration.

If you lived through that campaign or studied it in history, you'll recall how exciting the race was. Kennedy was the youngest man ever to run for the presidency of the United States; he exuded life. I was very young at the time but I still remember the fun of it all. All the adults were excited and looked forward to the opportunity to vote for the man that exemplified change in America. He was a celebrity. We kids got caught up in all the excitement; we understood it was a special time in history. We prepared ourselves, as our parents did, to open the door when destiny knocked. We were ready to accept the responsibility of making sure that destiny did its work.

You will notice that I said "we." When our parents voted we considered it a vote for us as well, until we were old enough to do it ourselves. I can still remember the theme song of the Kennedy Campaign recorded by Frank Sinatra, Ol' Blue Eyes, to the tune of his 1959 hit single, *High Hopes*:

> "Everyone is voting for Jack
> Cause he's got what all the rest lack
> Everyone wants to back – Jack
> Jack is on the right track.
> 'Cause he's got high hopes
> He's got high hopes
> Nineteen Sixty's the year for his high hopes..."

Sinatra used the song effectively to promote the candidacy of his friend. Only 1000 copies of the song were pressed for public use. Voters heard the name of Jack Kennedy on the radio as they went about their daily lives at home, in their cars, shopping centers, hair salons, bowling lanes, parks, and anywhere else a radio could be heard. The 45 rpm was never sold in stores. It would have been a wonderful memento. The campaign song enhanced Kennedy's name recognition across the country.

In addition, seventy million homes watched the first televised presidential debate ever between Jack Kennedy and Richard Nixon on September 26, 1960. Kennedy had practiced using television media, which was still relatively new, to promote his agenda. As a result, he appeared to be the better communicator.

His opponents said he could never win the White House because he was too young—the constitutional age requirement is 35 years old; he lacked foreign affairs experience — his experience derived from working with his father, Ambassador of Great Britain, as World War II erupted in Europe was irrelevant to them; and he was a Catholic—political spin, even back then, suggested that the United States would be run by the Pope if a Catholic became President. But he overcame those objections and the traditional assumption that a winning candidate must have the support of entrenched party leaders from states with large blocs of electoral votes. An impressive victory in predominantly Protestant West Virginia launched him to a first ballot victory at the Democratic National Convention in Los Angeles. He received the 761 votes required for the nomination when Wyoming voted—the final state in the roll call.

"The New Frontier of which I speak is not a set of promises—it is a set of challenges. It sums up not what I intend to offer the American people, but what I intend to ask of them." — **Acceptance Speech as the Democratic presidential nominee on July 15, 1960.**

"If by a "Liberal" they mean someone who looks ahead and not behind, someone who welcomes new ideas without rigid reactions, someone who cares about the welfare of the people — their health, their housing, their schools, their jobs, their civil rights, and their civil liberties — someone who believes we can break through the stalemate and suspicions that grip us in our policies abroad, if that is what they mean by a "Liberal," then I'm proud to say I'm a "Liberal." — **Acceptance of the New York Liberal Party nomination on September 14, 1960.**

"For of those to whom much is given, much is required. And when at some future date the high court of history sits in judgment on each of us, recording whether in our brief span of service we fulfilled our responsibilities to the state, our success or failure, in whatever office we hold, will be measured by the answers to four questions: First, were we truly men [women] of courage... Second, were we truly men [women] of judgment... Third, were we truly men [women] of integrity... Finally, were we truly men [women] of dedication?"— **Speech to Massachusetts State Legislature on January 9, 1961.**

"So let us begin anew — remembering on both sides that civility is not a sign of weakness, and sincerity is always subject to proof. Let us never negotiate out of fear. But let us never fear to negotiate." — **Inaugural Address, Washington D.C, January 20, 1961**

"We decided long ago that the dangers of excessive and unwarranted concealment of pertinent facts far outweighed the dangers which are cited to justify it. Even today, there is little value in opposing the threat of a closed society by imitating its arbitrary restrictions. Even today, there is little value in ensuring the survival of our nation if our traditions do not survive with it. And there is very grave danger that an announced need for increased security will be seized upon by those anxious to expand its meaning to the very limits of official censorship and concealment. That I do not intend to permit to the extent that it is in my control." — **Address before the American Newspaper Publishers Association on April 27, 1961.**

"Terror is not a new weapon. Throughout history it has been used by those who could not prevail, either by persuasion or example. But inevitably they fail, either because men are not afraid to die for a life worth living, or because the terrorists themselves came to realize that free men cannot be frightened by threats, and that aggression would meet its own response." Mankind must put an end to war or war will put an end to mankind." — **Address before the General Assembly of the United Nations, September 25, 1961.**

In short, we must face problems which do not lend themselves to easy or quick or permanent solutions. And we must face the fact that the United States is neither omnipotent nor omniscient, that we are only six percent of the world's population, that we cannot impose our will upon the other ninety-four percent of mankind, that we cannot right every wrong or reverse each adversity, and that therefore there cannot be an American solution to every world problem." — **Speech at the University of Washington, Seattle, November 16, 1961**

"The United States, as the world knows, will never start a war. We do not want a war. We do not now expect a war. This generation of Americans has already had enough — more than enough — of war and hate and oppression. We shall be prepared if others wish it. We shall be alert to try to stop it." — **Address at American University, Washington D.C, June 10 1963.**

Milestones in the Presidency of John F. Kennedy
Source - Kennedy Library and Museum

November 8, 1960
Senator John F. Kennedy is elected 35th President of the United States of America.

January 20, 1961
John F. Kennedy is inaugurated President—"Ask not what your country can do for you, ask what you can do for your country."

January 21 and 24, 1961
President signs Executive Orders increasing quantity and quality of surplus food distributed to jobless Americans and expanding Food for Peace Program to aid overseas needy.

January 30, 1961
President asks Congress to include health insurance in Social Security Program.

February 2, 1961
President asks Congress for program to help end recession, including food stamps, extended benefits for unemployed workers and welfare payments for their children.

February 9, 1961
President requests legislation to assist medical and dental colleges and students.

February 15, 1961
President warns Soviets to avoid interfering with United Nations pacification of the Congo.

March 1, 1961
President initiates Peace Corps to take American skills and idealism to new and developing countries.

March 13, 1961
President proposes a long-term Alliance for Progress between the United States and Latin America, emphasizing democratic reform and economic development.

March 22, 1961
President calls for long-term Foreign Aid program with new emphasis on self-help.

March 23, 1961
President warns Communists that ceasefire must precede negotiations for a neutral and independent Laos.

March 28, 1961
President initiates the largest and most rapid defense buildup in United States' peacetime history, doubling Polaris missile program, increasing armed bomber and other missile programs, adding five combat ready divisions and quadrupling anti-guerilla forces.

April 20, 1961
President assumes responsibility for failed Bay of Pigs invasion, says policies and procedures will be changed.

May 1, 1961
President signs long-sought Area Redevelopment Bill to aid communities with chronic unemployment.

May 25, 1961
President proposes an American space effort greater than all previous efforts combined, and designed to put an American space team on the moon within the decade.

June 3, 1961
President opens channels of communication with Chairman Khrushchev of the Soviet Union in an informal conference in Vienna.

June 30, 1961
President signs bill extending Social Security benefits to five million people and permitting people to retire with benefits at age 62. President signs most comprehensive Housing Bill in history, initiating aid to middle income families and mass transportation users, and increasing urban renewal and elderly housing.

July 20, 1961
President signs bill doubling Federal effort to halt water pollution.

July 25, 1961
President tells nation of determination to deter war in West Berlin, increasing military might and manpower—Soviet deadline for East German Treaty subsequently passes.

August 7, 1961
President signs first of three bills creating National Seashore Parks, the first major addition to the National Park System in 16 years.

August 8, 1961
President signs most comprehensive wheat and feed grain bill since 1938, resulting in higher farm income and lower food surpluses.
September 3, 1961
President signs $1.25 Minimum Wage Bill, expanding coverage for the first time since original passage.
September 22, 1961
President signs bill committing United States to unprecedented search for economic breakthrough in the conversion of salt water to fresh.
President signs bill establishing first Federal program to help combat juvenile delinquency.
September 25, 1961
President, in speech to United Nations General Assembly, endorses complete and general disarmament and challenges Soviets to a "peace race."
September 26, 1961
President signs bill establishing the first full-scale, full-time Disarmament Agency in the world.
December 15, 1961
President renews American commitment to preserve independence of Vietnam.
March 2, 1962
President announces that Soviet resumption of atmospheric nuclear testing makes American testing necessary in late April unless effective treaty is signed.
March 15, 1962
President signs first major Federal bill to retrain jobless victims of automation and chronic unemployment.
April 5, 1962
President calls for overhaul of Federal transportation policy, emphasizing increased and equal competition instead of regulation—also renews request for urban mass transportation program.
April 11, 1962
President urges reconsideration of inflationary steel price increase—increase was rescinded shortly thereafter.
July 12, 1962
President couples depreciation reform with tax credit to spur greater investment in plant and industry.

July 26, 1962
President signs the most far-reaching revision of public welfare legislation since enactment in 1935, emphasizing family rehabilitation and training instead of dependency.

September 26, 1962
President signs bill enabling construction of world's largest atomic power plant in Hanford, Washington.

September 30, 1962
President announces action by Federal Government to carry out court order, admitting James Meredith to the University of Mississippi.

October 2, 1962
President signs United Nations bond issue bill authorizing American participation in financing United Nations peacekeeping operations in the Congo and elsewhere.

October 10, 1962
President signs first major improvement in Food and Drug laws since 1938, protecting families against untested and ineffective drugs.

October 11, 1962
President signs Trade Expansion Act granting unprecedented authority to end American protectionism and build free world economic unity.

October 22, 1962
President announces naval quarantine to halt Soviet missile buildup in Cuba—Khrushchev subsequently withdraws missiles under United States inspection.

November 20, 1962
President signs Executive Order to prevent racial discrimination in Federal housing.

January 14, 1963
President calls for massive tax reduction and tax reform, accurately predicting longest, strongest economic expansion in American peace-time history to that time.

March 22, 1963
President urges final action on Constitutional Amendment outlawing poll tax as a bar to voting—it became the 24th Amendment.

June 10, 1963
President, in speech at American University, calls on American people to reexamine their attitude toward Cold War.

June 11, 1963
President mobilizes Alabama National Guard to admit two blacks to the University of Alabama as ordered by the court.

June 22, 1963
President proposes most sweeping Civil Rights legislation in history to give all Americans equal opportunity in education, employment, public accommodations, voting and access to Federal programs.

July 18, 1963
President presents latest in series of administrative and legislative programs to stabilize United States balance of payments and stem outflow of gold

September 20, 1963
President, in address to the United Nations General Assembly, proposes additional cooperation with Soviet Union, including outer space exploration—United States and Soviet Union subsequently agree on outer space disarmament move.

September 24, 1963
President signs first major program assisting construction of higher education classrooms.

October 7, 1963
President signs Nuclear Test Ban Treaty, first disarmament agreement of the nuclear age.

October 9, 1963
President announces agreement with Soviet Union to open private negotiations for sale of American wheat.

October 24, 1963
President signs bill launching first major national drive against mental illness and mental retardation.

November 21, 1963
President asks economic advisers to prepare "War on Poverty" program for 1964.

These ideas and accomplishments are of a man thought by many unprepared to be President of the United States based on some of the same biases and prejudices of the old political playbook that's still in use today. But now we have modern technology—the Internet, cable TV, 24-hour news networks, and cell phones—to assist us in making a decision. We have the technology to see and to hear it all.

Kennedy's Democratic opponents, when confronted with his ability to actually win the primary, was generous enough to offer him the vice-presidency. But he knew what destiny required of him — he had already stepped into the shoes of President of the United States of America for the cause of human redemption. His opponents saw evidence of it, and he knew it in his heart. The battle for the Democratic nomination was fierce and the general election was fiery too. The Republicans used the same tactics that his fellow Democrats had used during the primary. The sense of déjà vu occurred often during the 2008 campaign.

Many in my community thought President Kennedy was a noble man. And it was validated when he went on national television to apologize to the nation when he felt that he had not done his job well—isn't that refreshing!

It happened on April 20, 1961, after being in office only ninety days. The President spoke to the nation and took responsibility for the failed Bay of Pigs Invasion which was a plan conceived by the CIA to overthrow the Castro government of Cuba, a dictatorship ninety miles off the coast of Florida which appeared to have had a cozy relationship with Nikita Khrushchev, the Soviet Premier of the USSR, our opponent in the Cold War. In March 1960, President Eisenhower gave the CIA permission to train 1400 Cuban exiles, dubbed the 2506 Brigade, to invade their homeland. Well, logistics went bad and approximately 1200 members of the brigade were captured and imprisoned for 20 months as the Kennedy Administration negotiated their release with the help of the American people. Castro finally agreed to trade the prisoners for baby food and pharmaceuticals.

I believe that failed attempt and his humility before the nation aided his success in the Cuban Missile Crisis, which occurred as the Kennedy administration was still negotiating for the return of the Cuban exiles. Photos from a U2 reconnaissance plane revealed that the Soviets had begun to build an offensive medium-range ballistic missile base near San Cristobal, Cuba, with missiles aimed at the United States. The Soviets had amassed 40,000 troops in Cuba and the CIA thought it was only 2,000 to 3,000. For thirteen days in October of 1962, the world watched, hoped and prayed for a peaceful solution as President Kennedy through negotiations, diplomacy and a show of readiness — a naval blockade, a ring of ships, around Cuba — averted what many thought would be World War III, the first nuclear war of obliteration. By December the missiles were removed and the sites were destroyed, which led the way to peaceful negotiations between the two countries that culminated in the Limited Nuclear Test Ban Treaty and a "hotline" between the White House and the Kremlin—a direct line of communication between the superpowers, making it unlikely one would dehumanize the other. When we talk to our enemies, true or imagined, their value as human beings elevates in our eyes; the stereotypical thoughts and the myths go away.

Prior to the Cuban Missile Crisis, public opinion polls had shown that more than half of all Americans thought war with the Soviets was inevitable. However, destiny was in place and ready to prevent such a catastrophe. And I am sure that those who were persuaded to vote for Nixon, only because Kennedy was a young Catholic who lacked experience in foreign affairs by their standard of measurement were equally pleased and comforted by the outcome.

No doubt the elder Chairman Khrushchev had heard of the young Kennedy who was unprepared to be President and lacked foreign affairs experience, according to members of his own party and the opposing party. Here was his chance to gain preeminence in the Western Hemisphere — the Bay of Pigs had proven Kennedy. After all, Eisenhower was a military general; Kennedy was just the officer of PT109. The Soviet Premier, however, met America's gift of destiny for that chosen time, who was destined to win that battle between good and evil on behalf of the entire world. Had Republican Vice President Richard Nixon of California, Republican Senator Barry Goldwater of Arizona, Republican Governor Nelson Rockefeller of New York, Democratic Senate Majority Leader Lyndon B. Johnson of Texas — then Vice President, Democratic Senator Hubert Humphrey of Minnesota or Democratic Governor Adlai Stevenson of Illinois been President, the outcome could have been disastrous. President Kennedy had stepped into the shoes of destiny long before the crisis arose:

"A man does what he must — in spite of personal consequences, in spite of obstacles and dangers, and pressures — and that is the basis of all human morality." **John F. Kennedy - Profiles in Courage (1956)**

Destiny has knocked at the door of the United States of America once again, as it did with Thomas Jefferson, Abraham Lincoln, Franklin Roosevelt, John Kennedy, and now Barack Obama. Americans have allowed destiny an opportunity to restore this country to morality, peace, security and prosperity.

Destiny never calls without a cause and never engages without a plan, though every eye cannot see it. The responsibility of adoption and fulfillment lies with those who do through spiritual insight, because they are called to action, they will join the coalition, they will do the work and complete the task. It's not a job for one; it's a job for many — yet, it's a job for all.

Called to Service

Hillary Rodham Clinton has taken her place in the framework of the Obama administration, as Joe Biden, Teddy Kennedy—the Great Statesman who has moved on, Al Gore, John Kerry and others have done. Her time has come to serve our country as Secretary of State, a position that I believe was negotiated during the Democratic National Convention. Nevertheless, she is already showing signs of aptitude by seeking to expand the State Department through special envoys and the Diplomatic Corps. I still believe that many of her attacks on President Obama during the primary were baseless, but here we are today—forgiving all and getting along just as we should. I believe that she will be a loyal and selfless public servant. And her husband, President Clinton, is moving ever closer to becoming "the Statesman" that he should be.

CHOOSE

Overrule, overrule
My thoughts of deceit.
Forbid my soul to avenge
Wrong done to me.

The Rock is struck;
Waters of peace be released
To wash away the remembrance
Of wrong done to me.

Light the lamp of my feet;
Anguish to the dross.
Blot out the hatred
And the insults hurled at me.

I beseech you my soul
Arise and be free;
Live by my decree.
I choose life, life eternally.

Chapter 9

THE 2008 PRESIDENTIAL CAMPAIGN

"The problem of power is how to achieve its responsible use rather than its irresponsible and indulgent use – of how to get men of power to live for the public rather than off the public."
Robert F. Kennedy, 'I Remember, I Believe,' The Pursuit of Justice, 1964

Fear - vs. - Hope

Historic, lengthy, and unpredictable could describe the Presidential Campaign of 2008. Two prominent candidates emerged and we began the general election with vigor—the gloves were off, on one side at least. They tried to make it look pretty, but it was ugly. The candidates were as different as day and night.

The brightness of day brings hope and confidence; one can see clearly — solutions are unveiled; but the darkness of night brings hopelessness and despair; it impairs the vision, creates illusions, and holds secrets — fears crescendo.

9/11 taught us what fear can do to a nation. It can paralyze a nation into helplessness and wrongfully subjugate God to man. President Franklin D. Roosevelt saw its destructive nature during the Great Depression and revealed it to the people—"We have nothing to fear but fear itself," he said. Our official motto is "In God We Trust," not "In Man We Trust." The bible says fear not; be strong and courageous. But we passed laws in fear, we went to war in fear, and we voted for a president in fear. As a nation, we began to shrink. And every decision we made in fear has been proven to be wrong and/or costly in many ways. And those who told us to fear began to exercise greater authority over us; unconstitutional authority. Our government had been warned that al Qaeda was coming, but they chose to ignore it; perhaps disdain had set in.

Consequently, the referendum of the 2008 Presidential Election became "return to our roots." Americans wanted to return to the core principles of our Founding Fathers from which we had strayed. Americans wanted to return to our constitutional rule of law. We are not a country which has to make it up as we go along. We have a constitution that is based on Godly principles which has served us well for two hundred thirty-three years. We want to stick with it. Therefore, our choice for President was a very decisive one in 2008. We sought someone who would lead us back to our promised land of freedom, peace, and prosperity, so that we could then move on to realizing the evidentiary truths of our Constitution.

The Decision-Making Process

The process of choosing a President was not an easy one for me. The scope and magnitude of our problems were increasing as the campaign went on. This required the candidates to offer more credible solutions, which perhaps they didn't have. I, and many other citizens, have viable solutions to many of our problems, but we have to be heard and included in their implementation. Our greatest value to our political representatives is that we think outside the Washington-box. While candidates are telling us of their great solutions, by the thousands we are saying in our communities, "that won't take us over the mountain, that will only get us to the base." Yet, they continually leave us out of the loop; we want to be in the loop. We desire to pour into them, not only draw from their well, which may not respond to priming. A wise leader knows he doesn't have all the answers, nor does his circle. After a while they begin to mimic one another. Perhaps that restricted social network is how the majority of members of our Washington government has gotten so haughty and low-performing?—from the elected officials to the appointees to the civil servants to the lifers. We are indeed thankful for those who are very productive public servants; those who have contributed for most of their adult life because of their love for our country. We honor and applaud their service.

So my first question was, "Which candidate would work with me as I participate in the growth and betterment of my country at the national level, along with other like-minded citizens? I determined that perhaps one of them would. Then I narrowed my scope of decision—Who would be the best transitional President?

The spirit of collaboration and compromise took over, and I thought with a chuckle, of the then current administration's claim to perpetual secrecy for the purpose of national security. Well, some of us bought it, but most of us did not. Washington, our national capital, had become the whole of the United States of America. Those who wanted to continue that policy could not be on the short list nor could embellishers and assassins of character. The short list then became very short.

Finally I asked, who would be a President of all the people? As I said earlier, we have seasons for disagreements along party lines. Thereafter, we should only have general disagreements followed by all-American solutions. Could we endure another four years of millions of American citizens being disenfranchised because their party's nominee did not win the general election? My answer was an unequivocal no. Thereafter, the short list consisted of only one name.

I didn't factor in the opinions of news reporters or political pundits who expressed their opinions readily. I considered my opinion more valuable because it guides my vote for which I am responsible.

Voting carries responsibility and that responsibility requires us to use our most valuable commodity — time. This time is spent for the good of our family, our community, our state, and our nation.   Yet again, I remind you that what elected officials do in Washington and around the world affect our lives. And as voters, we bear some of the responsibility. It's easy to blame them solely for mistakes made in governance. But if you voted for them, you should share in the blame too. You can't vote with impunity. If your choices win, you must stick with them—pray and help. You can't walk away and delegate your responsibilities to someone else, especially if your selections turn out to be bad choices for whatever reason. Don't criticize them; that only makes it worse. Double your prayers for them instead. Those who didn't vote for them should come alongside and do the same. That due-diligence process will lead you to choose better elected officials by setting appropriate parameters for making your decisions, asking pertinent questions of the candidates, doing adequate research of any previous public service to establish their stance on issues of concern to you, and debating the issues with others to clarify your beliefs.

Appendix C - Directory of the 111th Congress gives you the phone number and email address of each member of Congress. So if you have questions, concerns or suggestions about governance, you may write or call them. If you need a job, contact your representatives to ask about immediate job-creation programs and training. If you need healthcare, ask about universal healthcare goals and timetables. If you need a good retirement plan, ask about retirement plans, pensions, and subsidies. If you need cleaner air to breathe, ask about plans to revamp the Environmental Protection Agency and schedule town hall meetings with an EPA representative to discuss local issues. If you need money for your college education, ask about money for tuition and plans to restructure the student loan program. If you need saving grace to keep your home, ask about immediate plans to help stop foreclosures. If you have a son or daughter in Iraq or Afghanistan serving a second or third tour of duty, ask for a reprieve. Ask relevant questions, and above all *offer solutions.* Oh, by the way, bury the "tude" forever; it doesn't serve you well.. After the election, become a viable partner with your new representatives and reinforce your relationships with the existing ones—they represent you. Make a political folder and keep copies of your correspondences to manage your efforts. Include a calling log to track your calls and comments. Stay in touch even if all is well. Give a verbal high-five, or a verbal pat on the back for a job well-done. Be appreciative; balance positive and negative feedback. Your involvement and contact with their office could keep them grounded and serve as a reminder of their reason for being in Washington. They would be motivated to stay connected to reality and be less inclined to gravitate to the Washington "bubble" for acceptance.

In addition, *Chapter 16, "Yes, Mr. President, It Would Be My Pleasure!"* tells you how to stay in touch with the President and how to receive special courtesies from the White House.

Put your hope on display. Stay informed. Don't be a "low-info" citizen who lacks due diligence and makes decisions based on emotion, bias, prejudice, ignorance, malice, jealousy, bigotry, crudeness, haughtiness, and injustice. And if you have hatred that dies hard; starve it and let it die nevertheless. You deserve to live in prosperity with all the privileges and liberties guaranteed by the Constitution of the United States of America. You are an American citizen.

Collaboration and Compromise

Some Democrats and Republicans did not vote in the 2008 Presidential Election because they didn't like either candidate. To you I say, "not voting was not an option." Wasting your vote with a spoiler candidate was not wise. Again, voting is a responsibility of citizenship. If you don't vote, you knowingly and willingly transfer your citizenship to inactive status; you choose not to be represented and not to have your children represented—no one is obliged to listen to you or any non-voting member of your household. You lose your voice in your own country.

Our republic cannot function effectively if its citizens spoil or pervert the democratic process. It leads to corruption—a decision not to vote is an attempt to corrupt the process. In making such a decision, ask yourself, "How will not voting affect me and my family?" Will it teach my children and my grandchildren to honor their citizenship and their country?

Furthermore, don't be a sore loser; be gracious. Learn the art of collaboration and compromise; let your voice become one of reason and reconciliation during this season of restoration in our country.

Whether you are counting a million votes or a million dollars, the count begins with one; therefore, one is very important — it's the beginning. You could be number one.

Changing Our Ways

We are part of the reason why government, as a whole, doesn't get things done. And if you don't believe it, just look at the kinds of campaigns we have allow politicians to run. If we had rejected them, they would have changed long ago. Campaign strategies have consistently caused us to vote *against our own interest,* which they are designed to do in some cases. They are intended to take our focus away from real issues onto those that are irrelevant. Such campaigns are also intended to increase our emotional levels to the point that we don't think soundly.

A large percentage of the electorate is known for making quick decisions based on sound bites, political rhetoric, innuendo, and rumor. Oh, we have our "feel good moments" of arrogance when we take our opinions over the top and require candidates to answer *insignificant questions while we are losing jobs, benefits, pensions, savings, homes, college tuition funds, family cohesiveness, and self-esteem.* The honorable guy is asking himself, "Why am I being asked such irrelevant questions? On the other hand, the less honorable guy loves it; he gets to walk away having said nothing of importance.

During the 2008 Presidential Election season, I was more concerned about our behavior as citizens, rather than that of the candidates. We seem to have developed the "battered citizen syndrome." Election after election, we vote and get the same result— representatives who disregard and disrespect our agreement of representation. Perhaps we have forgotten the real reason for the process—to choose a candidate who will represent our ideas in government by speaking and voting on our behalf to foster domestic and foreign prosperity as we pursuit happiness.

But thanks to the information age, we made a change by altering our thoughts and behavior. We heard the candidates for ourselves and made our decision based on facts and proposals that were put forth in earnest. Our quality of life, and that of our posterity were at stake, so we made every effort to exercise sound moral judgment in our vote for president especially.

We sought a president of change; we have one. We sought a president who reflects America's values and principles; we have one. We sought a president with reasonable foreign policies; we have one. We sought a president with a plan to keep jobs here at home; we have one. We sought a president who would give us universal healthcare; we have one. We sought a president who would advance our pursuit of happiness; we have one. We sought a president who would continue to perfect the union; we have one. We sought a president who would maintain our domestic tranquility; we have one. We sought a president who would restore our moral standing around the world; we have one. We sought a president who would end the war in Iraq; we have one. We sought a president who would treat our veterans with dignity; we have one. We sought a president who would preserve, protect, and defend the Constitution of the United States of America; we have one.

"I'm asking you to believe. Not just in my ability to bring about real change in Washington... I'm asking you to believe in yours," is President Obama's request of us. The challenge is ours; it has always been ours, and it shall always be ours.

DAYSPRING

Awake my soul alive
To the dawning of grace,
Who pours into life
Minuets of lace.

Walk on mountaintops ablaze,
Amid panacean showers of praise.
Row, as the sea billows roar,
To treasure unfolding as they raise.

Shouting in my mind resign
To thoughts forever green,
Stayed by roots of hope
Sunk in the torrid desire to ween.

Symphony of my heart resound,
As I pillow my head to string,
The rhapsodies of my soul;
Till I awake again to reprise my
Dayspring.

Chapter 10

MR. PERFECT
PRESIDENT?

"I am not here as a public official, but as a citizen of a troubled world who finds hope in a growing consensus that the generally accepted goals of society are peace, freedom, human rights, environmental quality, the alleviation of suffering, and the rule of law." President James (Jimmy) Carter, Nobel Peace Prize Lecture, 2002

Complementing the People

Have you ever been in a battle in which you were assured of victory — you only had to show up and apply a few tactical blows and it was o-v-e-r! Be assured; we are not in that kind of socioeconomic battle in our country today. We face a battle that is multifaceted; one that requires simultaneous attacks on several fronts. There are many wild cards at play; therefore, multiple strategies are being applied. But be of good cheer, President Franklin D. Roosevelt did the same and got good results. He was radical, however, in his thinking and in his deeds. If one strategy didn't work, he tried another, and continued until he found one that did. Doing nothing was not an option for him.

Not since the Great Depression, have we faced such a plethora of problems: a depressed economy, war in Afghanistan, war in Iraq, diplomatic conflict with Iran and North Korea, the Palestinian/Israeli conflict, Russian aggression, global warming, declining education, increased dependence on foreign oil, runaway deficits, rising unemployment, lower wages, massive foreclosures, insufficient healthcare, massive deregulation, retirement deprivation, Social Security Fund depletion, Medicare Fund depletion, blatant corporate greed, budgetary assaults on our borders, and overt circumvention of constitutional rights of American citizens by their government.

There are people in this world who wish to topple our democracy and harm us, and would think they do God a favor. They cannot be convinced that they are actually fighting against God Almighty himself, who built and preserves this country because the righteous among us ask him to on a daily basis. We don't have enough military power to solve every disagreement and conflict. We must use diplomacy—the art of compromise. "If you nuke me, I'll nuke you," is not a reasonable compromise. It doesn't work. It didn't work during the Cuban Missile Crisis, nor will it work now.

As American corporations move jobs overseas to enhance their profits, and eliminate millions of other jobs to adjust to our shrinking economy; the middle-class of the United States is beginning to feel the uneasiness of lack on a daily basis. And it will get worse, as it has since the election, before it gets better.

We can take comfort in knowing that we have, at least, elected a president who has developed and executed a plan of action to create millions of jobs immediately. But the task is ours. It has always been ours—the citizens of the United States of America. We had to rise up and take matters into our own hands because our latent politicians never would. So we have chosen a leader who complements our vision of rebuilding our republic.

Do you recall the preamble to the Constitution? *"We the People of the United States, in Order to form a more perfect Union, establish Justice, insure domestic Tranquility, provide for the common defence, promote the general Welfare, and secure the Blessings of Liberty to ourselves and our Posterity, do ordain*

and establish this Constitution for the United States of America."
It does not say, "We the Elected Officials of the United States"
or "We the Representatives of the People of the United States."
It says, "We the People of the United States."

For the first time in recent history, we have a president
who has not been purchased by lobbyists. He is free to do the
work of the people with the people — Teams America. It's an
accomplishment to be celebrated.

We begin with increased deficits; projected for four or five
years followed by deceases, to finally a balanced budget as our
economy become more robust. Many Republicans in Congress
defy increased deficits. But if you were to examine the
*National Debt From 1950 — 2010 in Chapter 6 – Who Controls
America*? you would discover that deficits are a long-standing policy
of this country. They were started back in the 1930s and continued
during peaceful and prosperous times under both Republican and
Democratic administrations—Republicans having generated the
greatest increases. So the current deficit spending generated to put
Americans back to work is a strategic move to stimulate immediate
economic growth. Remember, we've lost over 14,000,000 jobs in
this recession so far. That amounts to billions of dollars of
goods and services that are not being purchased, billions of
dollars that are not circulating in our economy, and billions of
dollars of lost tax revenue—Americans must get back to work.
This is the first step in reconstituting the vision of America.

So we'll take the bus; we won't be traveling by plane or
train. TARP (*Troubled Asset Relief Program*) funds traveled by
plane without filing a flight plan and parachuted from high
attitudes with great accuracy from one end of the country to the
other. Billions of dollars landed securely, but we can't account
for much of it. We can't even get information from the black
boxes; there weren't any.

None of us wants our taxes increased, but in due time we
will have to curb deficit spending by curtailing runaway
budgets like those of the Department of Defense which waste
billions of dollars a year on faulty contracts alone.
Suggestively, if we were to get rid of twenty to twenty-five
percent of annual wasteful spending, if we were to eliminate
tax breaks for the wealthiest Americans, if we were to stop

corporate welfare, if we were to keep the minimum wage above the poverty index; we could maintain a balanced budget and a vibrate economy without raising taxes on the middle-class and still have sufficiency in all things.

We have borrowed money from Japan, China, Great Britain and other nations to sustain our spending. We have not exercised sound fiscal policies that are essential to a prosperous economy. And even though the Clinton administration moved to the center and changed those policies; leaving us a substantial surplus when they left office; the Bush-43 administration squandered it and resumed business as usual — irresponsible fiscal policies. Now, instead of having billion dollar deficits; we have trillion dollar deficits.

Large chucks of America are now owned by foreign entities. Some have said it gives new meaning to the words "our country." Are you comfortable with someone who doesn't believe in democracy owning large parts of our country?

President Obama was elected because we trust him to keep his campaign promises and to boost the economy by creating jobs. His priorities have changed slightly because of the changing economy. Healthcare and the Iraq war were at the top of his agenda in October. Now job creation, foreclosure curtailment, and market stability are at the top of the list, and the President is adjusting accordingly.

For years, government has given the appearance of helping average Americans in times of quandary, but never really doing so. During the Kennedy administration, I saw monetary evidence of the economic prosperity he had generated. Up to January 20, 2009, we got psychological dramatizations staged for the nightly newscast to convince us that we were being cared for. That's all we ever got — scripted drama. Millions of Americans citizens had mortgage problems—our government's solution initially was to hold a press conference to say that they were helping a hundred thousand of them while ridiculing millions of others for bad fiscal management—the government's ridicule of its citizens for bad fiscal management is laughable considering its own.

I don't hear such ridicule or see such low performance in response to corporations' cries for help—$700 billion for a few financial institutions verses an estimated $130 billion for millions of families in foreclosure. The government bailed out the financial giants that caused the housing crisis, and it appears that bailout two and three are forthcoming.

A vote for Barack Obama was a vote against this pattern of injustice. One might concede that it would take a perfect president to peel away the layers of misdoings which have taken hold of our government for such a long time. Applying a layer of integrity over layers of deception and mismanagement will not form a lasting fix — it won't work. Invigoration will require spring cleaning from the attic to the basement.

The charge given to President Obama by the American people is the same charge we have given ourselves.

The Presidential Campaign is Suspended

Of course the news media has strong opinions about everything, that's the nature of their work. I just wish they wouldn't editorialize so much. Most people tune in to news programs to get the facts; they are not seeking to be indoctrinated. They are fully capable of forming their own opinions. Some reporters would feel remiss in their job if they didn't try to sway their listeners just a bit, very much like politicians. I do admit, though, that they are right in their editorial comments about fifty percent of the time.

Since the 2008 campaign is over, I ask every Republican who did not vote for Barack Obama to suspend their campaign and to work with him and all prudent Americans to rebuild our country. If there are still issues that you feel strongly about, we would like to hear them, not as a campaign issue, but as an issue facing your community or our country as a whole. We can still agree to disagree as Americans. Our goal is not to rehash old arguments; it is to reconcile what we can and continue to build viable coalitions.

The Republican/Democratic feud of the last twenty years is over. Any vestiges of it that dares to raise its ugly head will be beaten into the dust. President Obama will serve and will be honored as President of all the people of the United States of America.

Change has come; it is time to rebuild our country, as I have said repeatedly, for the good of all Americans. And it need not be reiterated that you did not vote for our current President; that is irrelevant now and will be until November 2012. The state of our morals and the state of our economy are what matter most. We must unite under the banner of loyal Americans and continue the work of the republic. To do otherwise, would call your patriotism into question.

Consider momentarily that it was not only Democrats, Independents and Moderates who elected President Obama; it was Republicans too – citizens of high moral standing who put country before party. And you should replicate their acts of patriotism if you are contrary. Should you stumble upon something that is less than stellar in our government, in your humble opinion; try your best to fix it. Should you see a crack in President Obama's armor, get your best material and plug it up. If you want to use it in the 2012 Presidential Election, it's fair game, but not now. If you decide, after reflection, to use it in the next election, remember to judge yourself before you judge him and measure your character before you measure his. That's God's protection to each of us so that we do not harm ourselves. Actually, you'll have to walk a mile in his shoes to understand truly what he is facing. In doing so, you might eventually become the man or woman you think you are. You won't allow your integrity to be determined by whether you can affect an election.

You've had eight years to do as you pleased—and you did. Now help us clean up the mess.

Democrats, welcome those who have not been in your favor for the last decade. You too must suspend your campaign and begin the work of the republic. One must be gracious in winning. Because the 2008 Presidential Election was a grassroots campaign, millions of you were instrumental in getting President Obama elected. Countless millions of you gave 100% of what you had. Others gave 10% of what they had. According to biblical principles those who gave all gave more, even if the dollar value was less. If you fall into that category, you among all others know your sacrifice, which you will probably never share with others — it's between you and God. Therefore, your emotions will run very deeply. So don't feel slighted if you don't get phone calls anymore or handshakes in abundance. That which you have worked for has come to pass – you loved your country enough to get a visionary elected President. And during his days in the oval office as leader of the free world – the testament of your hope – he will think of you all with thanksgiving. He is the son of working-class Americans.

I encourage you now to look at your children and your grandchildren during the next four years and know that they will have better lives because of your efforts. However, your work is not yet done, the second phase has just begun—restoring the American dream.

Mr. Perfect President?

President Obama has been given a very tall order as President of the United States. As someone commented, "he seems to be President of the World," but that is not the case. He seems to be a decent, moral and honest man who believes in inclusion. And it can certainly be said that he is a man of unusual courage.

He went to work on November 5, 2008 because of his love for the American people – those who voted for him and those who did not. He is already being spent to ensure that the America that once was will be again – only greater. So we must include his wife and children in our daily prayer as we do him. The bible tells us that we must pray for our leaders to do well. He is just a man, like all others, but an endowed man. If you see flaws, pray for God's mercy to enable him. He will, no doubt, become somewhat isolated in his role as President, so we must make every effort to keep him connected. It will be lonely for him sometimes, I am sure. He may even look at his girls some days and question his decision to run for President, but in due process he will remember that it's his destiny; therefore it's theirs. People are happiest when they are doing what they were born to do, regardless of how difficult it is.

His tasks as President are as daunting as they were for President Roosevelt. He's been preparing, however, for this moment in history all of his life. From the time his mom got him up early in the morning to tutor him before school to his entrance into Illinois politics.

I'm sure many have asked the question, "Of all the cities in the United States of America , why did he choose Chicago? Why did he choose Illinois?—considered by many to be the roughest political landscape in the country. Yet he chose it and succeeded there.

"Can any good thing come out of Illinois politics?" The answer is a resounding, yes! — by way of Hawaii.

The change which we sought and brought about in this country for the last two years will continue from the Atlantic to the Pacific and around the world. It must not die, but live on through the next generation. We must teach our children and have them understand what we faced in the first decade of the twenty-first century — a loss of freedom, liberty, morality, and prosperity as we have always known it in America.

Through coalition power, the new administration has vowed to welcome everyone to the table. Anyone who wants to participate, can participate; everyone with great ideas can be heard—it's an irrefutable asset. And we can be assured that the greatest of ideas will come from homes across America from California to Virginia, from South Dakota to Texas, from Washington to Florida, from Arizona to Maine, and from Alaska to Hawaii. From every town and every city, the ideas and solutions will come; they are expected at the White House.

President Obama understands better than anyone that his orders are taller than him. His first fundamental task was to develop a cohesive first team of players, who will in turn develop teams, who will also develop teams. The process will continue until every willing citizen is assigned to a team and tasked with clear responsibilities to bring about the success of the whole—a giant schematic with timetables. Here are the names of those on the Obama First Team in order of succession to the Presidency:

Vice President of the United States—Joseph R. Biden
Secretary of State—Hillary Rodham Clinton
Secretary of the Treasury—Timothy F. Geithner
Secretary of Defense—Robert M. Gates
Attorney General—Eric H. Holder, Jr.
Secretary of the Interior—Kenneth L. Salazar

Secretary of Agriculture—Thomas J. Vilsack
Secretary of Commerce—Gary F. Locke
Secretary of Labor—Hilda L. Solis
Secretary of Health &Human Services—Kathleen Sebelius
Secretary of Housing & Urban Development—Shaun Donovan
Secretary of Transportation—Raymond L. LaHood
Secretary of Energy—Steven Chu
Secretary of Education—Arne Duncan
Secretary of Veterans Affairs—Eric K. Shinseki
Secretary of Homeland Security—Janet A. Napolitano

Other Cabinet-rank Positions:

Chairman of the Council of Economic Advisors—Christina Romer
Administrator of Environmental Protection Agency—Lisa P. Jackson
Director of the Office of Management & Budget—Peter R. Orszag
United States Trade Representative—Ronald Kirk
United States Ambassador to the United Nations—Susan Rice
White House Chief of Staff—Rahm I. Emanuel

Executive Office Positions and Other White House Staff:

Director of the National Economic Council—Lawrence Summers
National Security Advisor—James Jones
White House Deputy Chief of Staff—Jim Messina
White House Deputy Chief of Staff—Mona Sutphen
White House Press Secretary—Robert Gibbs
White House Senior Advisor—David Axelrod
White House Senior Advisor—Valerie Jarrett
White House Senior Advisor—Pete Rouse

The President has chosen senators, representatives, governors, veteran bureaucrats, scientists, and close advisors — Democrats and Republicans — to help him confront the challenges of a deepening recession, a crippled financial system, two wars, healthcare, and approximately nineteen other items on his agenda. Although they are an exceptional first team, they are part of a much larger team that extends from the local level to the national level and abroad.

Our new president has reflected pragmatism in his choices, even in choosing "Bo," the first dog — the most adorable PWD (Portuguese water dog) most of us have ever seen.

So, is he the perfect president? Is he the best guy for the job at this time in history? If the answer is yes, then we have chosen a perfect president. Is he perfect in deeds? — probably not. Is he perfect in thought? — probably not. But Barack Obama is our perfect choice. He is not a president of convenience, or a dynastic president; he is a president of destiny – the ultimate choice. He is God's mercy to this country to give us opportunity to return to our Christian roots, to love our neighbors as we love ourselves, and to become our brother's keeper again — not his exploiter.

A MOMENT IN THOUGHT

DESTINY'S FAITH

Destiny says dream;
When I want to beam.

Destiny says believe;
When I want to achieve.

Destiny says seed;
When I want to deed.

Destiny says love;
When I want to shove.

Destiny says prepare;
When I want to compare.

Destiny says connect;
When I want to protect.

Destiny says finish;
When I want to diminish.

Copyright © 2000 by Linda E. Schexnayder
From the Poetry of the Heart Collection

Chapter 11

RACE IDENTIFICATION IN AMERICA

"Each and every one of us, in our own way, must assume personal responsibility — not only for ourselves and our families, but for our neighbors and our nation. Our greatest responsibility is to embrace a new spirit of community for a new century. For any one of us to succeed, we must succeed as one America.

The challenge of our past remains the challenge of our future — will we be one nation, one people, with one common destiny, or not? Will we all come together, or come apart?

The divide of race has been America's constant curse. And each new wave of immigrants gives new targets to old prejudices. Prejudice and contempt, cloaked in the pretense of religious or political conviction are no different. These forces have nearly destroyed our nation in the past. They plague us still. They fuel the fanaticism of terror. And they torment the lives of millions in fractured nations all around the world.

These obsessions cripple both those who hate and, of course, those who are hated, robbing both of what they might become. We cannot, we will not, succumb to the dark impulses that lurk in the far regions of the soul everywhere. We shall overcome them. And we shall replace them with the generous spirit of a people who feel at home with one another. Our rich texture of racial, religious and political diversity will be a Godsend in the 21st century. Great rewards will come to those who can live together, learn together, work together, forge new ties that bind together." President William Jefferson Clinton - Inaugural Address, January 20, 1997

Who Am I?

"Who am I?" is the question asked by most children during their teenage years and explored well into their adult life. It's not a difficult question to answer ordinarily, but it can be in light of a racially charged society where many are expecting you to identify yourself as being of one race, rather than a blend of two or more. At a time when you may be celebrating the blend of who you are, society says choose. And if you were to succumb to societal pressure, which part of you would you discard—as though such a process were possible. Actually we are of one race; the human race, designations have to do with origin or as some would have it—class or social standing. Nevertheless, let us look at origins.

If you are the son or daughter of a black man and a white woman, you might be an African/European American or Hamitic/Caucasian American or if you choose, just an American, which is sufficient to say—we only need to consider your citizenship to establish your allegiance and your responsibility to this country. Being an American is sufficient to have you join a "perfecting the union" team. But let's go on. If you are the son or daughter of a yellow man and a black woman, then you might be an Asian/African (Afroasian) American or Mongolian/Hamitic American or if you prefer, just an American. If you are the son or daughter of a red man and a brown woman, then you might be a Native American/Latino American or Amerindian/Malay or just an American. If you are the son or daughter of a white man and a red woman, then you might be a European/Native American or Caucasian/Amerindian American or just an American.

Let's take it another step; if you are a son or daughter of a black/white man and a red/brown woman, you might be an African/European/Native American/Latino American or Hamitic/Caucasian/Amerindian/Malay American — a citizen of the United States of America or suffice it to say, just an American. Folks we could go on and on! Within each designation of origin are many subcategories. For instance, Asian could be Chinese, Japanese, Burmese, Tibetans and many others.

Those designations are personally important to archive your cultural history for your posterity. They are not socially relevant in our society except to record the history of diversity in this country as proof that the United States of America was a model to the world that the ignorance of man could be overcome through moral conscience, education and a desire to eradicate it; and to supply our government with necessary data for lawful actions.

How vain can mankind become if ignorance goes unchecked by the wise? Just look back about sixty-five years to World II for your answer. Scientific racism has tried to give validity to such ignorance for generations. It has only proven that scientific theory is only as pure as the soul of the person forming the hypothesis. In all of history, we have not applied color as the gauge of performance, worth, skill or intuitiveness for any other part of creation except to mankind—the intellect of God. Yet our skin hue is the most superficial of all our parts; it's only a covering under which all of mankind is basically the same. We love and cherish the diversity of color in all other parts of creation.

Have you ever pondered the colors of the human race and our use of them as a pseudo-reality? Have you considered it to be a spirit of division perpetuated against the intellect of God for the purpose of amassing self-worth, wealth and power?

The tenets of racism and bigotry are dehumanization, devaluation, degradation, and minimization of others and in contrast to humanize, overvalue, upgrade and maximize oneself in the eyes of others, thereby implying superiority. And in our politically-correct society we need to be aware of these dog whistles as they are being blown. For the sake of our union we need to be aware, so that we are not drawn into deception either publicly or privately.

Millions of Americans are blended races; they are not one or the other. They are as much of one race as they are of the other.

Some may call themselves black, others may call themselves brown, still others may call themselves red, while others call themselves white, as others call themselves yellow. Some may say "I'm biracial" or "I'm multiracial." Yet, some don't feel obliged to define themselves at all. It's their decision; it's their choice. I would only hope that their definition is not based on social pressure, but truly reflect and celebrate who they are whether their outward appearance validates it or not. After all, according to OMB, Office of Management and Budget, 63 possible combinations of racial categories exist; 57 of those categories are for combinations of two or more races.

To simplify it all, according to the bible, we can all be traced back to one of the three sons of Noah.

Racial Classifications Used in Census 2000

Some have begun to use the word, "ethnics," to describe non-European races. Everyone is part of an ethnic group which is different from man's groupings of the human race according to origin. Ethnic groupings relate to cultural traditions and traits, language, religion and beliefs.

You may recall nine years ago during Census 2000, the categories of racial groups were American Indian or Alaska Native, Asian, Black or African American, Native Hawaiian or Other Pacific Islander, White, and Some Other Race (Hispanic can be of any race). "White" alone is not an origin designation, it's a color designation. And if it were to be by color designation, it should have read: black, brown, red, yellow, white and other. Or it should have appropriately read: African American, Alaskan Native American, Asian American, Australian American, European American, Mexican American, Native American, Cuban American, Canadian American, Latin American, Pacific Islander American, and Some Other Race (you could have chosen to list your origin in that category as Italian/German American, Chilean/Brazilian American, Ethiopian/Nigerian American, Japanese/Korean American, Native Hawaiian/Indonesian American). After all, we all came here and joined the Native American. Let the Census Bureau make that distinction in the 2010 Census in respect of all Americans, if our intent is to record the origins, history and backgrounds of America's people. Many citizens were insulted by a single color designation.

So let OMB, the Census Bureau, and the Interagency Committee for the Review of Racial and Ethnic Standards (individuals from 30 government agencies) reconvene and finish the job. Let's respect the heritage of all Americans.

Race in American Politics

Was race or gender important in the 2008 Presidential Campaign? For most Americans, it was not a consideration. It was instigated and perpetuated by many in the news media from the beginning of the campaign — those who didn't see the harm of peddling division. Conflict rules their business. They sought to polarize the black race and antagonize the white race through divisive words and propaganda, but by the end of the campaign very few were listening. Decency and harmony had taken over. The majority of Americans had decided that they would no longer be tainted by the hatred of other Americans because of that God-given factor of hue. Nor would they uphold it in their heritage.

The issue of race and gender was settled in this country long ago. We even declared it in writing: *We hold these Truths to be self-evident, that all Men are created equal, that they are endowed, by their Creator, with certain unalienable Rights, that among these are Life, Liberty, and the Pursuit of Happiness.* The Declaration of Independence, The Constitution and the Bill of Rights of the United States, all speak to the issue. They declare who we are and what we believe. And as recently as the fifties and sixties, we confirmed our beliefs again during the civil rights movement — all colors, all races, both genders, all religions. We have taken the wisdom of the past and applied it to our future — *evil thrives when good men and women do nothing*. We will not allow the seed of hatred of another human being to threaten the existence of our country. To premeditatedly seek to destroy another human being requires the destruction of oneself. Malice and hatred carry within themselves the destruction of the host.

The 2008 Presidential Campaign brought us once again to a point of confirmation and validation of our core values and beliefs as

Americans. We encouraged our hearts, strengthened our souls, and reestablished the cause of truth — we are one nation under God.

On January 20, 2009, we closed the door to a questionable past in our country, locked it with our "national key" and sealed it for history to ever teach us how low the human soul can sink when we fail to love others as we love ourselves and to treat others as we would have them treat us.

Parents of this country will never again teach hatred at the dinner table after thanking God for his bountiful blessing—blessing and cursing from the same mouth. Never again will we infest our children's hearts with destruction and allow every decision of their lives to be tainted with hatred. Never again!

I was not taught hatred at home or at school; I was thought to love and to forgive — it was modeled for me. And I can tell you today that it worked. I live in peace. Today, we as a nation choose to do what's right. We choose it through moral conscience. *To see a middle-aged white woman hate a young black child, to such a degree that she spits on her without provocation, is a visual of a dark soul;. one that we never want to see again. One human being should not see another in such a sinister and self-destructive moment.* Hatred is not innate to children, they must be taught it. They don't understand it, nor do they cope with it very well when its projected at them.

Nowadays, children's responses to hatred normally simulate rebellion and anger because they are unable to process an adult being mean to them for no apparent reason. And if it happens in a classroom through an authority figure, as I have seen, anger and rebellion rev up a few notches.

We are one America. It is time that the black race, the brown race, the red race, the white race, and the yellow race release racial descriptions from their everyday vernacular such as: I was speaking with an African American gentleman; instead of, I was speaking with a gentleman ...Or I was speaking with an Anglo guy; instead of, I was speaking with a guy... Or I was speaking with an Asian girl; instead of, I was speaking with a girl... Or I was speaking with a Latina lady; instead of, I was speaking with a lady. We must stop prefacing our statements with the race of a person. If we do, we will find that a lot of our biases, if any, will disappear with little effort, because the preface itself advocates division.

Have you noticed that the human race is a shade of brown from light to dark with hues of other colors intermingled — a little red, a little gold, and a little yellow. Is one color of eyes better than another? Absolutely not. All that matters is that they function perfectly — that you see well with them.

I have heard stories of how U.S. soldiers injected divisiveness into Iraqi communities after the invasion of 2003 by constantly referencing ethnicity when speaking of Iraqi people and grouping them accordingly. Soon after the invasion there was a piece on one of the networks that showed an Iraqi woman in utter despair asking, "Why do they (American soldiers) ask us who we are?" "We are Iraqis," she said. That constant infusion of separation awakened internal conflict within the country that had been dormant for at least a generation.

Sources: United States Office of Management and Budget, Census Bureau, Census 2000 and Report of the Interagency Committee for the Review of Racial and Ethnic Standards

DAYS OF NIGHT

Darkness engages morning, as I lay to see
If the Light of day will give me strength to leap.
Once, twice, then thrice—more required of patience's might,
Reserved to whet the dream sprouts in times of lullaby flights.

Wave upon wave douse my shroud as I stand the gale,
Peering the distant Lighthouse certified to hale.
Riding the tide as it rises high to its final halt;
To stretch, stretch, and stretch again to step into the catapult.

Pause reflections; gauge affections; harness reactions—
Retreat within to clear the paths of former timed infractions.
Moments taken, moments given in shades of grayish cover.
Some to stay; some to go; some to rediscover.

I avow myself a believer—Light has come to favor.
Thoughts be yielded to the inlet of my Savior.
No time to spare to declare, "Light bid darkness flee,
Come brighter than first I saw—eclipse my days of night to glee,"

To embrace at daybreak, the sun upon my face—
Renewal aglow, fading the unwonted chase.
Days of Night have been a leap of faith for me.
A gift forever into Days of Light to be.

Chapter 12

POETRY OF AMERICA

"When power leads men towards arrogance, poetry reminds him of his limitations. When power narrows the areas of man's concern, poetry reminds him of the richness and diversity of his existence. When power corrupts, poetry cleanses. For art establishes the basic human truth which must serve as the touchstone of our judgment."
President John (Jack) F. Kennedy - Speech at Amherst College, Amherst, Massachusetts, October 26, 1963

America's poetry is as powerful as any on earth. It's etched into our spirits and souls and carved into our buildings and statutes to magnify our existence. It is not the poetry of one man, but the poetry of a people. It is poetry developed over generations that we have hallowed in times of difficulty and struggle. These are words penned from the heart of a courageous soul in love with their country — a country that symbolizes truth, principle, and freedom. We didn't consider these words so at their inception, but through time they revealed themselves to be the cry of the masses because they exemplified the essence of our hearts – the heart of an American.

America is a dream manifested in the hearts of her citizens which causes her to stay alive and vibrant. And as long as we the people live the dream, the dream lives in us. It's not a dream that can be given, but one that every true American has to take to heart; to become that dream; to live that dream out in their personal thoughts and actions, thereby becoming an American. Please note that some words were spelled differently during the time of the original writings than they are today. This is the American Anthology:

Liberty Bell
Cast by Whitechapel Foundry in London, England
Arrived in Philadelphia, Pennsylvania, September 1, 1752
Inscription

By order of the Assembly of the Province of Pensylvania for the State house in the City of Philada 1752

"Proclaim Liberty thro' all the Land to all the Inhabitants thereof. - Levit. XXV.10"
[Leviticus 25:10 "And ye shall hallow the fiftieth year, and proclaim liberty throughout all the Land unto all the Inhabitants thereof."]

Declaration of Independence of the Second Continental Congress
Independence Hall, Philadelphia, Pennsylvania, July 4, 1776

"When, in the Course of human Events, it becomes necessary for one People to dissolve the Political Bands which have connected them with another, and to assume, among the Powers of the Earth, the separate and equal Station to which the Laws of Nature and of Nature's God entitle them, a decent Respect to the Opinions of Mankind requires that they should declare the Causes which impel them to the Separation.
We hold these Truths to be self-evident, that all Men are created equal, that they are endowed, by their Creator, with certain unalienable Rights, that among these are Life, Liberty, and the Pursuit of Happiness.—*That to secure these Rights, Governments are instituted among Men, deriving their just Powers from the Consent of the Governed, that whenever any Form of Government becomes destructive of these Ends, it is the Right of the People to alter or to abolish it, and to institute new Government, laying its Foundation on such Principles, and organizing its Powers in such*

Form, as to them shall seem most likely to effect their Safety and Happiness. Prudence, indeed, will dictate, that Governments long established, should not be changed for light and transient Causes; and accordingly all Experience hath shewn, that Mankind are more disposed to suffer, while Evils are sufferable, than to right themselves by abolishing the Forms to which they are accustomed. But when a long Train of Abuses and Usurpations, pursuing invariably the same Object, evinces a Design to reduce them under absolute Despotism, it is their Right, it is their Duty, to throw off such Government, and to provide new Guards for their future Security. Such has been the patient Sufferance of these Colonies; and such is now the Necessity which constrains them to alter their former Systems of Government."

Preamble to the Constitution of the United States of America
Philadelphia, Pennsylvania, September 17, 1787

"We the People of the United States, in Order to form a more perfect Union, establish Justice, insure domestic Tranquility, provide for the common defence, promote the general Welfare, and secure the Blessings of Liberty to ourselves and our Posterity, do ordain and establish this Constitution for the United States of America."

Thomas Jefferson - Third President of the
United States of America to George Hammond in 1792

"A nation, as a society, forms a moral person, and every member of it is personally responsible for his society."

James Madison - Fourth President of the
United States of America to W.T. Barry, August 4, 1822

"Knowledge will forever govern ignorance: and a people who mean to be their own governours, must arm themselves with the power which knowledge gives."

Abraham Lincoln - Sixteenth President of the
United States of America
Soldiers' National Cemetery in Gettysburg, Pennsylvania
November 19, 1863

"Four score and seven years ago our fathers brought forth on this continent a new nation, conceived in Liberty, and dedicated to the proposition that all men are created equal. Now we are engaged in a great civil war, testing whether that nation, or any nation, so conceived and so dedicated, can long endure. We are met on a great battlefield of that war. We have come to dedicate a portion of that field, as a final resting place for those who here gave their lives that that nation might live. It is altogether fitting and proper that we should do this.

But, in a larger sense, we can not dedicate—we can not consecrate—we can not hallow—this ground. The brave men, living and dead, who struggled here, have consecrated it, far above our poor power to add or detract. The world will little note, nor long remember what we say here, but it can never forget what they did here. It is for us the living, rather, to be dedicated here to the unfinished work which they who fought here have thus far so nobly advanced. It is rather for us to be here dedicated to the great task remaining before us—that from these honored dead we take increased devotion to that cause for which they gave the last full measure of devotion—that we here highly resolve that these dead shall not have died in vain—that this nation, under God, shall have a new birth of freedom—and that government of the people, by the people, for the people, shall not perish from the earth..."

Franklin D. Roosevelt - Thirty-Second President of the
United States of America
National Industrial Recovery Act, June 16, 1933

"No business which depends for existence on paying less than living wages to its workers has any right to continue in this country."

Motto of the United States of America
Washington, D.C., July 30, 1956
Proclamation

On July 20, 1956, Congress proclaimed that the national motto of the United States of America is "In God We Trust," and that motto is inscribed above the main door of the Senate, behind the Chair of the Speaker of the House of Representatives, and on the currency of the United States of America. On July 30, 1956, President Dwight Eisenhower signed the law officially establishing "In God We Trust," as the national motto of the United States of America.

John F. Kennedy – Thirty-Fifth President of the
United States of America
Inaugural Address in Washington, D.C., January 20, 1961

"The same revolutionary beliefs for which our forebearers [forebears] fought — are still at issue around the globe — the belief that the rights of man come not from the generosity of the state but from the hand of God."

James (Jimmy) Carter - Thirty-Ninth President of the
United States of America
Speech to Parliament of India June 2, 1978

"Democracy is like the experience of life itself - always changing,, infinite in its variety, sometimes turbulent and all the more valuable for having been tested by adversity."

Ronald Wilson Reagan - Fortieth President of the
United States of America
First Inaugural Address, January 20, 1981

"No arsenal or no weapon in the arsenals of the world is so formidable as the will and moral courage of free men and women."

William Jefferson Clinton - Forty-Second President of the United States of America
John Kerry Presidential Campaign Rally, October 25, 2004

"Now, one of Clinton's laws of politics is this: If one candidate's trying to scare you and the other one's trying to get you to think, if one candidate's appealing to your fears and the other one's appealing to your hopes, you better vote for the person who wants you to think and hope."

George W. Bush - Forty-Third President of the United States of America
50th Anniversary of Our National Motto, "In God We Trust," Proclamation 8038, July 27, 2006

"On the 50th anniversary of our national motto, 'In God We Trust,' we reflect on these words that guide millions of Americans, recognize the blessings of the Creator, and offer our thanks for His great gift of liberty.

"From its earliest days, the United States has been a Nation of faith. During the War of 1812, as the morning light revealed that the battle-torn American flag still flew above Fort McHenry, Francis Scott Key penned, "And this be our motto: 'In God is our trust!'" His poem became our National Anthem, reminding generations of Americans to 'Praise the Power that hath made and preserved us a nation.' On July 30, 1956, President Dwight Eisenhower signed the law officially establishing 'In God We Trust' as our national motto.

"Today, our country stands strong as a beacon of religious freedom. Our citizens, whatever their faith or background, worship freely and millions answer the universal call to love their neighbor and serve a cause greater than self.

"As we commemorate the 50th anniversary of our national motto and remember with thanksgiving God's mercies throughout our history, we recognize a divine plan that stands above all human plans and continue to seek His will.

"Now, Therefore, I, George W. Bush, President of the United States of America, do hereby proclaim July 30, 2006, as the

50th Anniversary of our National Motto, 'In God We Trust.' I call upon the people of the United States to observe this day with appropriate programs, ceremonies, and activities.

"In Witness Whereof, I have hereunto set my hand this twenty-seventh day of July, in the year of our Lord two thousand six, and of the Independence of the United States of America the two hundred and thirty-first."

Barack H. Obama - Forty-Fourth President of the United States of America
First Inaugural Address, January 20, 2009

"For as much as government can do and must do, it is ultimately the faith and determination of the American people upon which this nation relies. It is the kindness to take in a stranger when the levees break, the selflessness of workers who would rather cut their hours than see a friend lose their job which sees us through our darkest hours. It is the firefighter's courage to storm a stairway filled with smoke, but also a parent's willingness to nurture a child, that finally decides our fate.

"Our challenges may be new. The instruments with which we meet them may be new. But those values upon which our success depends — hard work and honesty, courage and fair play, tolerance and curiosity, loyalty and patriotism — these things are old. These things are true. They have been the quiet force of progress throughout our history. What is demanded then is a return to these truths. What is required of us now is a new era of responsibility — a recognition, on the part of every American, that we have duties to ourselves, our nation, and the world, duties that we do not grudgingly accept but rather seize gladly, firm in the knowledge that there is nothing so satisfying to the spirit, so defining of our character, than giving our all to a difficult task.

"This is the price and the promise of citizenship. This is the source of our confidence — the knowledge that God calls on us to shape an uncertain destiny."

THE PAST

The past.
The wise teacher
Lessons of the completer
Reservoir of empirical wisdom
Heralded rewards of courage random.

The past.
Breathless cost of freedom
Musty ruins of differences and martyrdom
Perils of unharnessed power
Seeds of today's flowers

The past.
Ineffable graces smitten
Living memoirs written
Mendaciousness lamented
Signatures of history witnessed.

The past.
Ground swell of hued inhumanity
Reveille of brotherhood and profanity
Undaunted heroes discovered
Scores of united friends uncovered.

The past.
Enamored life to treasure
Efflorescent wealth to measure
Guide of gratuitous living
Progenies of philanthropic giving.

Chapter 13

SONGS OF AMERICA

*Songs can implant words and ideas in the minds of millions
of people that a million speeches cannot.*
Linda E. Schexnayder, Author, CEO and Teacher

Patriotic songs stir our hearts, swell our national pride and remind us
of our responsibility as Americans. Honor your country by learning
and singing these songs daily. If you are not familiar with the tune,
they can be heard every Fourth of July — Independence Day. These
songs were penned through the expressed hopes of our forebears,
who sought to build a nation that would require the efforts of future
generations to energize it and to perfect it. They were written and
sometimes revised to reflect the tribulations, victories, and triumphs
of a generation so that subsequent generations would understand the
challenges of our Republic, accept the charge of freedom, and
deliver the flaming torch of democracy to the next generation.
Democracy requires a constant forward motion in morality,
education, and hope to survive; to be stagnant is to cease to be.

Star Spangled Banner
"Defence of Fort McHenry," poem written by Francis Scott Key
during *The War of 1812*
Baltimore, Maryland, September 17, 1814
Congress proclaimed it the U.S. National Anthem in 1931

Oh, say can you see by the dawn's early light
What so proudly we hailed at the twilight's last gleaming?
Whose broad stripes and bright stars thru the perilous fight,
O'er the ramparts we watched were so gallantly streaming?
And the rocket's red glare, the bombs bursting in air,
Gave proof through the night that our flag was still there.
Oh, say does that star-spangled banner yet wave
O'er the land of the free and the home of the brave?

On the shore, dimly seen through the mists of the deep,
Where the foe's haughty host in dread silence reposes,
What is that which the breeze, o'er the towering steep,
As it fitfully blows, half conceals, half discloses?
Now it catches the gleam of the morning's first beam,
In full glory reflected now shines in the stream:
'Tis the star-spangled banner! Oh long may it wave
O'er the land of the free and the home of the brave!

And where is that band who so vauntingly swore
That the havoc of war and the battle's confusion,
A home and a country should leave us no more!
Their blood has washed out their foul footsteps' pollution.
No refuge could save the hireling and slave
From the terror of flight, or the gloom of the grave:
And the star-spangled banner in triumph doth wave
O'er the land of the free and the home of the brave!

Oh! thus be it ever, when freemen shall stand
Between their loved home and the war's desolation!
Blest with victory and peace, may the heav'n rescued land
Praise the Power that hath made and preserved us a nation.
Then conquer we must, when our cause it is just,
And this be our motto: "In God is our trust."
And the star-spangled banner in triumph shall wave
O'er the land of the free and the home of the brave!

**God Bless America
by Irving Berlin, 1918 - Revised 1938**

*God bless America,
Land that I love,
Stand beside her and guide her
Thru the night with a light from above;*

*From the mountains, to the prairies,
To the oceans white with foam,
God bless America,
My home, sweet home.
God bless America,
My home, sweet home.*

**God Bless the USA
by Country Music Singer Lee Greenwood, 1984**

*If tomorrow all the things were gone
I'd worked for all my life,
And I had to start again
with just my children and my wife,
I'd thank my lucky stars
to be living here today,
'Cause the flag still stands for freedom
and they can't take that away.*

*From the lakes of Minnesota
to the hills of Tennessee,
Across the plains of Texas
from sea to shining sea.
From Detroit down to Houston
and New York to L.A.,
There's pride in every American heart
and it's time we stand and say:*

*I'm proud to be an American
where at least I know I'm free,
And I won't forget the men who died
who gave that right to me,
And I gladly stand up next to you
and defend her still today,
'Cause there ain't no doubt I love this land
God Bless the U.S.A.*

America, My Country, 'Tis of Thee
by Samuel F. Smith, 1832

My country, 'tis of Thee,
Sweet Land of Liberty
Of thee I sing;
Land where my fathers died,
Land of the pilgrims' pride,
From every mountain side
Let Freedom ring.

My native country, thee,
Land of the noble free,
Thy name I love;
I love thy rocks and rills,
Thy woods and templed hills,
My heart with rapture thrills
Like that above.

Let music swell the breeze,
And ring from all the trees
Sweet Freedom's song;
Let mortal tongues awake;
Let all that breathe partake;
Let rocks their silence break,
The sound prolong.

Our fathers' God to Thee,
Author of Liberty,
To thee we sing,
Long may our land be bright
With Freedom's holy light,
Protect us by thy might
Great God, our King.

Our glorious Land to-day,
'Neath Education's sway,
Soars upward still. Its hills of learning fair,
Whose bounties all may share,
behold them everywhere
On vale and hill!

Thy safeguard, Liberty,
The school shall ever be,
Our Nation's pride!
No tyrant hand shall smite,
While with encircling might
All here are taught the Right
With Truth allied.

*Beneath Heaven's gracious will
The stars of progress still
Our course do sway;
In unity sublime
To broader heights we climb,
Triumphant over Time,
God speeds our way!*

*Grand birthright of our sires,
Our altars and our fires
Keep we still pure!
Our starry flag unfurled,
The hope of all the world,
In peace and light impearled,
God hold secure!*

America, The Beautiful
by Katharine Lee Bates, 1913

*O beautiful for spacious skies,
For amber waves of grain,
For purple mountain majesties
Above the fruited plain!
America! America! God shed His grace on thee,
And crown thy good with brotherhood
From sea to shining sea!*

*O beautiful for pilgrim feet,
Whose stern impassion'd stress
A thoroughfare for freedom beat
Across the wilderness!
America! America! God mend thine ev'ry flaw,
Confirm thy soul in self-control,
Thy liberty in law!*

*O beautiful for heroes proved In liberating strife,
Who more than self their country loved,
And mercy more than life!
America! America! May God thy gold refine
Till all success be nobleness,
And ev'ry gain divine!*

*O Beautiful for patriot dream
That sees beyond the years
Thine alabaster cities gleam,
Undimmed by human tears!
America! America! God shed His grace on thee,
And crown thy good with brotherhood
From sea to shining sea!*

This is My Country
by Don Rave, 1940

This is my country! Land of my birth!
This is my country! Grandest on earth!
I pledge thee my allegiance, America, the bold,
For this is my country to have and to hold.

What difference if I hail from North or South
Or from the East or West
My heart is full of love for all of these.
I only know I swell with pride and deep within my breast,
I thrill to see old glory paint the breeze!

This is my country! Land of my choice!
This is my country! Hear my proud voice!
I pledge thee my allegiance, America, the bold,
For this is my country to have and to hold.

The Marines' Hymn
Author Unknown, Sung Early 1800s
Official Hymn of the Corps, 1929 - 4th Line Changed, 1942

From the Halls of Montezuma
To the shores of Tripoli,
We fight our country's battles
In the air, on land, and sea.
First to fight for right and freedom
And to keep our honor clean,
We are proud to claim the title
Of United States Marines.

"Our flag's unfurled to every breeze
From dawn to setting sun;
We have fought in every clime and place
Where we could take a gun.
In the snow of far-off Northern lands
And in sunny tropic scenes,
You will find us always on the job —
The United States Marines.

"Here's health to you and to our Corps
Which we are proud to serve;
In many a strife we've fought for life
And never lost our nerve.
If the Army and the Navy
Ever look on Heaven's scenes,
They will find the streets are guarded
By United States Marines."

Battle Hymn of the Republic
by Julia Ward Lowe, 1862

Mine eyes have seen the glory of the coming of the Lord
He is trampling out the vintage where the grapes of wrath are stored,
He has loosed the fateful lightning of His terrible swift sword
His truth is marching on.
Glory! Glory! Hallelujah!
Glory! Glory! Hallelujah!
Glory! Glory! Hallelujah!
His truth is marching on.

I have seen Him in the watch-fires of a hundred circling camps
They have builded Him an altar in the evening dews and damps
I can read His righteous sentence by the dim and flaring lamps
His day is marching on.
Glory! Glory! Hallelujah!
Glory! Glory! Hallelujah!
Glory! Glory! Hallelujah!
His truth is marching on.

I have read a fiery gospel writ in burnish`d rows of steel,
"As ye deal with my contemnors, so with you my grace shall deal;"
Let the Hero, born of woman, crush the serpent with his heel
Since God is marching on.
Glory! Glory! Hallelujah!
Glory! Glory! Hallelujah!
Glory! Glory! Hallelujah!
His truth is marching on.

He has sounded from the trumpet that shall never call retreat
He is sifting out the hearts of men before His judgment-seat
Oh, be swift, my soul, to answer Him! Be jubilant, my feet!
Our God is marching on.
Glory! Glory! Hallelujah!
Glory! Glory! Hallelujah!
Glory! Glory! Hallelujah!
His truth is marching on.

In the beauty of the lilies Christ was born across the sea,
With a glory in His bosom that transfigures you and me:
As He died to make men holy, let us die to make men free,
While God is marching on.
Glory! Glory! Hallelujah!
Glory! Glory! Hallelujah!
Glory! Glory! Hallelujah!
His truth is marching on.

The Stars and Stripes Forever
Official National March by John Philip Sousa, 1897

Let martial note in triumph float
And liberty extend its mighty hand
A flag appears 'mid thunderous cheers,
The banner of the Western land.
The emblem of the brave and true
Its folds protect no tyrant crew;
The red and white and starry blue
Is freedom's shield and hope.
Other nations may deem their flags the best
And cheer them with fervid elation
But the flag of the North and South and West
Is the flag of flags, the flag of Freedom's nation.

Hurrah for the flag of the free!
May it wave as our standard forever,
The gem of the land and the sea,
The banner of the right.
Let despots remember the day
When our fathers with mighty endeavor
Proclaimed as they marched to the fray
That by their might and by their right
It waves forever.

Let eagle shriek from lofty peak
The never-ending watchword of our land;
Let summer breeze waft through the trees
The echo of the chorus grand.
Sing out for liberty and light,
Sing out for freedom and the right.
Sing out for Union and its might,
O patriotic sons.
Other nations may deem their flags the best
And cheer them with fervid elation,
But the flag of the North and South and West
Is the flag of flags, the flag of Freedom's nation.

Hurrah for the flag of the free.
May it wave as our standard forever
The gem of the land and the sea,
The banner of the right.
Let despots remember the day
When our fathers with mighty endeavor
Proclaimed as they marched to the fray,
That by their might and by their right
It waves forever.

The Air Force Song
Written by Major Robert Crawford
for Army Air Corps Song Contest, 1938
(Some changes to the original lyrics are reflected)

Off we go into the wild blue yonder,
climbing high into the sun;
Here they come, zooming to meet our thunder,
at 'em boys, give 'er the gun!
Down we dive, spouting our flame from under,
off with one Hell-of-a roar!
We live in fame or go down in flame. Hey!
Nothing'll stop the U.S. Air Force!

Minds of men fashioned a crate of thunder,
Sent it high into the blue;
Hands of men blasted the world asunder,
How they lived God only knew!
Souls of men dreaming of skies to conquer
Gave us wing, ever to soar!
With scouts before and bombers galore. Hey!
Nothing'll stop the US Air Force!

Here's a toast to the host of those who
love the vastness of the sky,
To a friend we send this message
of his brother men who fly.
We drink to those who gave their all of old,
Then down we roar to score the rainbow's pot of gold.
A toast to the host of men we boast
The US Air Force!

Off we go into the wild sky yonder,
Keep the wing level and true;
If you'd live to be a grey-haired wonder
Keep the nose out of the blue!
Flying men, guarding our nation's borders,
We'll be there followed by more!
In echelon, we carry on. Hey!
Nothing'll stop the US Air Force!

"The Army Goes Rolling Along,"
Official Song of the U.S. Army, 1952
Originally written by Brigadier General Edmund L. Gruber, 1908

March along, sing our song, with the Army of the free
Count the brave, count the true, who have fought to victory
We're the Army and proud of our name
We're the Army and proudly proclaim

First to fight for the right,
And to build the Nation's might,
And The Army Goes Rolling Along
Proud of all we have done,
Fighting till the battle's won,
And the Army Goes Rolling Along.

Then it's Hi! Hi! Hey!
The Army's on its way.
Count off the cadence loud and strong (TWO! THREE!)
For where e'er we go,
You will always know
That The Army Goes Rolling Along.

Valley Forge, Custer's ranks,
San Juan Hill and Patton's tanks,
And the Army went rolling along
Minute men, from the start,
Always fighting from the heart,
And the Army keeps rolling along.

Then it's Hi! Hi! Hey!
The Army's on its way.
Count off the cadence loud and strong (TWO! THREE!)
For where e'er we go,
You will always know
That The Army Goes Rolling Along.

Men in rags, men who froze,
Still that Army met its foes,
And the Army went rolling along.
Faith in God, then we're right,
And we'll fight with all our might,
As the Army keeps rolling along.

Then it's Hi! Hi! Hey!
The Army's on its way.
Count off the cadence loud and strong (TWO! THREE!)
For where e'er we go,
You will always know
That The Army Goes Rolling Along.

The Navy Hymn
"Eternal Father, Strong to Save"
Lyrics by Rev. William Whiting, Winchester, England, 1860
Music by Rev. John B. Dyke, 1861
(Certain verses have been changed from the original.
Google "naval hymn" to download for ceremonies.)

Eternal Father, strong to save,
Whose arm hath bound the restless wave,
Who bidd'st the mighty ocean deep,
Its own appointed limits keep.

Oh hear us when we cry to Thee,
For those in peril on the sea! Amen.

Eternal Father, lend Thy grace To
those with wings who fly thro' space,
Thro wind and storm, thro' sun and rain,
Oh bring them safely home again.

Oh Father, hear an humble prayer,
For those in peril in the air! Amen.

Oh Trinity of love and pow'r,
Our brethren shield in danger's hour,
From rock and tempest, fire and foe,
Protect them where so e'er they go.

Thus evermore shall rise to Thee
Glad hymns of praise from land and sea! Amen.

Hail to the Chief
Official Anthem of the President of the United States
Lyrics by Albert Gamse adapted from Sir Walter Scott's, "Lady of
the Lake" - Music by James Sanderson, 1810
The President receives preceding fanfare of four ruffles (drums) and flourishes (bugles)
before *"Hail to the Chief"*— four are the highest honor. Lyrics are rarely sung.

Hail to the Chief we have chosen for the nation,
Hail to the Chief! We salute him, one and all.
Hail to the Chief, as we pledge cooperation
In proud fulfillment of a great, noble call.
Yours is the aim to make this grand country grander,
This you will do, that's our strong, firm belief.
Hail to the one we selected as commander,
Hail to the President! Hail to the Chief!

Official Song of the National Guard
The National Guard is the oldest component of the Armed Forces of the United States.
It celebrated its 372nd birthday on December 13, 2008, dating back to 1636.

I was a minuteman at Concord Bridge
The shot heard 'round the world
and I was there on Bunker Hill
When "Old Glory" was unfurled
And when my country called me
From within or from afar
I'll be first to answer
Proud to be the Guard

Defending Freedom protecting dreams
This is the spirit of what it means to me
For my God and my home that I love
I GUARD AMERICA

And in the eyes of my enemies
Or the eye of a storm
I face the dangers as they come
In any shape or form
I am your sons, your friends, your fathers
And your daughters working hard
To be the best and keep us strong
Proud to be the Guard

Defending Freedom protecting dreams
This is the spirit of what it means to me
For my God and my home that I love
I GUARD AMERICA

Defending Freedom protecting dreams
This is the spirit of what it means to me
For my God and my home that I love
I GUARD AMERICA

Guarding AMERICA

AMERICA

Lift Every Voice and Sing
Poem by James Weldon Johnson,
Music by John Rosamond Johnson, 1900
(The first verse is most commonly sung.)

Lift ev'ry voice and sing, 'til earth and heaven ring,
Ring with the harmonies of Liberty;
Let our rejoicing rise, high as the listening skies,
Let it resound loud as the rolling sea.
Sing a song full of the faith that the dark past has taught us,
Sing a song full of the hope that the present has brought us;
Facing the rising sun of our new day begun,
Let us march on 'til victory is won.

Stony the road we trod, bitter the chast'ning rod,
Felt in the days when hope unborn had died;
Yet with a steady beat, have not our weary feet,
Come to the place for which our fathers sighed?
We have come over a way that with tears has been watered,
We have come, treading our path through the blood of the
slaughtered,
Out from the gloomy past, 'til now we stand at last
Where the white gleam of our bright star is cast.

God of our weary years, God of our silent tears,
Thou Who has brought us thus far on the way;
Thou Who has by Thy might, led us into the light,
Keep us forever in the path, we pray.
Lest our feet stray from the places, our God, where we meet Thee;
Lest our hearts, drunk with the wine of the world, we forget Thee;
Shadowed beneath Thy hand, may we forever stand,
True to our God, true to our native land.

Chapter 14

OLD GLORY ETIQUETTE AND DISPLAY

"I pledge allegiance to the Flag of the United States of America, and to the Republic for which it stands, one Nation under God, indivisible, with liberty and justice for all.," should be rendered by standing at attention facing the flag with the right hand over the heart. When not in uniform men should remove any non-religious headdress with their right hand and hold it at the left shoulder, the hand being over the heart. Persons in uniform should remain silent, face the flag, and render the military salute."

From the U.S. Code Online via GPO Access [wais.access.gpo.gov]

Stars and Stripes

For more than 200 years, the American flag has been the symbol of our nation's strength and unity, a source of pride and inspiration for American citizens, and a prominent icon in our national history. Here are the highlights of its unique past.

On January 1, 1776, *the Continental Army was reorganized in accordance with a Congressional resolution which placed American forces under George Washington's control. On that New Year's Day, the Continental Army was laying siege to Boston which had been taken over by the British Army. Washington ordered the Grand Union flag hoisted above his base at Prospect Hill. It had 13 alternate red and white stripes and the British Union Jack in the upper left-hand corner (the canton).*

In May of 1776, *Betsy Ross reported that she had sewn the first American flag.*

On June 14, 1777, *in order to establish an official flag for the new nation, the Continental Congress passed the first Flag Act: "Resolved, That the flag of the United States be made of thirteen stripes, alternate red and white; that the union be thirteen stars, white in a blue field, representing a new Constellation."*

Between 1777 and 1960, *Congress passed several acts that changed the shape, design and arrangement of the flag and allowed for additional stars and stripes to be added to reflect the admission of each new state.*

Act of January 13, 1794 *provided for 15 stripes and 15 stars after May 1795.*

Act of April 4, 1818 *provided for 13 stripes and one star for each state, to be added to the flag on the 4th of July following the admission of each new state, signed by President Monroe.*

Executive Order of President Taft dated June 24, 1912 *established the proportions of the flag and provided for the arrangement of the stars in six horizontal rows of eight stars each, the single point of each star to be upward.*

Executive Order of President Eisenhower dated <u>January 3, 1959</u> provided for the arrangement of the stars in seven rows of seven stars each, staggered horizontally and vertically.

Executive Order of President Eisenhower dated <u>August 21, 1959</u> provided for the arrangement of the stars in nine rows staggered horizontally and eleven rows staggered vertically.

Today the flag of the United States of America consists of thirteen horizontal stripes, seven red alternating with six white. The stripes represent the thirteen original colonies; the stars represent the fifty states of the Union. The colors of the flag are symbolic as well: <u>*Red*</u> symbolizes *Hardiness and Valor*, <u>*White*</u> symbolizes *Purity and Innocence* and <u>*Blue*</u> represents *Vigilance, Perseverance and Justice.*

Old Glory Protocol and Etiquette

Did you know that federal law stipulates many aspects of flag protocol and etiquette? The section of law dealing with American Flag etiquette is generally referred to as the *Flag Code*. Some general guidelines from the code may answer many of your most common questions:

  * ★   The flag should be lighted at all times, either by sunlight or by an appropriate light source.

  * ★   The flag should be flown in fair weather, unless the flag is designed for inclement weather use.

  * ★   The flag should never be dipped to any person or thing. It is flown upside down only as a distress signal.

  * ★   The flag should not be used for any decoration in general. Bunting of blue, white and red stripes is available for these purposes. The blue stripe of the bunting should be on the top.

★   The flag should never be used for any advertising purpose. It should not be embroidered, printed or otherwise impressed on such articles as cushions, handkerchiefs, napkins, boxes, or anything intended to be discarded after temporary use. Advertising signs should not be attached to the staff or halyard.

★   The flag should not be used as part of a costume or athletic uniform. A flag patch may be used on the uniforms of military personnel, firemen, policemen and members of patriotic organizations.

★   The flag should never have any mark, insignia, letter, word, number, figure or drawing of any kind placed on it or attached to it.

★   The flag should never be used for receiving, holding, carrying or delivering anything.

★   When the flag is lowered, no part of it should touch the ground or any other object; it should be received by waiting hands and arms.

★   To store the flag, fold it neatly and ceremoniously.

★   The flag should be cleaned and mended when needed.

★   When a flag is so worn that it is no longer fit to serve as a symbol of our country, it should be destroyed by burning in a dignified manner.

Rules for Display of the American Flag Outdoors

Over the Middle of the Street
The flag should be suspended vertically with the union to the north on an east and west street or to the east on a north and south street.

Flown at Half-Staff

"Half-staff" is the lowering of the flag to one-half the distance between the top and bottom of the staff. The flag should be first hoisted to the peak for an instant and then lowered to the half-staff position. The flag should be again raised to the peak before it is lowered for the day. Crepe streamers may be affixed to spearheads or flagstaffs in a parade only by order of the President of the United States.

Flown on the Same Halyard with Non-Nation Flags

The flag of the United States of America should always be at the peak of the staff.. When other flags are flown from adjacent staffs, the American flag should be hoisted first and lowered last. No other flag or pennant may be placed above the American flag or to the right of it.

Suspended Over a Sidewalk

The flag may be suspended from a rope extending from a house to a pole at the edge of the sidewalk. The flag should be hoisted out, union first, from the building.

From a Staff Projecting Horizontally or at an Angle

The flag may be projected from the window sill, balcony, or front of a building, with the union of the flag placed at the peak of the staff unless the flag is at half-staff.

In a Parade with Other Flags

When the flag is carried in a procession with other flags, it should be either on the marching right (the flag's own right) or in front of the center line of other flags.

With Non-National Flags

The flag of the United States of America should be centered at the highest point when it is displayed with a group of flags of states, localities or pennants of societies on other staffs.

With Other National Flags
When flags of two or more nations are displayed, they should be of approximately equal size and flown from separate staffs of the same height. International agreements do not allow the display of the flag of one nation above that of another in time of peace.

With Another Flag Against a Wall from Crossed Staffs
The flag should be on the right (the flag's own right which is the viewer's left) with its staff in front of the staff of the other flag.

Rules for Display of the American Flag Indoors

From a Staff in a Church or Public Auditorium on a Podium
The flag of the United States of America should hold the position of superior prominence, in advance of the audience, and in the position of honor at the clergyman or speaker's right as he faces the audience. Any other flag so displayed should be placed on the left of the clergyman or speaker (to the right of the audience).

From a Staff in a Church or Public Auditorium Off the Podium
Custom, not flag code, establishes that the flag of the United States of America should hold the position of superior prominence and honor at the audience's right as part of the audience.

Used to Cover a Casket
The flag should be so placed that the union is at the head and over the left shoulder. The flag should not be lowered into the grave or allowed to touch the ground.

Other Than Being Flown from a Staff
The flag should be displayed flat, whether indoors or outdoors. When displayed either horizontally or vertically against a wall, the union should be uppermost and to the flag's own right, that is, to the observer's left. When displayed in a window it should be displayed in the same way, that is with the union or blue field to the left of the observer in the street. When festoons, rosettes or draping are desired, bunting of blue, white

and red should be used, but never the flag. Remember, you don't need a holiday to display your flag. There are 365/366 days in a year. Be free. Follow your heart.

Sources: [Laws in effect as of January 3, 2006] [CITE: 4USC4] TITLE 4--FLAG AND SEAL, SEAT OF GOVERNMENT, AND THE STATES CHAPTER 1--THE FLAG Sec. 4. Pledge of allegiance to the flag; manner of delivery of "The Pledge of Allegiance to the Flag:" (Added Pub. L. 105-225, Sec. 2(a), Aug. 12, 1998, 112 Stat. 1494; amended Pub. L. 107-293, Sec. 2(a), Nov. 13, 2002, 116 Stat. 2060.), http://www.usflag.org, and http://www.usa-flag-site.org

TRUST

Turn your face to the sun
With eyelids shut tight,
To see the beautiful hues of red,
The color line of life.

Then go inside and close your eyes—
See the gravity of shade.
Though the walls are frosty white,
Sable strikes and fades.

Chapter 15

RESTORATION AND THE FUTURE

"We have faith that future generations will know that here, in the middle of the twentieth century [twenty-first century], there came a time when men of good will found a way to unite, and produce, and fight to destroy the forces of ignorance, and intolerance, and slavery, and war."
President Franklin Delano Roosevelt - Address to White House Correspondents' Association, Washington, D.C., February 1943

If you are one who thinks that the President will alone change the country, you are mistaken. *"Leaders are followers of what is true, what is fair, what is right."* That can be said of our President, I'm sure, but it should also be said of us. A noble President inspires, unifies, and calls to action the citizens of the country to achieve our high ideals through moral excellence. Repeatedly, I have said that we are one nation—a team of many teams. It will take the President and his administration; it will take Congress; it will take you; and it will take me; all working together according to our plan of action. Never again should we follow the plan of a man. Hereafter, we should follow the plan of God for this nation; the fundamentals of which are clearly outlined in our Constitution and Bill of Rights. Change was the mandate of the 2008 Presidential Election, but it was really restoration that we sort; restoration of those things we hold dear which we will never change— freedom of speech, freedom to follow our destiny; freedom to participate in the political process and to choose our leaders without retaliation; freedom to prosper spiritually, physically, financially, and socially; freedom to occupy our dwellings without intrusion; freedom to live peacefully anywhere in this country. These are things we seek to maintain and to perfect because they are our rights and privileges as American citizens by design.

The Work Order

If we are going to maximize our efforts in the next four years, we must scrutinize every tier of government and remove the obstructionists — those whose agendas are clearly contrary to the blessings of liberty. Those congressional seats that have been abandoned by Republicans and those that should be abandoned by Democrats must be filled with forthright people of high moral character — not subject to arrogance, bias, bigotry and hatred of the poor — to move legislation thru expeditiously without regard to partisanship. The tainted voices of congressional leaders whose actions are entangled with cords of corporate gold should be eradicated. Let them speak, if they will, as private citizens and not as representatives of the people.

American Consumer Confidence?

It doesn't surprise me that the jobless rate increased in the months preceding the 2008 Presidential Election and as well as after the election — over 500,000 in the month of November and in the month of December of 2008, and in each of the months of January, February, March, and April of 2009. May 2009 came in lower at 345,000. Fourteen and a half million Americans are unemployed which is 9.4% of our workforce and represent a huge loss of tax revenue at every governmental level. Though the rich of our country possess a disproportional amount of its wealth, they do not pay a disproportional amount of its taxes. Our national budget is funded mainly by the working-class whose wages are garnished by the government before they receive them.

So as the new administration gears up, the Department of Labor still projects that through 2015, thousands more jobs will be shipped overseas *to increase the profit margin of big business,* and millions more will be eliminated due to a deepening recession unless the substantial stimulus package instituted by the Obama administration takes hold.

The products and services generated by the jobs that are shipped overseas will be funneled back into the United States at top dollar for the triple whammy to the American economy — fewer jobs, lower wages and higher prices. So should we continue to buy their products and services? Should we support the fleecing of America by corporations, which in some cases pay less taxes than the average American wage-earner. Am I against "Corporate World?" Absolutely not! I am against their profit-making strategies which land squarely on the backs of working-class Americans. Moreover, they seek to keep it that way by monopolizing markets to limit our choices—they seek wealth a-n-d control. That's why it's vital to cutoff their Washington connection.

There are honorable means for corporations to obtain substantial wealth in this country and around the world. Fairness is due them, yes, but it is also due the small business owner, whom we must support on a daily basis. "Mom and Pop" businesses are the "bread and butter" of the American economy. Remember that the next time you shop at the all-American discount store which shops abroad and brings the bargains to us. Your savings of a few dollars are an unauthorized courtesy of their workers and those they provide for. And while you are there, walk the aisles and count the items that were made here in America.

Restoring the Blessing of Prosperity

It does appear that certain segments of our economy are trying to slow down the recovery. Such activity could be considered political posturing—a pursuit of power. While some companies are lowering their prices on goods and services to aid the recovery; others are raising their prices. Still others are faking it— they lower prices on a few items and unfairly mark-up others beyond competitiveness. Perhaps if the working-class consumers would turn their pockets inside out and tell them they need a break, they'd slow the squeeze—maybe. It makes me think of the ole phone-chain hypothesis applied to the previous administration when the leading economic indicators were reported. Someone from the White House would make the first call and say "Pass this message on to at least ten people and what you say will come true — 'Jobs are plentiful, wages are increasing, money is bountiful; take a nap now and see that it is true.'"

We now know that the middle-class of this country was facing financial difficulties then and continues to do so as the cream keeps floating to the top 1% of the population. The eight-year run of the previous administration resulted in exponential wealth for a few and an unprecedented downturn for the masses. But through our efforts, and a cooperative President and Congress, the next eight years will be a season of prosperity for all.

Some Americans seek judgment and punishment for deeds done during the previous administration, but it would take a great deal of time, money, and effort; none of which we can spare now. So we submit them to God's discretion and move on in peace as we endeavor to extract ourselves from two wars, reestablish our moral standing in the world, restore our moral commitment to each other, and rebuild our nation.

In response to such a large number of job losses to date, we will have to encourage and fund — through private and public sources — thousands of new startups, as I said in my introduction. New startups mean thousands of new jobs, and millions of dollars in our treasury. So, if you feel that you are destined to be an entrepreneur, now is the time. If you feel that you are destined to invent a product that will make the world better, now is the time. If you feel that you are destined to be a school teacher, now is the time. If you feel that you are destined to be a politician that serves his/her country, now is the time. If you feel that you are destined to be an enabler of those who answer a call — to fund and to support them, now is the time (See Chapter 16, pages 185-187).

It's a new and exciting beginning; one that every citizen must participate in, including the young and the senior—the young to receive knowledge and wisdom, the senior to give knowledge and wisdom. It's the dawning of a new day in the lives of Americans!

Righteousness Exalts a Nation

Immeasurable rewards shall rain on us again as we restore and maintain our righteous stance in God. History reflects the magnitude of blessings of provision and protection manifested to us in our homeland because of our deeds of righteousness at home and around the world.

As a nation, we have sent messengers and missionaries around the world to demonstrate our love of humanity, to teach the Godly principles of our Constitution, and to share our wealth. That's why so many insist on joining our ranks. To other nations, we give billions of dollars; provide medical aid; build hospitals and shelters; provide food, clothing, entrepreneurial training and small business funding to provide sustainable prosperity to their citizens.

On the other hand, we have not received a significant gift from another country since the Statue of Liberty arrived on our shores from France back in 1886. Wouldn't it be a kind and noble gesture if Saudi Arabia and other countries were to send a $100 gas card to every vehicle-owning adult in the United States as a thank-you for making them wealthy? It would be a nice gesture, wouldn't it!—especially if they don't try to hike prices to immediately get it back.

It would also be commendable if our government were to take every homeless person off the streets of our nation by supplying them with housing vouchers to live wherever they please, and by providing them green-job training to jumpstart their prosperity. The Section 8 program is not doing an adequate job in that segment of our society. And it displeases God that we don't shelter our own.

We should also consider providing more assistance to families of elderly parents to ensure their care, which would only require a shift in funding. A senior's last days on earth should be spent in sufficiency and comfort with their families, not in nursing homes. We have to fix such areas of neglect here at home by funding special offices to handle these matters with discretion.

In addition, most government regulations designed to help the poor have also been designed to breakup the family unit. We must be more creative in our approach to assisting our citizens in sustaining prosperity. Instead of requiring recipients of aid to go to work for minimum wage; let's require them to go to college instead; one year for every three years of aid. Some of you pompous ones will say, "Working for minimum wage is better than nothing." Well, to you I would simply say, God loves cheerful givers who give their best, not their least. Productive middle-class taxpayers are what we are striving for. And if you don't mind others joining your ranks to assist in achieving an annual balanced budget, work with us.

Fireside chats or email?

I enjoyed receiving emails from the presidential candidates and party leaders for a year. It suits me well. Wouldn't it be wonderful if that could continue as the President's weekly mode of communication to us from now on? Radio programs are okay, but they are restrictive. I can read an email at my convenience. I would also like to receive quarterly progress reports on television to keep us connected as we institute change in our communities. It would enhance our relationships from the national level to the local level as we travel the road of oneness again. Wouldn't it be encouraging if Congress were to also communicate with their constituents by weekly email on the issues at hand?

The Four Freedoms that were set forth by President Franklin Roosevelt in his State of the Union Address to the 77th Congress on January 6, 1941, as goals for the American people and citizens around the world to broaden their hope as they faced a challenge of great magnitude, as we do today, were reiterated during his "fireside chats" and spoken into the consciousness of the American people by the President himself:

"In the future days, which we seek to make secure, we look forward to a world founded upon four essential human freedoms.

The first is freedom of speech and expression—*everywhere in the world.*

The second is freedom of every person to worship God in his own way—*everywhere in the world.*

The third is freedom from want—*which,   translated into universal terms , means economic understandings which will secure to every nation a healthy peacetime life for its inhabitants—everywhere in the world.*

The fourth is freedom from fear—*which, translated into world terms, means a world-wide reduction of armaments to such a point and in such a thorough fashion that no nation will be in a position to commit an act of physical aggression against any neighbor—anywhere in the world. That is no vision of a distant millennium. It is a definite basis for a kind of world attainable in our own time and generation."*

President Roosevelt's speech was so celebrated that it inspired the United Nations Declaration of Human Rights, the Four Freedoms Monument, Norman Rockwell's Four Freedoms Paintings, the Four Freedoms Award, essays, postage stamps, games, and comics. The same could be accomplished today through emails and quarterly television reports.

SUSTAINED

Reach forth O hope, my branch of strength
And draw from deep your source of drink.
Infuse my heart with dawning light
And water my memories with love shone bright.

Blow wind blow—the chaff to take away—
Set to die, then to live;
To be nourished, then to flourish;
To receive, then to give life in full array.

Arisen from the ashes,
Pulled from the throes,
To embrace and to celebrate
The wellspring of my soul.

I stand beneath my tree of life,
Forever to remain
Sustained by faith in Love,
Sustained by His eternal flame.

Chapter 16

YES, MR. PRESIDENT, IT WOULD BE MY PLEASURE!

"I think this is the most extraordinary collection of talent, of human knowledge, that has ever been gathered together at the White House, with the possible exception of when Thomas Jefferson dined alone."
President John F. Kennedy - Address at a White House Dinner Honoring Nobel Prize Winners, April 1962

The Office of the President of the United Sates of America embodies the citizens of the Republic — you and me. If the President is going to represent us effectively, he must share our hopes and dreams. He must become a part of us, and we a part of him — there must be a union. Unions are consummated only after people spend time with each other; it's a process etched in time. This may be the first time since 1961 that a President understands his true position and function in the office. Most men who occupied the office since then thought is was about their power and their authority over others. But all along, it has been about the people's power and authority. (It's not about the legacy of a man; it's about the legacy of a people. It's not about the agenda of a man; it's about the agenda of the people.) The President of the United States speaks for the people of the United States of America. How can one speak for a people he has not heard? Let this Presidency be the model for all history.

Do you recall when first lady Jacqueline Kennedy invited us to the White House and gave us an unforgettable tour? We were enamored of her charm. We have not been invited back since, except perhaps those with a wad in their pocket.

I suspect, however, that many of us will be invited to the White House to share our thoughts and ideas as the President and Congress consider the ongoing direction of our country in the many areas that must be addressed to return America to greater glory. After all, the richest ideas and resources of America are found in her people of all walks of life from the Pacific Ocean to the Atlantic Ocean, from the Canadian border to the Gulf of Mexico, who are ready to share, listen, and work alongside the President and Congress to complete our task of restoration so that the next generation of Americans can continue on a clear path of perfecting the union.

So in light of such anticipation, I thought perhaps we might get ready for our evening by brushing up on our social and dining etiquette. The way you handle your silverware; the way you handle yourself; and most importantly, how you converse with others, tell others much about you.

The following tips will help you feel comfortable in any setting at the White House or any other setting of business. Remember, etiquette is for the purpose of honoring the host and making you and those around you comfortable. Generally speaking you will:

RSVP immediately
Dress appropriately
Follow social etiquette
Follow dining etiquette
Be self-confident and knowledgeable
Forward a thank-you note by mail within 24 hours

So here's my short lesson for practically any occasion. Just modify it as needed and make it your own. Let's start with a few definitions:

★ *Etiquette:* The rules of decorum etiquette. The usual word for the code governing manners, conduct, and for observance of these rules.

★ *Decorum:* Decency, propriety, dignity. All of these are a code of rules respecting what is right, fitting, or honorable.

★ *Manners:* A customary way of acting. Usually polite and distinguished.

★ *Protocols:* The rules prescribing the etiquette in ceremonies of state. The code prescribing preference to rank and strict adherence to due order of preference and correct procedure, as in diplomatic exchange and ceremonies.

According to Ball State University Career Center in Muncie, Indiana, dining manners play an important part in making favorable impressions. Social manners are just as important. They signal the state of your manners whether you are having dinner with the President, Warren Buffet, Queen Elizabeth II, your congressperson, a potential business client, a new employer, or others in a professional environment. If one looks at you favorably for any reason, it could engender goodwill. And that's certainly a valuable commodity in any arena of life.

In our more perfect union, one never knows when he will be called upon to serve his country. It is not only those in the military, the Diplomatic Corps, the legislative branch of government, the judicial branch of government, and the executive branch of government who must serve; we all must. Whether it is for a day, a week, a month, or a few years; everyone must serve. In calm times or frenzied times, we all must serve. At every level, we must serve.

So start contemplating today how your forte can best benefit your country, and then at the appropriate time and at the appropriate level offer your services where the need is the greatest. It's important to know your niche.

By the way, in the interest of broadening your knowledge in dining etiquette, I've included a section on ordering. Even if you feel comfortable in this area, a few tips may still be helpful.

You might be asking yourself now with a chuckle, "Can etiquette enhance my life to a valuable degree? But that's not me!" In our own way, it is everybody! No one is born with etiquette and manners; it's learned behavior and skill. So it can become you! Even the President has to be trained in social decorum and protocol. If he refers to another head of State by his first name as they respond to news reporters during an international summit, he will not be favored in his negotiations. The public insult will linger even in private. Heads of State may call each other by their first name privately with permission, but never publicly. In this country, as in most, we honor the office of the President, so our President should always be an example of social etiquette at home and abroad. Now let's get started by practicing at home with the entire family, even if it consists of one.

DINING ETIQUETTE:

Table Manners -
   ★   Sit up fairly straight. Relax.
   ★   Keep your elbows in.
   ★   A toast or blessing may be suggested before everyone eats. It is polite to give thanks for the food and to the host and hostess for their hospitality. Also, it can help to start conversation around the table.
   ★   Pass to the right.
   ★   The servers will offer condiments and side dishes to everyone at the table. Once everything is passed around, you can expect the table to settle down. Wait until all are served before beginning to eat.
   ★   Taste your food before applying condiments. It is a huge insult to salt before you taste. Then if you still need salt, ask politely for a condiment; do not interrupt a conversation.

Removing Things From Your Mouth - The general rule for
removing food from your mouth is that it should go out the

same way it went in. So olive pits can be delicately dropped onto an open palm before putting them onto your plate, and a piece of bone discovered in a bite of chicken should be returned to the plate by way of the fork. Fish is an exception to the rule. It is fine to remove the tiny bones with your fingers, since they would be difficult to drop from your mouth onto the fork. If you need to spit out a fatty piece of meat, spit it into your napkin so that you can keep it out of sight.

Accidents - Don't clean up spills with your own napkin and don't touch items that have dropped on the floor. You may use your napkin to protect yourself from spills. Then, simply and politely ask your server to cleanup and to bring you a replacement for the soiled napkin or dirty utensil. If the item you dropped is obstructing a walkway, you may brush it out of the way with your foot until the server can remove it. The basic reasoning behind the hands-off rule is that a pill shouldn't disrupt the meal for too long, and while you are eating you shouldn't be cleaning things that will make your hands dirty.

Napkin Use - The meal begins when the host unfolds his or her napkin. This is your signal to do the same. Place your napkin on your lap, completely unfolded if it is a small luncheon napkin or in half lengthwise, if it is a large dinner napkin. Typically, you should put your napkin on your lap soon after sitting down at the table (but follow your host's lead). The napkin remains on your lap throughout the entire meal and should be used to gently blot your mouth when needed. If you need to leave the table during the meal, place your napkin on your chair as a signal to your server that you will be returning. The host will signal the end of the meal by placing his or her napkin on the table. Once the meal is over, you too should place your napkin neatly on the table to the right of your dinner plate. Do not wad up or refold your napkin.

Ordering - If, after looking over the menu, there are items you are uncertain about, ask your server any questions you might have. Answering your questions is part of the server's job. It is better to find out before you order that a dish is prepared with something you do not like or are allergic to than to spend the entire meal picking tentatively at your food. An employer will generally suggest that your order be taken first; his or her order will be taken last.

Sometimes, however, the server will decide how the ordering will proceed. Often, women will order first, then men.

As a guest, you should not order one of the most expensive items on the menu or more than two courses unless your host indicates that it is all right. If the host says, "I'm going to try this delicious looking white chocolate cheesecake; why don't you try dessert too?" or "The prime rib has been voted the best in the city; I think you'd enjoy it," then it is all right to order that item if you would like.

Reading the Table Setting - Should you be attending a formal dinner or banquet with pre-set place settings, it is possible to gain clues about what may be served by "reading" the place setting. Start by drawing an imaginary line through the center of the serving plate (the plate will be placed in the center of your dining space). To the *right* of this imaginary line all of the following will be placed; glassware, cup and saucer, knives, and spoons— as well as a seafood fork, if the meal includes seafood. It is important to place the glassware or cup back in the same position after its use in order to maintain the visual presence of the table. To the *left* of this imaginary line all of the following will be placed; bread and butter plate — including a small butter knife placed horizontally across the top of the plate, salad plate, napkin, and forks. Remembering the rule of *"liquids on your right"* and *"solids on your left"* will help in allowing you to quickly become familiar with the place setting.

Use of Silverware - Handle your silverware with ease. Don't grip your fork or knife as though you are about to launch them into space or to crave a turkey. Gently wrap your hands around the knife and fork, with your index finger leading down the backside.

Choosing the correct silverware from the variety in front of you is not as difficult as it may first appear. Start with the knife, fork, or spoon that is farthest from your plate and work your way in using one utensil for each course. The salad fork is on your outermost *left*, followed by your dinner fork. Your soupspoon is on your outermost *right*, followed by your beverage spoon, salad knife and dinner knife. Your dessert spoon and fork are *above* your plate or brought out with dessert. If you remember the rule, to *work from the outside in*, you'll be fine.

There are two ways to use a knife and fork to cut and eat your food: the American style and the European or Continental style. Either style is considered appropriate. In the *American style*, one cuts the food by holding the knife in the right hand and the fork in the left hand with the fork tines piercing the food to secure it on the plate. The knife is then placed across the top edge of your plate with the sharp edge of the blade facing in. The fork is placed in your right hand to eat, tines facing up — if you are left-handed, keep your fork in your left hand, tines facing up. The *European or Continental style* is the same as the American style in that you cut your meat by holding your knife in your right hand while securing your food with your fork in your left hand. The difference is your fork remains in your left hand, tines facing down, and the knife remains in your right hand. Simply eat the cut pieces of food by picking them up with your fork still in your left hand.

Food Tips -

★ Chicken is eaten with a fork and knife.

★ Clams and oysters in the half shell are eaten by holding the shell with the left hand and lifting the clam out of the shell with an oyster fork in your right hand.

★ Crab, shrimp and lobster cocktails are eaten with a cocktail fork.

★ Fried Fantail Shrimp are picked up by the tail and eaten with the fingers.

★ Crab and lobster claws are cracked with a nutcracker, broken with the fingers, and the meat eaten with an oyster fork.

★ Butter is placed on a baked potato with a fork, not with a knife.

★ Baked potatoes are eaten by scooping out the insides bite by bite. Do not take the insides out and put the skin aside or take the foil off.

★ French fries are eaten with a fork and chips are eaten with the fingers. Never pick up a whole piece and bite part of it off.

★   Soup is eaten by dipping the spoon into the soup and moving it away from the body until it is about two-thirds full. Sip the liquid, without slurping, from the side of the spoon. Do not insert the whole bowl of the spoon into the mouth. It is perfectly fine to tilt the bowl away from the body to get the last spoonful or two of soup.

***When You Have Finished* -** Do not push your plate away from you when you have finished eating. Leave your plate where it is in the place setting. The common way to show that you have finished your meal is to lay your fork and knife diagonally across your plate. Place your knife and fork side by side, with the sharp side of the knife blade facing inward and the fork tines down, to the left of the knife. The knife and fork should be placed as if they are pointing to the numbers 10 and 4 on a clock face. Make sure they are placed in such a way that they do not slide off the plate as it is being removed. Once you have used a piece of silverware, never place it back on the table. Do not leave a used spoon in a cup, place it on the saucer. You may, however, leave a soupspoon in a soup plate. Any unused silverware is simply left on the table. Replace your chair after the meal.

***Freshen the Breath and Clean the Teeth* -** Do not chew gum; use mints instead. Check your teeth for food particles in the restroom, not at the table.

Let's move on now to introductions. Since making a good first impression is invaluable, let's fine-tune our skills.

SOCIAL ETIQUETTE:

***When Meeting People* -** Stand up when meeting people. Go around furniture or anything else that is between you and the person you are being introduced to. Give attention to the other person. Be alert and interested, which helps you to remember their name.

***Deference to Introductions* -** Deference refers to common courtesy that is extended to one another. With regard to introductions, juniors are always presented to seniors. A common rule is to introduce the highest ranking person first, and then introduce everyone to him/her. Deference is based on rank in a company and not on gender. Also, remember that a client ALWAYS outranks someone from within your company (even your supervisor). First, avoid referring to individuals by their first name. This assumes a friendly relationship and often is not appropriate. Next, use the name that was given during the introduction. "Susan is Susan, NOT Sue." Name tags should ALWAYS be placed on the right side, so an individual may easily look at your name when shaking your hand. Furthermore, if you forget someone's name, take the embarrassment upon yourself. Say something like, "Forgive me, I know that we met earlier, you are...?" Finally, remember to close an introduction by saying, "It was nice to have met you." Never simply walk away.

Rules For Shaking Hands - First, extend your hand in an open vertical, flat position. Men should always wait for a woman to extend her hand first. Next, tilt your fingers down with your thumb up, exposing the web of your hand towards the other person. Then, go in for the handshake, grabbing the other person's hand firmly, but not crushingly. Never pat the top of the hand. Finally, take your hand back. The length of the handshake should be 2-3 seconds. Now, that's simple, isn't it? There's no need to wait, find someone to practice with now.

Social Conversation - Learn the art of social conversation and appropriate topics of conversation for formal and informal occasions. Social conversation is very important. Often social conversation can be boring if we are uninterested in talking or if the talk does not pertain to us. It is important to always be attentive. Here are some basic rules regarding social conversation:

* ★ Keep it short! After all, it is social conversation.
* ★ Be a good listener
* ★ Use academic vocabulary
* ★ Do not interrupt others when they are speaking.
* ★ Do not attempt to finish the statements of others.
* ★ Speak only of what you know.
* ★ Use titles unless you are instructed by the person to do otherwise — *do not ask to do otherwise* (Example: Mr. President, Madam Speaker, Madam/Mr. Ambassador Madam/Mr. Secretary, Senator, Dr., Sir, Mr., Ms., Congressman, Congresswoman).

★ Do not monopolize the conversation.
★ If you experience rudeness in conversation, ignore it and forget it. If appropriate and under extreme circumstances, address it in private with the individual.
★ If someone extends you a compliment, accept it humbly and discreetly — it is not your cue to applaud yourself. Also, if you're the one extending the compliment; be sincere.
★ Always think twice about criticizing someone. Always ask yourself, "Is it my place to be critical?"
★ Be constructive publicly; express your disapproval privately.
★ Never complain. If you are experiencing a problem, deal with it yourself.

Possible Topics of Conversation -
★ Current events
★ Positive news
★ Books, trade publications, and the event at hand
★ Personal hobbies
★ The sports and entertainment world
★ Topics in your line of work

Communication Barriers - There are many barriers to effective communication. If you are tired, hungry, or angry, you will not be an effective communicator. It could show in your posture, facial expressions, and body language. Bad grammar can also minimize effective communication. Therefore, make physical and mental adjustments prior to your arrival and maintain them throughout the evening. Deal with the negatives after you have had a wonderful evening, if you still care to.

Social Manners - Social manners are crucial to a successful dinner at the White House. The following helpful hints regarding social manners will ensure that you leave a positive and lasting impression —and, who knows, perhaps a trip back.

★ When invited to the White House respond by mail within twenty-four hours by the means requested. If you are out of town, call the White House Social Secretary to express your response verbally. An invitation from the White House is considered to be a command invitation and is expected to be accepted unless you are ill, getting marriage, or out of the country. If you are unable to attend, please give a reason — be honest.

★ If your name is the only one on the invitation, you are the only guest — *do not take anyone with you and do not call to request to take someone.*

★ If you are not sure what to wear to the gathering, call the White House Social Secretary and inquire. If you are unclear about the scope of the category, ask for more details.

★ Arrive ten to fifteen minutes early. In other words, "BE ON TIME!" Being "fashionably late" is not an option.

★ If you are presenting a host gift, which is customary, consider a community gift that could be tied to some legislation that the president has passed in education, environmental protection, or children healthcare. I also suggest that you have your gift framed, encased, and embossed professionally.

★ Use your evening to strengthen community relationships, thereby, allowing everyone in your community to share in the experience.

★ Business is normally the purpose of the invitation, so don't arrive starved.

★ If you are a smoker, call ahead to get your options. Don't be offended if you are asked to smoke outside. Follow the instructions and never smoke near an entrance. If it's windy adjust accordingly. It's been proven that second hand smoke kills and makes everything it contacts smells, which would cause a timely and costly cleanup.

★   If you decide to drink, you should limit yourself
    to one alcoholic beverage per hour, sipped throughout
    the hour. If you do not drink alcohol, please do
    not start then.

★   When you write thank-you notes, you should always
    hand-address the envelope unless you have bad
    handwriting. You should always use a stamp instead
    of metered mail, and send the thank-you within
    twenty-four hours.

★   When sending a more formal, professional thank-you,
    type it on the computer in a business letter format.
    Make sure to correctly spell the President and his
    wife's name. It also may be advantageous to send a
    thank-you to the President's liaison and others that
    served as hosts at the dinner.

Appropriate Dress -

★   White Tie: Ultra formal—women wear formal gowns;
    men wear tailcoats w/matching trousers, white vests,
    bowties, and white or gray gloves—this is not seen
    often today.

★   Black Tie: Black tuxedos for men or an elegant
    black suit, white shirt and black necktie as long as it
    is formal. Women wear formal evening or cocktail
    dresses.

★   Black Tie Optional: Men wear tuxedos or dark
    conservative suits. Women wear cocktail or formal
    dresses.

★   Semi-formal: Men wear dressy business attire.
    Women wear either dressy business or cocktail attire.

CONTACTING THE WHITE HOUSE

Mailing Address
The White House
1600 Pennsylvania Avenue NW
Washington, DC 20502

Phone Numbers
Comments: 202-456-1111
Switchboard: 202-456-1414
FAX: 202-456-2461

TTY/TDD
Comments: 202-456-6213

E-Mail
To send questions, concerns, comments or well-wishes to the President or his staff, please use the contact form at www.whitehouse.gov/contact/. Due to the large volume of e-mail received, the White House may not be able to respond to every message. For up-to-date information on Presidential initiatives, current events, and topics of interest to you, please use the White House website: www.whitehouse.gov

Vice President: vice_president@whitehouse.gov

Problems Using the Website
If you experience problems making an online request, please make your request by fax or mail.

To Extend an Invitation

Everyday, the White House receives a large volume of e-mail. To ensure timely processing, The White House ask instead that you mail your invitation. Please make sure to include your full name, complete address, and telephone number.

Communications With Other Federal Government Agencies

If you have a question about a particular government benefit, program or service, contact USA.gov, the official gateway to all government information and is a catalyst for a growing electronic government.

Gifts and Items Sent to the White House

Items sent to the White House often experience a significant delivery delay and can be irreparably harmed due to the security screening process. Therefore, please do not send items of personal importance, such as family photographs, or gifts of a consumable nature, such as food, flowers, and perishable items. While the President and his wife and the Vice President and his wife appreciate your thoughtfulness, they request that you look instead to your local community for opportunities to assist your neighbors in need.

WHITE HOUSE GREETING REQUEST

The White House Greetings Office receives and processes all requests in accordance with long-standing guidelines. Please carefully review the guidelines below prior to submitting your request. Requests that do not comply with the guidelines or do not contain sufficient information will not be fulfilled.

U.S. Citizens
The White House will send greetings only to United States citizens for special occasions as outlined below.

Required Information
Please provide the following information when making your request:
Name of honoree(s)
Address of honoree(s
Form of address (Mr., Mrs., Ms., Miss)
Date (month, day, year) of
birthday, wedding, or anniversary.
Requestor's name and daytime phone number

Number of Requests Limited
The number of requests you can submit per day is limited, though unspecified. Institutional requests for multiple greetings must be submitted by fax or mail on official letterhead with the required information listed above.

When to Expect Your Greeting

For birthdays and anniversaries, greetings will be mailed from the White House approximately 14 days prior to the event. Wedding and baby's birth greetings will be sent after the event.

Please Make a Request From the Following:

Baby's Birth Greeting

A baby's birth card will be sent within a year of the birth. Please make your request after the baby is born.

Birthday Greeting

A birthday card will be sent to individuals celebrating their 80th (or greater) birthday. Please make your request at least 6 weeks in advance of the birthday.

Wedding Greeting

A wedding card will be sent to couples after the event. Please make your request after the wedding.

Anniversary Greeting

An anniversary card will be sent to couples who are celebrating their 50th (or greater) wedding anniversary. Please make your request at least 6 weeks in advance of the anniversary.

Your Greeting Request Can Also Be Made By:

FAX: 202-395-1232

MAIL: The White House
Attn: Greetings Office
Washington, D.C. 20502-0039

Well, if you don't get that invitation, isn't it a wonderful dream. To hope that any American of any income level and any political party could be invited to the White House for dinner to be heard on issues that are important to them is a big step toward a brighter future. We pay the bills; should we not be welcomed in our house. And to know that it would not be done just as a publicity stunt or for monetary gain is commendable.

The Office of Public Liaison & Intergovernmental Affairs (www.whitehouse.gov/administration/eop/opl) is seen as the front door to the White House through which every citizen can participate and inform the work of the President. White House Senior Advisor, Valerie Jarrett, has oversight of this entity—to bring new voices to the table and to build relationships through the government's engagement of its citizens, thereby stimulating honest dialogue with the assurance that our government works with us. We certainly expect our government to come to our communities, but we also expect to be received graciously at the house of our nation.

I hope the President will consider a monthly dinner with the people of the nation and call it *"The People's Night at the White House."* He could have citizens from across the country who are willing to represent their communities submit a "letter of request" to have dinner with the President to present a self-help community plan of action to improve or alleviate a designated economic, social, or environmental problem in their community within one year. A detailed report should be submitted to the President of their achievement. Such a self-help plan could be used by other communities to solve similar problems. The plan must be developed through community organization and town hall meetings that are inclusive of everyone. The plan should include methods by which they will have everyone in the community cross the victory line simultaneously. I offer a few words of advice here to those who are saying, "That's a great idea!" — administrators are not good managers; managers are not good administrators, so don't confuse the two. I've seen it happen on many occasions. It causes big problems, yet it's an easy fix. Remember, leaders and followers are equal; only their jobs are different. An administrator is a person that follows integrity, honesty, and equality and focuses on the big picture — the end result. A manager sees in more detail and operates with the nuts and bolts of a plan.

This is the kind of grassroots organization that built America; this is the kind of grassroots organization that can restore America. The local community is the bedrock of our country. We must become community-minded again. We must help one another again. When a neighbor is in need, perhaps you can't help sufficiently, but pooling resources of 10, 20, 50, 100, or a 1000 people could buy groceries, make mortgage payments, and make car payments when jobs are lost or sickness is extended. Forming gasoline coops, food coops, childcare coops and healthcare coops can reduce every family's overall cost of living. Everyone's dollar has more purchasing power — from the worker at Burger King to the attorney on main street. It is not unheard of nowadays that a well-educated person can go from making $100,000 a year to making $30,000 a year because his job was shipped overseas or his company downsized.

You will also have to extend a hand to single parent households — men and women — who have become accustomed to suffering in silence along with their children.

Begin to mobilize your community today! Set up a communitywide Rainy Day Fund now with the guidance of an unbiased reputable law and accounting firm who doesn't charge exorbitant fees and who submits monthly statements to every citizen who has contributed. You will be surprised how fast $20.00, more or less, from everyone in the community on a monthly basis can generate huge sums of money to be distributed *fairly* as needed without robbing the recipients of their dignity. Remember, they will have contributed too. Only 9.4% of the population is unemployed, that leaves 90.6% that's doing okay and would be willing to contribute a small sum.

You will also be amazed at the buying power of a community that pools its resources. Freeze or decrease gasoline, grocery, and utility prices by negotiating prices well into the future—include a clause to lower your cost if prices fall five percent below your negotiated cost. Develop alternative energy sources, such as solar panels on vacant properties and on every rooftop throughout the community.

Form citizen committees for each endeavor and assign tasks by teams. Take copious notes and archive everything. Your projects could be the test models for other communities. I recommend that you task your elected officials with procuring public and private funding for infrastructure upgrades or replacements. Don't limit your resources.

To showcase community development, I would suggest that the President divide the country into 25 regions, appoint a czar, assign a Presidential Liaison to each region, and have the liaison draw a "letter of request" from the pool on a monthly basis. A detailed proposal must accompany the letter. The proposal must include a mission statement, the signatures of the citizens who have agreed to participate in the project, the percentage of community participation, the organizational structure, the source of funding — public and private — and an estimated time of completion.

The feeling of ownership and camaraderie that could emanate from such an endeavor could prove to be monumental in getting us back on track morally, educationally, financially, and environmentally.

Wouldn't it be grand to see patriotism oozing out of Americans again, as they begin to feel the richness of American citizenship that is unlike any other in the world? And when that happens, they will sing her songs and read her poetry with new fervor and new life. I also hope that it would be one of the President's best and most relaxing evenings of the month.

I hope—

Sources: Official White House Website, <u>Dining Etiquette</u>-Ball State University Career Center Website, <u>Emily Post's Etiquette</u>, Letitia Baldridge's <u>New Manners for New Times</u>, and <u>Etiquette for Dummies</u>.

SNOWFLAKE

"Anew, anew," my heart cried aloud.
Expectations are high; I don't know why.
All around things seem the same,
But within change beckons by name.

"Anew, anew," my heart cried again.
"What could it be?" my soul exclaimed.
Shall I understand; could I surrender me?
Thought upon thought—surely more effort to see.

Anew, anew—I sat to ponder,
As my eyes gazed through the window yonder
To streaming torrents of shivering calmness
That stilled my soul hour upon hour.

"Anew, anew,"—whispered I in silence;
As the renascence began to shower.
Moment by moment each revealed
The purity of my heart repealed.

"Anew, anew,"—let it stay! Oh, let beauty hold!"—
But what could I do and not impose!
So, in my mind forever; forever I framed,
God's snowflake and myself the same.

Appendix A

Procedural Guide to the Electoral College

Source: The Office of the Federal Register

The Electoral College in Brief

The Electoral College was established by the founding fathers as a compromise between election of the president by Congress and election by popular vote. The electors are a popularly elected body chosen by the States and the District of Columbia. The Electoral College consists of *538 electors (one for each of 435 members of the House of Representatives and 100 Senators; and 3 for the District of Columbia by virtue of the 23rd Amendment). Each State's allotment of electors is equal to the number of House members to which it is entitled plus two Senators.* The decennial census is used to reapportion the number of electors allocated among the States.

State laws vary on the appointment of electors. The States prepare a list of the slate of electors for the candidate who receives the most popular votes on a *Certificate of Ascertainment* and sends them the Archivist of the United States at the *National Archives and Records Administration (NARA).* The Archivist transmits the originals to NARA's *Office of the Federal Register (OFR).* A *majority of 270 electoral votes* is required to elect the President and Vice President. No Constitutional provision or Federal law requires electors to vote in accordance with the popular vote in their State. But many states have enacted laws that do require their electors to vote as pledged. The electors prepare Certificates of Vote and annex Certificates of Ascertainment to them. Each Certificate of Vote lists all persons voted for as President and the number of electors voting for each person and separately lists all persons voted for as Vice President and the number of electors voting for each person. If no presidential candidate wins a majority of electoral votes, the 12th Amendment to the Constitution provides for the presidential election to be decided by the House of Representatives. The House would select the President by majority vote, choosing from the three candidates who received the greatest number of electoral votes. The vote would be taken by State, with each State delegation having one vote. If no vice-presidential candidate wins a majority of electoral votes, the Senate would select the Vice President by majority vote, with each Senator choosing from the two candidates who received the greatest number of electoral votes.

Role of the States
The United States Constitution and Federal law place certain responsibilities relating to the Presidential election upon State executives and the electors for President and Vice President. Neither the Constitution nor Federal law prescribe the manner in which each State appoints its electors other than directing that they be appointed on the Tuesday after the first Monday in November. The Constitution forbids a Senator, Representative, or person holding an office of trust or profit under the United States from being appointed as an elector.

In most States, the electors are appointed by state-wide popular election. The slate of electors for the candidate who receives the most popular votes is appointed. The slates of electors are generally chosen by the political parties. However, the States' laws vary on the appointment of electors. In Maine and Nebraska, two electors are chosen at-large by state-wide popular vote and the rest are selected by the popular vote in each congressional district. As a result, the electoral procedure in these States permits a split slate of electors to be chosen.

After the general election, the Governor of each State and the Mayor of the District of Columbia prepare a Certificate of Ascertainment of the electors appointed (herein, the term "Governor" includes the Mayor of the District of Columbia). The Certificate of Ascertainment must list the names of the electors appointed and the number of votes received by each. It must also list the names of all other candidates for elector and the number of votes received by each. The Certificate must be signed by the Governor and carry the seal of the State. The format of the Certificate is not dictated by Federal law, but conforms to the law or custom of the submitting State.

The Governor must prepare seven original Certificates of Ascertainment. One original, along with two authenticated copies (or two additional originals) must be sent by registered mail to the Archivist of the United States, National Archives and Records Administration. The Certificates should be sent as soon as practicable after the election, but must be submitted to the Archivist no later than the day after the meetings of the electors. The other six originals must be delivered to the State's electors no later than the day after the meetings of the electors.

On the first Monday after the second Wednesday in December, the electors meet in their respective States. The State legislature may designate where in the State the meeting will take place. It usually takes place in the State capital, often in the capitol building. At this meeting, the electors vote by ballot for President and Vice President. There must be distinct ballots for President and Vice President. The electors' votes are recorded on a Certificate of Vote. This Certificate must contain a list of all persons voted for as President and the number of electors voting for each. It must also contain a list of persons voted for as Vice President and the number of electors voting for each. The names of candidates receiving no electoral votes do not appear on the Certificate of Vote. As said in the brief, there is no Constitutional provision or Federal law requiring electors to vote in accordance with the popular vote in their States. In the 1976 election, a Washington elector pledged to President Gerald Ford voted for Ronald Reagan. In the 1988 election, a West Virginia elector voted for Senator Lloyd Bentsen as President and for Governor Michael Dukakis as Vice President. But some State laws require electors to cast their votes according to the popular vote and provide that so-called "faithless electors" may be subject to fines or may be disqualified for casting an invalid vote and be replaced by a substitute elector.

The format of the Certificate is not dictated by Federal law, but is determined by the law or custom of each State. Six original Certificates of Vote must be prepared by the electors. Each Certificate must be signed by all of the electors. One of the six Certificates of Ascertainment forwarded to the electors by the Governor must be attached to each of the six Certificates of Vote. Each of the six pairs of Certificates must be sealed and certified by the electors to be the list of votes of that State.

The six pairs of Certificates are distributed as follows:

- ★ One pair, by registered mail, to the President of the United States Senate, The Capitol, Washington, DC 20510;
- ★ Two pairs, by registered mail, to the Archivist of the United States, National Archives and Records Administration, c/o Office of the Federal Register (NF), 8601 Adelphi Road, College Park, MD 20740-6001;
- ★ Two pairs to the Secretary of State of the State, one of which is held subject to the order of the President of the United States Senate, the other to be preserved by the Secretary for public inspection for one year;
- ★ One pair to the chief judge of the Federal district court of the district in which the electors meet.

Since there is a very short time between the meetings of the electors in the States and the counting of the electoral votes by Congress, and the meetings of electors coincides with the December holiday mail season, it is imperative that these Certificates be delivered as soon as possible. After the Certificates of Ascertainment and Certificates of Vote are delivered to the appropriate persons, the States' functions in the electoral process are completed.

Role of NARA and the Office of the Federal Register
The Archivist of the United States is required by law to perform certain functions relating to the electoral college (3 U.S.C. sections *6, 11, 12, 13*). The Archivist has delegated to

the Director of the Federal Register the authority to carry out the administration of the electoral college process.

Prior to the General Election
In October of each Presidential election year, the Archivist sends a letter to the Governor of each State and the Mayor of the District of Columbia along with an instruction package prepared by the Office of the Federal Register (OFR) that sets out the States' responsibilities regarding the electoral college. The package also includes a quantity of booklets containing applicable Federal Constitutional and statutory provisions regarding presidential elections to be distributed to each elector.

Also in the month prior to the election, the OFR contacts the Assistant Secretary of the Senate and the House Parliamentarian to make arrangements for the delivery of the electoral college certificates to Congress. And finally, in the month prior to the election, the OFR prepares to receive the electoral college certificates from the States. The OFR makes special arrangements with the Archivist's mailroom staff and messenger service to establish procedures for handling the Certificates and transmitting them from the Archives to the OFR.

After the General Election
During the week following the general election, the OFR calls the Governor's Office in each State and the Mayor's Office in the District of Columbia to make a personal contact with a person responsible for the electoral college process. In some States, the Secretary of State is the official designated to administer the electoral college, but other State officials may be assigned this responsibility according to State law or custom. The OFR confirms that materials mailed in October have arrived and reviews the States' plans for carrying out their responsibilities.

Receipt of Certificates of Ascertainment
Certificates should begin arriving at NARA shortly after the general election. The Archives makes a record of the Certificates of Ascertainment it receives and transmits them to the OFR's Legal

Affairs and Policy Staff by special delivery. The OFR logs in a record of the Certificates and checks them for facial legal sufficiency. If there are any problems with a Certificate, an OFR attorney calls the contact person in the State to advise them of the defect. The OFR makes copies of the Certificates of Ascertainment available for public inspection and secures the originals.

Receipt of Certificates of Vote
Certificates of Vote should begin arriving at NARA shortly after the State meetings of the electors. Certificates of Vote are recorded on a log sheet when received at the Archivist's office and at the OFR. Each Certificate is checked for facial legal sufficiency, and if there are any problems with a Certificate, an OFR attorney calls the contact person in that State and the Assistant Secretary of the Senate to inform them of the problems and offer advice as to a solution. After the Certificates of Vote have been determined to be facially sufficient, the OFR makes copies of them available for public inspection and secures the originals.

Certificates of Ascertainment Transmitted to Congress
The OFR prepares cover letters for the Archivist's signature to accompany the Certificates of Ascertainment transmitted to Congress. The OFR hand delivers the Certificates and cover letters to the Vice President's Office in the Senate (the Vice President is the President of the Senate) and the Speaker's Room on the House side of the Capitol and obtains a receipt. If all the Certificates of Ascertainment are received in a timely fashion, they are sent to Congress in one group. However, late arriving Certificates may also be hand delivered separately to Congress so that transmittal of the other Certificates is not delayed.

Certificates of Vote Subject to the Call of the President of the Senate
The OFR holds one of the two original Certificates of Vote subject to the call of the President of the Senate in the event that one or more Certificates fail to reach the Senate in a timely manner. If the Archivist does not receive a Certificate of Vote from a State by a week after the electors meet, the OFR calls that State's contact

person to make sure the Certificates were mailed. If the Certificates were not mailed, the OFR advises the State to transmit the Certificates by express mail. If the Certificates were mailed and are overdue in arriving, the OFR calls the Postal Service to request that it trace the package. Finally, if no Certificate of Vote is received from a State by the fourth Wednesday in December after the election, the OFR employs the procedural steps set forth at 3 U.S.C. sections 12 and 13 by securing a duplicate from the Secretary of State of the State or by dispatching a special messenger to obtain the duplicate held by a Federal District judge and hand carrying it to Washington, D. C.

Preserving the Certificates
After Congress has met in joint session for the official counting of electoral votes, all Certificates of Ascertainment and Certificates of Vote in OFR's files are combined into one file. Each file contains all Certificates from a State, any cover letter accompanying the Certificates, and any envelopes bearing certifications of electors' votes. The files are placed in archival boxes and made available for public inspection at the OFR for one year and then transferred to NARA for permanent retention.

Role of Congress
House and Senate staff come to the Office of the Federal Register (OFR) to inspect the Certificates of Vote in late December. Because the statutory procedure prescribes that the Certificates of Vote sent to the President of the Senate be held under seal until Congress opens and counts them in joint session, the Congress depends on the OFR to ensure the facial legal sufficiency of Certificates. If any State's Certificate fails to reach the President of the Senate, the President of the Senate calls on OFR to deliver duplicate originals in its possession to complete the set held by Congress. After the 1988 general election, the President of the Senate called for nineteen of the Certificates of Vote held by the OFR. For the 1992 election, the OFR supplied the Congress with two missing Certificates of Vote.

The Congress is scheduled to meet in joint session in the House of Representatives on January 6 of the year following the popular vote to conduct the official tally of electoral votes. The Vice President, as President of the Senate, is the presiding officer. Two tellers are appointed to open, present and record the votes of the States in alphabetical order. The President of the Senate announces the results of the vote and declares which persons, if any, have been elected President and Vice President of the United States. The results are entered into the official journals of the House and Senate. The President of the Senate then calls for objections to be made. If any objections are registered, they must be submitted in writing and be signed by at least one member of the House and Senate. The House and Senate would withdraw to their respective chambers to consider the merits of any objections according the procedure set out under 3 U.S.C. section 15.

2008 Presidential Election

Summary of Key Dates, Events and Information on State Electors

Registered voters chose the electors on November 4, 2008 during the General Election.

June thru October 2008
  ★ **Preparation Stage**
    The Federal Register prepared letters and instructional materials for the Archivist to send to the Governors of the 50 States and the Mayor of the District of Columbia. The materials included pamphlets on Federal election law and detailed instructions on how to prepare and submit the electors' credentials *(Certificates of Ascertainment)* and the electoral votes *(Certificates of Vote)*. In October, the Federal Register began contacting Governors and Secretaries of State to establish contacts for the November 4 Presidential Election.

November 4, 2008
  ★ **General Election**
    Registered voters in each State and the District of Columbia

voted for President and Vice President. They cast their vote by selecting a pair of candidates listed on a single Presidential/Vice-Presidential ticket. By doing so, they also chose slates of Electors to serve in the Electoral College. Forty-eight of the fifty States and the District of Columbia are *"winner-take-all"* (ME and NE are the exceptions).

Mid-November thru December 15, 2008
★ **Transmission of Certificates of Ascertainment to NARA**
The Ascertainment lists the names of the electors appointed and the number of votes cast for each person. The States prepared seven originals authenticated by the Governor's signature and the State Seal. One original and two certified copies were sent to the Federal Register (the remaining six originals were attached to the electoral votes at the State meetings). The Governors submitted the certificates "as soon as was practicable," after their States certified election results. They were transmitted no later than December 15 (but Federal law sets no penalty for missing the deadline).

December 9, 2008
★ **Date for Determination of Controversy as to Appointment of Electors**
States made final determinations of any controversies or contests as to the appointment of electors at least six days before December 15 meetings of electors for their electoral votes to be presumptively valid when presented to Congress. Determinations by States' lawful tribunals were conclusive, if decided under laws enacted prior to election day.

December 15, 2008
★ **Meetings of Electors and Transmission of Certificates of Vote to NARA**
The electors met in their State to select the President and Vice President of the United States. No Constitutional provision or Federal law requires electors to vote in accordance with the popular vote in their States. NARA's

website lists the States that have laws to bind electors to candidates. The electors recorded their votes on six "Certificates of Vote," which were paired with the six remaining Certificates of Ascertainment. The electors signed, sealed and certified packages of electoral votes and immediately sent one set of votes to the President of the Senate and two sets to the Archivist. The Federal Register preserved one archival set and held the reserve set subject to the call of the President of the Senate to replace missing or incomplete electoral votes.

December 24, 2008
★ **Deadline for Receipt of Electoral Votes at NARA**
The President of the Senate and the Archivist had the electoral votes in hand by December 24, 2008 (States face no legal penalty for failure to comply). If votes had been lost or delayed, the Archivist would have taken extraordinary measures to retrieve duplicate originals.

On or Before January 3, 2009
★ **Transmission of Certificates of Ascertainment to Congress**
The Archivist transmitted copies of the Certificates of Ascertainment to the new Congress as they assembled. This occurred in late December or early January when the Archivist and/or representatives from the Federal Register met with the Secretary of the Senate and the Clerk of the House in a ceremonial occasion. Informal meetings took place earlier.

January 6, 2009
★ **Counting Electoral Votes in Congress**
The Congress met in joint session to count the electoral votes (Congress may pass a law to change the date). The President of the Senate was the presiding officer. If a Senator and a House member had jointly submitted an objection, each House would have retired to its chamber to consider it. The President and Vice President had to achieve a majority

of electoral votes (270) to be elected. In the absence of a majority, the House would have selected the President, and the Senate would have selected the Vice President. If a State had submitted conflicting sets of electoral votes to Congress, the two Houses acting concurrently would have accepted or rejected the votes. If they had not concurred, the votes of the electors certified by the Governor of the State would have been counted in Congress.

January 20, 2009 at Noon
★ **Inauguration**
The President-Elect took the Oath of Office and became the U.S. President.

General Authority
The Archivist of the United States, as the head of the National Archives and Records Administration (NARA), is responsible for carrying out ministerial duties on behalf of the States and the Congress under 3 U.S.C. sections 6, 11, 12, and 13. NARA is primarily responsible for coordinating the various stages of the electoral process by helping the States prepare and submit certificates that establish the appointment of electors and validate the electoral votes of each State. The Archivist delegates operational duties to the Director of the Federal Register. The Federal Register Legal Staff ensures that electoral documents are transmitted to Congress, made available to the public, and preserved as part of our nation's history. The Legal Staff reviews the electoral certificates for the required signatures, seals and other matters of form, as specified in Federal law. Only the Congress and the Courts have the authority to rule on substantive legal issues.

Source: Office of the Federal Register, National Archives and Records Administration

Distribution of 2004 and 2008 Electoral Votes
Votes are allocated based on the 2000 Census.

State	2004 - 2008
Alabama	9
Alaska	3
Arizona	10
Arkansas	6
California	55
Colorado	9
Connecticut	7
Delaware	3
District of Columbia	3
Florida	27
Georgia	15
Hawaii	4
Idaho	4
Illinois	21
Indiana	11
Iowa	7
Kansas	6
Kentucky	8
Louisiana	9
Maine	4
Maryland	10
Massachusetts	12
Michigan	17
Minnesota	10

Mississippi	6
Missouri	11
Montana	3
Nebraska	5
Nevada	5
New Hampshire	4
New Jersey	15
New Mexico	5
New York	31
North Carolina	15
North Dakota	3
Ohio	20
Oklahoma	7
Oregon	7
Pennsylvania	21
Rhode Island	4
South Carolina	8
South Dakota	3
Tennessee	11
Texas	34
Utah	5
Vermont	3
Virginia	13
Washington	11
West Virginia	5
Wisconsin	10
Wyoming	3

Source: U.S. Federal Election Commission Last Update: 10/3/03
Allocation of the 2012 Electoral Votes Will Be Based on the 2010 Census

Presidential Election Laws

PROVISIONS OF THE CONSTITUTION

Article II

Section 1. The executive Power shall be vested in a President of the United States of America. He shall hold his Office during the Term of four Years, and, together with the Vice President, chosen for the same Term, be elected, as follows:

Each State shall appoint, in such Manner as the Legislature thereof may direct, a Number of Electors, equal to the whole Number of Senators and Representatives to which the State may be entitled in the Congress: but no Senator or Representative, or Person holding an Office of Trust or Profit under the United States, shall be appointed an Elector.

The Congress may determine the Time of choosing the Electors, and the Day on which they shall give their Votes; which Day shall be the same throughout the United States.

Twelfth Amendment

The Electors shall meet in their respective states, and vote by ballot for President and Vice President, one of whom, at least, shall not be an inhabitant of the same state with themselves; they shall name in their ballots the person voted for as President, and in distinct ballots the person voted for as Vice President, and they shall make distinct lists of all persons voted for as President, and of all persons voted for as Vice President, and of the number of votes for each, which lists they shall sign and certify, and transmit sealed to the seat of the government of the United States, directed to the President of the Senate; The President of the Senate shall, in the presence of the Senate and House of Representatives, open all the certificates and the votes shall then be counted;—The person having the greatest number of votes for President, shall be the President, if such number be a majority of the whole number of Electors appointed; and if no person have such majority, then from the persons having the highest numbers not exceeding three on the list of those voted for as President, the House of Representatives shall choose immediately, by ballot, the President. But in choosing the President, the votes shall be taken by states, the representation from each state having one vote; a quorum for this purpose shall consist of a member or members from two-thirds of the states, and a majority of all the states shall be necessary to a choice. The person having the greatest number of votes as Vice President, shall be the Vice President, if such number be a majority of the whole number of Electors appointed, and if no person have a majority, then from the two highest numbers on the list, the Senate shall choose the Vice President; a quorum for the purpose shall consist of two-thirds of the whole number of Senators, and a majority of the whole number shall be necessary to a choice. But no person constitutionally ineligible to the office of President shall be eligible to that of Vice President to the United States.

Fourteenth Amendment

Section 3. No person shall be... elector of President and Vice President... who, having previously taken an oath, as a member of Congress, or as an officer of the United States, or as a member of any State legislature, or as an executive or judicial officer of any State, to support the Constitution of the United States, shall have engaged in insurrection or rebellion against the same, or given aid or comfort to the enemies thereof. But Congress may by a vote of two-thirds of each House, remove such disability.

Fifteenth Amendment

Section 1. The right of citizens of the United States to vote shall not be denied or abridged by the United States or by any State on account of race, color, or previous condition of servitude.

Nineteenth Amendment

The right of citizens of the United States to vote shall not be denied or abridged by the United States or by any State on account of sex.

Twentieth Amendment

Section 1. The terms of the President and Vice President shall end at noon on the 20th day of January, and the terms of Senators and Representatives at noon on the 3d day of January, of the years in which such terms would have ended if this article had not been ratified; and the terms of their successors shall then begin.

Section 2. The Congress shall assemble at least once in every year, and such meeting shall begin at noon on the 3d day of January, unless they shall by law appoint a different day.

Section 3. If, at the time fixed for the beginning of the term of the President, the President elect shall have died, the Vice President elect shall become President. If a President shall not have been chosen before the time fixed for the beginning of his term, or if the President elect shall have failed to qualify, then the Vice President elect shall act as President until a President shall have qualified; and the Congress may by law provide for the case wherein neither a President elect nor a Vice President elect shall have qualified, declaring who shall then act as President, or the manner in which one who is to act shall be selected, and such person shall act accordingly until a President or Vice President shall have qualified.

Section 4. The Congress may by law provide for the case of the death of any of the persons from whom the House of Representatives may choose a President whenever the right of choice shall have devolved upon them, and for the case of the death of any of the persons from whom the Senate may choose a Vice President whenever the right of choice shall have devolved upon them.

Twenty-Second Amendment

Section 1. No person shall be elected to the office of the President more than twice, and no person who has held the office of President, or acted as President, for more than two years of a term to which some other person was elected President shall be elected to the office of the President more than once. But this Article shall not apply to any person holding the office of President when this Article was proposed by the Congress, and shall not prevent any person who may be holding the office of President, or acting as President, during the term within which this Article becomes operative from holding the office of President or acting as President during the remainder of such term.

Twenty-Third Amendment

Section 1. The District constituting the seat of Government of the United States shall appoint in such manner as the Congress may direct: A number of electors of President and Vice President equal to the whole number of Senators and Representatives in Congress to which the District would be entitled if it were a State, but in no event more than the least populous State; they shall be in addition to those appointed by the States, but they shall be considered, for the purposes of the election of President and Vice President, to be electors appointed by a State; and they shall meet in the District and perform such duties as provided by the twelfth article of amendment.

Twenty-Fourth Amendment

Section 1. The right of citizens of the United States to vote in any primary or other election for President or Vice President, for electors for President or Vice President, or for Senator or Representative in Congress, shall not be denied or abridged by the United States or any State by reason of failure to pay any poll tax or other tax.

Twenty-Fifth Amendment

Section 1. In case of the removal of the President from office or of his death or resignation, the Vice President shall become President.

Section 2. Whenever there is a vacancy in the office of the Vice President, the President shall nominate a Vice President who shall take office upon confirmation by a majority vote of both Houses of Congress.

Section 3. Whenever the President transmits to the President pro tempore of the Senate and the Speaker of the House of Representatives his written declaration that he is unable to discharge the powers and duties of his office, and until he transmits to them a written declaration to the contrary, such powers and duties shall be discharged by the Vice President as Acting President.

Section 4. Whenever the Vice President and a majority of either the principal officers of the executive departments or of such other body as Congress may by law provide, transmit to the President pro tempore of the Senate and the Speaker of the House of Representatives their written declaration that the President is unable to discharge the powers and duties of his office, the Vice President shall immediately assume the powers and duties of the office as Acting President. Thereafter, when the President transmits to the President pro tempore of the Senate and the Speaker of the House of Representatives his written declaration that no inability exists, he shall resume the powers and duties of his office unless the Vice President and a majority of either the principal officers of the executive department or of such other body as Congress may by law provide, transmit within four days to the President pro tempore of the Senate and the Speaker of the House of Representatives their written declaration that the President is unable to discharge the powers and duties of his office. Thereupon Congress shall decide the issue, assembling within forty-eight hours for that purpose if not in session. If the Congress, within twenty-one days after receipt of the latter written declaration, or, if Congress is not in session, within twenty-one days after Congress is required to assemble, determines by two-thirds vote of both Houses that the President is unable to discharge the powers and duties of his office, the Vice President shall continue to discharge the same as Acting President; otherwise, the President shall resume the powers and duties of his office.

Twenty-Sixth Amendment

Section 1. The right of citizens of the United States, who are eighteen years of age or older, to vote shall not be denied or abridged by the United States or by any State on account of age.

UNITED STATES CODE

The following provisions of law governing Presidential Elections are contained in Chapter 1 of Title 3, United States Code (62 Stat. 672, as amended):

TITLE 3 THE PRESIDENT
Chapter 1. Presidential Elections and Vacancies
Section

1. Time of appointing electors.
2. Failure to make choice on prescribed day.
3. Number of electors.
4. Vacancies in electoral college.
5. Determination of controversy as to appointment of electors.
6. Credentials of electors; transmission to Archivist of the United States and to Congress; public inspection.
7. Meeting and vote of electors.
8. Manner of voting.
9. Certificates of votes for President and Vice President.
10. Sealing and endorsing certificates.
11. Disposition of certificates.

12. Failure of certificates of electors to reach President of
    The Senate or Archivist of the United States; demand
    on State for certificate.
13. Same; demand on district judge for certificate.
14. Forfeiture for messenger's neglect of duty.
15. Counting electoral votes in Congress.
16. Same; seats for officers and Members of two Houses in
    joint meeting.
17. Same; limit of debate in each House.
18. Same; parliamentary procedure at joint meeting.
19. Vacancy in offices of both President and Vice
    President; officers eligible to act.
20. Resignation or refusal of office.
21. Definitions.

Chapter 1. Presidential Elections and Vacancies

Time of appointing electors
§ **1.** The electors of President and Vice President shall be appointed, in each State, on the Tuesday next after the first Monday in November, in every fourth year succeeding every election of a President and Vice President.
Failure to make choice on prescribed day
§ **2.** Whenever any State has held an election for the purpose of choosing electors, and has failed to make a choice on the day prescribed by law, the electors may be appointed on a subsequent day in such a manner as the legislature of such State may direct.
Number of electors
§ **3.** The number of electors shall be equal to the number of Senators and Representatives to which the several States are by law entitled at the time when the President and Vice President to be chosen come into office; except, that where no apportionment of Representatives has been made after any enumeration, at the time of choosing electors, the number of electors shall be according to the then existing apportionment of Senators and Representatives.

Vacancies in electoral college
§ 4. Each State may, by law, provide for the filling of any vacancies which may occur in its college of electors when such college meets to give its electoral vote.

Determination of controversy as to appointment of electors
§ 5. If any State shall have provided, by laws enacted prior to the day fixed for the appointment of the electors, for its final determination of any controversy or contest concerning the appointment of all or any of the electors of such State, by judicial or other methods or procedures, and such determination shall have been made at least six days before the time fixed for the meeting of the electors, such determination made pursuant to such law so existing on said day, and made at least six days prior to said time of meeting of the electors, shall be conclusive, and shall govern in the counting of the electoral votes as provided in the Constitution, and as hereinafter regulated, so far as the ascertainment of the electors appointed by such State is concerned.

Credentials of electors; transmission to archivist of the united states and to congress; public inspection
§ 6. It shall be the duty of the executive of each State, as soon as practicable after the conclusion of the appointment of the electors in such State by the final ascertainment, under and in pursuance of the laws of such State providing for such ascertainment, to communicate by registered mail under the seal of the State to the Archivist of the United States a certificate of such ascertainment of the electors appointed, setting forth the names of such electors and the canvass or other ascertainment under the laws of such State of the number of votes given or cast for each person for whose appointment any and all votes have been given or cast; and it shall also thereupon be the duty of the executive of each State to deliver to the electors of such State, on or before the day on which they are required by section 7 of this title to meet, six duplicate-originals of the same certificate under the seal of the State; and if there shall have been any final determination in a State in the manner provided for by law of a controversy or contest concerning the appointment of all or any of the electors of such State, it shall be the duty of the executive of such State, as soon as   practicable   after   such   determination,   to communicate under the seal of the State to the Archivist of the

United States a certificate of such determination in form and manner as the same shall have been made; and the certificate or certificates so received by the Archivist of the United States shall be preserved by him for one year and shall be a part of the public records of his office and shall be open to public inspection; and the Archivist of the United States at the first meeting of Congress thereafter shall transmit to the two Houses of Congress copies in full of each and every such certificate so received at the National Archives and Records Administration.

Meeting and vote of electors

§ 7. The electors of President and Vice President of each State shall meet and give their votes on the first Monday after the second Wednesday in December next following their appointment at such place in each State as the legislature of such State shall direct.

Manner of voting

§ 8. The electors shall vote for President and Vice President, respectively, in the manner directed by the Constitution.

Certificates of votes for president and vice president

§ 9. The electors shall make and sign six certificates of all the votes given by them, each of which certificates shall contain two distinct lists, one of the votes for President and the other of the votes for Vice President, and shall annex to each of the certificates one of the lists of the electors which shall have been furnished to them by direction of the executive of the State.

Sealing and endorsing certificates

§ 10. The electors shall seal up the certificates so made by them, and certify upon each that the lists of all the votes of such State given for President, and of all the votes given for Vice President, are contained therein.

Disposition of certificates

§ 11. The electors shall dispose of the certificates so made by them and the lists attached thereto in the following manner: *First.* They shall forthwith forward by registered mail one of the same to the President of the Senate at the seat of government. *Second.* Two of the same shall be delivered to the secretary of state of the State, one of which shall be held subject to the order of the President of the Senate, the other to be preserved by him for one year and shall be a part of the public records of his office and shall be open to public inspection.

Third. On the day thereafter they shall forward by registered mail two of such certificates and lists to the Archivist of the United States at the seat of government, one of which shall be held subject to the order of the President of the Senate. The other shall be preserved by the Archivist of the United States for one year and shall be a part of the public records of his office and shall be open to public inspection.

Fourth. They shall forthwith cause the other of the certificates and lists to be delivered to the judge of the district in which the electors shall have assembled.

Failure of certificates of electors to reach president of the senate or archivist of the united states; demand on state for certificate

§ 12. When no certificate of vote and list mentioned in sections 9 and 11 and of this title from any State shall have been received by the President of the Senate or by the Archivist of the United States by the fourth Wednesday in December, after the meeting of the electors shall have been held, the President of the Senate or, if he be absent from the seat of government, the Archivist of the United States shall request, by the most expeditious method available, the secretary of state of the State to send up the certificate and list lodged with him by the electors of such State; and it shall be his duty upon receipt of such request immediately to transmit same by registered mail to the President of the Senate at the seat of government.

Same; demand on district judge for certificate

§ 13. When no certificates of votes from any State shall have been received at the seat of government on the fourth Wednesday in December, after the meeting of the electors shall have been held, the President of the Senate or, if he be absent from the seat of government, the Archivist of the United States shall send a special messenger to the district judge in whose custody one certificate of votes from that State has been lodged, and such judge shall forthwith transmit that list by the hand of such messenger to the seat of government.

Forfeiture for messenger's neglect of duty

§ 14. Every person who, having been appointed, pursuant to section 13 of this title, to deliver the certificates of the votes of the electors to the President of the Senate, and having accepted such appointment, shall neglect to perform the services required from him, shall forfeit the sum of $1,000.

Counting electoral votes in congress

§ 15. Congress shall be in session on the sixth day of January succeeding every meeting of the electors. The Senate and House of Representatives shall meet in the Hall of the House of Representatives at the hour of one o'clock in the afternoon on that day, and the President of the Senate shall be their presiding officer. Two tellers shall be previously appointed on the part of the Senate and two on the part of the House of Representatives, to whom shall be handed, as they are opened by the President of the Senate, all the certificates and papers purporting to be certificates of the electoral votes, which certificates and papers shall be opened, presented, and acted upon in the alphabetical order of the States, beginning with the letter A; and said tellers, having then read the same in the presence and hearing of the two Houses, shall make a list of the votes as they shall appear from the said certificates; and the votes having been ascertained and counted according to the rules in this subchapter provided, the result of the same shall be delivered to the President of the Senate, who shall thereupon announce the state of the vote, which announcement shall be deemed a sufficient declaration of the persons, if any, elected President and Vice President of the United States, and, together with a list of the votes, be entered on the Journals of the two Houses. Upon such reading of any such certificate or paper, the President of the Senate shall call for objections, if any. Every objection shall be made in writing, and shall state clearly and concisely, and without argument, the ground thereof, and shall be signed by at least one Senator and one Member of the House of Representatives before the same shall be received. When all objections so made to any vote or paper from a State shall have been received and read, the Senate shall thereupon withdraw, and such objections shall be submitted to the Senate for its decision; and the Speaker of the House of Representatives shall, in like manner, submit such objections to the House of Representatives for its decision; and no electoral vote or votes from any State which shall have been regularly given by electors whose appointment has been lawfully certified to according to section 6 of this title from which but one return has been received shall be rejected, but the two Houses concurrently may reject the vote or votes when they agree that such vote or votes have not been so regularly given by electors whose appointment has been so certified. If more than one return or paper purporting to be a return from a State shall have been received by the President of the Senate, those votes, and those only, shall be counted which shall have been regularly given by the electors who are shown by the determination mentioned in section 5 of this title to have been appointed, if the determination in said section provided for shall have been made, or by such successors or substitutes, in case of a vacancy in the board of electors so ascertained, as have been appointed to fill such vacancy in the mode provided by the laws of the State; but in case there shall arise the question which of two or more of such State authorities determining what electors have been appointed, as mentioned in section 5 of this title, is the lawful tribunal of such State, the votes regularly given of those electors, and those only, of such State shall be counted whose title as electors the two Houses, acting separately, shall concurrently decide is supported by the decision of such State so authorized by its law; and in such case of more than one return or paper purporting to be a return from a State, if there shall have been no such determination of the question in the State aforesaid, then those votes, and those only, shall be counted which the two Houses shall concurrently decide were cast by lawful electors appointed in accordance with the laws of the State, unless the two Houses, acting separately, shall concurrently decide such votes not to be the lawful votes of the legally appointed electors of such State. But if the two Houses shall disagree in respect of the counting of such votes, then, and in that case, the votes of the electors whose appointment shall have been certified by the executive of the State, under the seal thereof, shall be counted. When the two Houses have voted, they shall immediately again meet, and the presiding officer shall then announce the decision of the questions submitted. No votes or papers from any other State shall be acted upon until the objections previously made to the votes or papers from any State shall have been finally disposed of.

Same; seats for officers and members of two houses in joint meeting

§ 16. At such joint meeting of the two Houses seats shall be provided as follows: For the President of the Senate, the Speaker's chair; for the Speaker, immediately upon his left; the Senators, in the body of the Hall upon the right of the presiding officer; for the Representatives, in the body of the Hall not provided for the Senators; for the tellers, Secretary of the Senate, and Clerk of the House of Representatives, at the Clerk's desk; for the other officers of the two Houses, in front of the Clerk's desk and upon each side of the Speaker's platform. Such joint meeting shall not be dissolved until the count of electoral votes shall be completed and the result declared; and no recess shall be taken unless a question shall have arisen in regard to counting any such votes, or otherwise under this subchapter, in which case it shall be competent for either House, acting separately, in the manner hereinbefore provided, to direct a recess of such House not beyond the next calendar day, Sunday excepted, at the hour of ten o'clock in the forenoon. But if the counting of the electoral votes and the declaration of the result shall not have been completed before the fifth calendar day next after such first meeting of the two Houses, no further or other recess shall be taken by either House.

Same; limit of debate in each house

§ 17. When the two Houses separate to decide upon an objection that may have been made to the counting of any electoral vote or votes from any State, or other question arising in the matter, each Senator and Representative may speak to such objection or question five minutes, and not more than once; but after such debate shall have lasted two hours it shall be the duty of the presiding officer of each House to put the main question without further debate.

Same; parliamentary procedure at joint meeting

§ 18. While the two Houses shall be in meeting as provided in this chapter, the President of the Senate shall have power to preserve order; and no debate shall be allowed and no question shall be put by the presiding officer except to either House on a motion to withdraw.

Vacancy in offices of both president and vice president; officers eligible to act

§ 19. (a) (1) If, by reason of death, resignation, removal from office, inability, or failure to qualify, there is neither a President nor Vice President to discharge the powers and duties of the office of President, then the Speaker of the House of Representatives shall, upon his resignation as Speaker and as Representative in Congress, act as President. (2) The same rule shall apply in the case of the death, resignation, removal from office, or inability of an individual acting as President under this subsection. (b) If, at the time when under subsection *(a)* of this section a Speaker is to begin the discharge of the powers and duties of the office of President, there is no speaker, or the Speaker fails to qualify as Acting President, then the President pro tempore of the Senate shall, upon his resignation as President pro tempore *(c)* An individual acting as President under subsection *(a)* or subsection *(b)* of this section shall continue to act until the expiration of the then current Presidential term, except that (1) if his discharge of the powers and duties of the office is founded in whole or in part on the failure of both the President-elect and the Vice President-elect to qualify, then he shall act only until a President or Vice President qualifies; and (2) if his discharge of the powers and duties of the office is founded in whole or in part on the inability of the President or Vice President, then he shall act only until the removal of the disability of one (d) (1) if, by reason of death, resignation, removal from office, inability, or failure to qualify, there is no President pro tempore to act as President under subsection (b) of this section, then the officer of the United States who is highest on the following list, and who is not under disability to discharge the powers and duties of the office of President shall act as President: Secretary of State, Secretary of the Treasury, Secretary of Defense, Attorney General, Secretary of the Interior, Secretary of Agriculture, Secretary of Commerce, Secretary of Labor, Secretary of Health and Human Services, Secretary of Housing and Urban Development, Secretary of Transportation, Secretary of Energy, Secretary of Education, Secretary of Veterans Affairs.(2) An individual acting as President under this subsection shall continue so to do until the expiration of the then current Presidential term, but not after a qualified and prior-entitled individual is able to act, except that the removal of the disability of an individual higher on the list contained in paragraph (1) of this subsection or the ability to qualify on the part of an individual higher on such list shall not terminate his service. (3) The taking of the oath of office by an individual specified in the list in paragraph (1) of this subsection shall be held to constitute his resignation from the office by virtue of the holding of which he qualifies to act as President.

(e) Subsections (a), (b), and (d) of this section shall apply only to such officers as are eligible to the office of President under the Constitution. Subsection (d) of this section shall apply only to officers appointed, by and with the advice and consent of the Senate, prior to the time of the death, resignation, removal from office, inability, or failure to qualify, of the President pro tempore, and only to officers not under impeachment by the House of Representatives at the time the powers and duties of the office of President devolve upon them. (f) During the period that any individual acts as President under this section, his compensation shall be at the rate then provided by law in the case of the President.

Resignation or refusal of office

§ 20. The only evidence of a refusal to accept, or of a resignation of the office of President or Vice President, shall be an instrument in writing, declaring the same, and subscribed by the person refusing to accept or resigning, as the case may be, and delivered into the office of the Secretary of State.

Definitions

§ 21. As used in this appendix the term –

(a) "State" includes the District of Columbia.

(b) "executives of each State" includes the Board of Commissioners of the District of Columbia — The functions of the Board of Commissioners of the District of Columbia are now performed by the Mayor of the District of Columbia. (Reorganization Plan No. 3 of 1967, Section 401, 81 Stat. 948: Pub. L. 93-198, Sections 422 and 711, 87 Stat. 790, 818.)

Appendix B

The Constitution of the United States of America

We the People of the United States, in Order to form a more perfect Union, establish Justice, insure domestic Tranquility, provide for the common defence, promote the general Welfare, and secure the Blessings of Liberty to ourselves and our Posterity, do ordain and establish this Constitution for the United States of America.

Article I

Section 1.

All legislative Powers herein granted shall be vested in a Congress of the United States, which shall consist of a Senate and House of Representatives.

Section 2.

The House of Representatives shall be composed of Members chosen every second Year by the People of the several States, and the Electors in each State shall have the Qualifications requisite for Electors of the most numerous Branch of the State Legislature.

No Person shall be a Representative who shall not have attained to the Age of twenty five Years, and been seven Years a Citizen of the United States, and who shall not, when elected, be an Inhabitant of that State in which he shall be chosen.

Representatives and direct Taxes shall be apportioned among the several States which may be included within this Union, according to their respective Numbers, which shall be determined by adding to the whole Number of free Persons, including those bound to Service for a Term of Years, and excluding Indians not taxed, three-fifths of all other Persons. (Note: changed by section 2 of the Fourteenth Amendment.) The actual Enumeration shall be made within three Years after the first Meeting of the Congress of the United States, and within every subsequent Term of ten Years, in such Manner as they shall by Law direct. The Number of Representatives shall not exceed one for every thirty Thousand, but each State shall have at Least one Representative; and until such enumeration shall be made, the State of New Hampshire shall be entitled to chuse three, Massachusetts eight, Rhode-Island and Providence Plantations one, Connecticut five, New-York six, New Jersey four, Pennsylvania eight, Delaware one, Maryland six, Virginia ten, North Carolina five, South Carolina five, and Georgia three. When vacancies happen in the Representation from any State, the Executive Authority thereof shall issue Writs of Election to fill such Vacancies.

The House of Representatives shall chuse their Speaker and other Officers; and shall have the sole Power of Impeachment.

Section 3.

The Senate of the United States shall be composed of two Senators from each State, chosen by the Legislature thereof, (Note: changed by the Seventeenth Amendment.) for six Years; and each Senator shall have one Vote.

Immediately after they shall be assembled in Consequence of the first Election, they shall be divided as equally as may be into three Classes. The Seats of the Senators of the first Class shall be vacated at the Expiration of the second Year, of the second Class at the Expiration of the fourth Year, and of the third Class at the Expiration of the sixth Year, so that one third may be chosen every second Year; and if Vacancies happen by Resignation, or otherwise, during the Recess of the Legislature of any State, the Executive thereof may make temporary Appointments until the next Meeting of the Legislature, which shall then fill such Vacancies. (Note: changed by the Seventeenth Amendment.)

No Person shall be a Senator who shall not have attained to the Age of thirty Years, and been nine Years a Citizen of the United States, and who shall not, when elected, be an Inhabitant of that State for which he shall be chosen.

The Vice President of the United States shall be President of the Senate, but shall have no Vote, unless they be equally divided.

The Senate shall chuse their other Officers, and also a President pro tempore, in the Absence of the Vice President, or when he shall exercise the Office of President of the United States. The Senate shall have the sole Power to try all Impeachments. When sitting for that Purpose, they shall be on Oath or Affirmation. When the President of the United States is tried, the Chief Justice shall preside: And no Person shall be convicted without the Concurrence of two thirds of the Members present. Judgment in Cases of Impeachment shall not extend further than to removal from Office, and disqualification to hold and enjoy any Office of honor, Trust or Profit under the United States: but the Party convicted shall nevertheless be liable and subject to Indictment, Trial, Judgment and Punishment, according to Law.

Section 4.

The Times, Places and Manner of holding Elections for Senators and Representatives, shall be prescribed in each State by the Legislature thereof; but the Congress may at any time by Law make or alter such Regulations, except as to the Places of chusing Senators. The Congress shall assemble at least once in every Year, and such Meeting shall be on the first Monday in December, (Note: changed by section 2 of the Twentieth Amendment.) unless they shall by Law appoint a different day.

Section 5.

Each House shall be the Judge of the Elections, Returns and Qualifications of its own Members, and a Majority of each shall constitute a Quorum to do Business; but a smaller Number may adjourn from day to day, and may be authorized to compel the Attendance of absent Members, in such Manner, and under such

Penalties as each House may provide. Each House may determine the Rules of its Proceedings, punish its Members for disorderly Behaviour, and, with the Concurrence of two thirds, expel a Member. Each House shall keep a Journal of its Proceedings, and from time to time publish the same, excepting such Parts as may in their Judgment require Secrecy; and the Yeas and Nays of the Members of either House on any question shall, at the Desire of one fifth of those Present, be entered on the Journal. Neither House, during the Session of Congress, shall, without the Consent of the other, adjourn for more than three days, nor to any other Place than that in which the two Houses shall be sitting.

Section 6.

The Senators and Representatives shall receive a Compensation for their Services, to be ascertained by Law, and paid out of the Treasury of the United States. They shall in all Cases, except Treason, Felony and Breach of the Peace, be privileged from Arrest during their Attendance at the Session of their respective Houses, and in going to and returning from the same; and for any Speech or Debate in either House, they shall not be questioned in any other Place. No Senator or Representative shall, during the Time for which he was elected, be appointed to any civil Office under the Authority of the United States, which shall have been created, or the Emoluments whereof shall have been encreased during such time; and no Person holding any Office under the United States, shall be a Member of either House during his Continuance in Office.

Section 7.

All Bills for raising Revenue shall originate in the House of Representatives; but the Senate may propose or concur with Amendments as on other Bills. Every Bill which shall have passed the House of Representatives and the Senate, shall, before it become a Law, be presented to the President of the United States; If he approve he shall sign it, but if not he shall return it, with his Objections to that House in which it shall have originated, who shall enter the Objections at large on their Journal, and proceed to reconsider it. If after such reconsideration two-thirds of that House shall agree to pass the Bill, it shall be sent, together with the Objections, to the other House, by which it shall likewise be reconsidered, and if approved by two thirds of that House, it shall become a Law. But in all such Cases the Votes of both Houses shall be determined by yeas and Nays, and the Names of the Persons voting for and against the Bill shall be entered on the Journal of each House respectively. If any Bill shall not be returned by the President within ten Days (Sundays excepted) after it shall have been presented to him, the Same shall be a Law, in like Manner as if he had signed it, unless the Congress by their Adjournment prevent its Return, in which Case it shall not be a Law. Every Order, Resolution, or Vote to which the Concurrence of the Senate and House of Representatives may be necessary (except on a question of Adjournment) shall be presented to the President of the United States; and before the Same shall take Effect, shall be approved by him, or being disapproved by him, shall be repassed by two thirds of the Senate and House of Representatives, according to the Rules and Limitations prescribed in the Case of a Bill.

Section 8.

The Congress shall have Power To lay and collect Taxes, Duties, Imposts and Excises, to pay the Debts and provide for the common Defence and general Welfare of the United States; but all Duties, Imposts and Excises shall be uniform throughout the United States;

- ★ To borrow Money on the credit of the United States;
- ★ To regulate Commerce with foreign Nations, and among the several States, and with the Indian Tribes;
- ★ To establish an uniform Rule of Naturalization, and uniform Laws on the subject of Bankruptcies throughout the United States;
- ★ To coin Money, regulate the Value thereof, and of foreign Coin, and fix the Standard of Weights and Measures;
- ★ To provide for the Punishment of counterfeiting the Securities and current Coin of the United States;
- ★ To establish Post Offices and post Roads;

★ To promote the Progress of Science and useful Arts, by securing for limited Times to Authors and Inventors the exclusive Right to their respective Writings and Discoveries;

★ To constitute Tribunals inferior to the supreme Court;

★ To define and punish Piracies and Felonies committed on the high Seas, and Offences against the Law of Nations;

★ To declare War, grant Letters of Marque and Reprisal, and make Rules concerning Captures on Land and Water;

★ To raise and support Armies, but no Appropriation of Money to that Use shall be for a longer Term than two Years;

★ To provide and maintain a Navy;

★ To make Rules for the Government and Regulation of the land and naval Forces;

★ To provide for calling forth the Militia to execute the Laws of the Union, suppress Insurrections and repel Invasions;

★ To provide for organizing, arming, and disciplining, the Militia, and for governing such Part of them as may be employed in the Service of the United States, reserving to the States respectively, the Appointment of the Officers, and the Authority of training the Militia according to the discipline prescribed by Congress;

★ To exercise exclusive Legislation in all Cases whatsoever, over such District (not exceeding ten Miles square) as may, by Cession of particular States, and the Acceptance of Congress, become the Seat of the Government of the United States, and to exercise like Authority over all Places purchased by the Consent of the Legislature of the State in which the Same shall be, for the Erection of Forts, Magazines, Arsenals, dock-Yards, and other needful Buildings;—And

★ To make all Laws which shall be necessary and proper for carrying into Execution the foregoing Powers, and all other Powers vested by this Constitution in the Government of the United States, or in any Department or Officer thereof.

Section 9.

The Migration or Importation of such Persons as any of the States now existing shall think proper to admit, shall not be prohibited by the Congress prior to the Year one thousand eight hundred and eight, but a Tax or duty may be imposed on such Importation, not exceeding ten dollars for each Person. The Privilege of the Writ of Habeas Corpus shall not be suspended, unless when in Cases of Rebellion or Invasion the public Safety may require it.

No Bill of Attainder or ex post facto Law shall be passed.

No Capitation, or other direct, Tax shall be laid, unless in Proportion to the Census or Enumeration herein before directed to be taken. (Note: see the Sixteenth Amendment.)

No Tax or Duty shall be laid on Articles exported from any State.

No Preference shall be given by any Regulation of Commerce or Revenue to the Ports of one State over those of another: nor shall Vessels bound to, or from, one State, be obliged to enter, clear, or pay Duties in another.

No Money shall be drawn from the Treasury, but in Consequence of Appropriations made by Law; and a regular Statement and Account of the Receipts and Expenditures of all public Money shall be published from time to time.

No Title of Nobility shall be granted by the United States: And no Person holding any Office of Profit or Trust under them, shall, without the Consent of the Congress, accept of any present, Emolument, Office, or Title, of any kind whatever, from any King, Prince, or foreign State.

Section 10.

No State shall enter into any Treaty, Alliance, or Confederation; grant Letters of Marque and Reprisal; coin Money; emit Bills of Credit; make any Thing but gold and silver Coin a Tender in Payment of Debts; pass any Bill of Attainder, ex post facto Law, or Law impairing the Obligation of Contracts, or grant any Title of Nobility.

No State shall, without the Consent of the Congress, lay any Imposts or Duties on Imports or Exports, except what may be absolutely necessary for executing its inspection Laws: and the net Produce of all

Duties and Imposts, laid by any State on Imports or Exports, shall be for the Use of the Treasury of the United States; and all such Laws shall be subject to the Revision and Controul of the Congress.

No State shall, without the Consent of Congress, lay any Duty of Tonnage, keep Troops, or Ships of War in time of Peace, enter into any Agreement or Compact with another State, or with a foreign Power, or engage in War, unless actually invaded, or in such imminent Danger as will not admit of delay.

Article II

Section 1.

The executive Power shall be vested in a President of the United States of America. He shall hold his Office during the Term of four Years, and, together with the Vice President, chosen for the same Term, be elected, as follows:

Each State shall appoint, in such Manner as the Legislature thereof may direct, a Number of Electors, equal to the whole number of Senators and Representatives to which the State may be entitled in the Congress: but no Senator or Representative, or Person holding an Office of Trust or Profit under the United States, shall be appointed an Elector. The Electors shall meet in their respective States, and vote by Ballot for two Persons, of whom one at least shall not be an Inhabitant of the same State with themselves. And they shall make a List of all the Persons voted for, and of the Number of Votes for each; which List they shall sign and certify, and transmit sealed to the Seat of the Government of the United States, directed to the President of the Senate. The President of the Senate shall, in the Presence of the Senate and House of Representatives, open all the Certificates, and the Votes shall then be counted. The Person having the greatest Number of Votes shall be the President, if such Number be a Majority of the whole Number of Electors appointed; and if there be more than one who have such Majority, and have an equal Number of Votes, then the House of Representatives shall immediately chuse by Ballot one of them for President; and if no Person have a Majority, then from the five highest on the List the said House shall in like Manner chuse the President. But in chusing the President, the Votes shall be taken by States, the Representation from each State having one Vote; A quorum for this Purpose shall consist of a Member or Members from two- thirds of the States, and a Majority of all the States shall be necessary to a Choice.

In every Case, after the Choice of the President, the Person having the greatest Number of Votes of the Electors shall be the Vice President. But if there should remain two or more who have equal Votes, the Senate shall chuse from them by Ballot the Vice President. (Note: changed by the Twelfth Amendment.) The Congress may determine the Time of chusing the Electors, and the Day on which they shall give their Votes; which Day shall be the same throughout the United States. No Person except a natural born Citizen, or a Citizen of the United States, at the time of the Adoption of this Constitution, shall be eligible to the Office of President; neither shall any Person be eligible to that Office who shall not have attained to the Age of thirty five Years, and been fourteen Years a Resident within the United States. In Case of the Removal of the President from Office, or of his Death, Resignation, or Inability to discharge the Powers and Duties of the said Office, the Same shall devolve on the Vice President, and the Congress may by Law provide for the Case of Removal, Death, Resignation or Inability, both of the President and Vice President, declaring what Officer shall then act as President, and such Officer shall act accordingly, until the Disability be removed, or a President shall be elected. (Note: changed by the Twenty-Fifth Amendment.) The President shall, at stated Times, receive for his Services, a Compensation, which shall neither be encreased nor diminished during the Period for which he shall have been elected, and he shall not receive within that Period any other Emolument from the United States, or any of them.

Before he enter on the Execution of his Office, he shall take the following Oath or Affirmation:—"I do solemnly swear (or affirm) that I will faithfully execute the Office of President of the United States, and will to the best of my Ability, preserve, protect and defend the Constitution of the United States."

Section 2.

The President shall be Commander in Chief of the Army and Navy of the United States, and of the Militia of the several States, when called into the actual Service of the United States; he may require the Opinion, in writing, of the principal Officer in each of the executive Departments, upon any Subject relating to the Duties of their respective Offices, and he shall have Power to grant Reprieves and Pardons for Offences against the United States, except in Cases of Impeachment. He shall have Power, by and with the Advice and Consent of the Senate, to make Treaties, provided two thirds of the Senators present concur; and he shall nominate, and by and with the Advice and Consent of the Senate, shall appoint Ambassadors, other public Ministers and Consuls, Judges of the Supreme Court, and all other Officers of the United States, whose Appointments are not herein otherwise provided for, and which shall be established by Law: but the Congress may by Law vest the Appointment of such inferior Officers, as they think proper, in the President alone, in the Courts of Law, or in the Heads of Departments. The President shall have Power to fill up all Vacancies that may happen during the Recess of the Senate, by granting Commissions which shall expire at the End of their next Session.

Section 3.

He shall from time to time give to the Congress Information of the State of the Union, and recommend to their Consideration such Measures as he shall judge necessary and expedient; he may, on extraordinary Occasions, convene both Houses, or either of them, and in Case of Disagreement between them, with Respect to the Time of Adjournment, he may adjourn them to such Time as he shall think proper; he shall receive Ambassadors and other public Ministers; he shall take Care that the Laws be faithfully executed, and shall Commission all the Officers of the United States.

Section 4.

The President, Vice President and all civil Officers of the United States, shall be removed from Office on Impeachment for, and

Conviction of, Treason, Bribery, or other high Crimes and Misdemeanors.

Article III

Section 1.

The judicial Power of the United States, shall be vested in one supreme Court, and in such inferior Courts as the Congress may from time to time ordain and establish. The Judges, both of the supreme and inferior Courts, shall hold their Offices during good Behaviour, and shall, at stated Times, receive for their Services, a Compensation, which shall not be diminished during their Continuance in Office.

Section 2.

The judicial Power shall extend to all Cases, in Law and Equity, arising under this Constitution, the Laws of the United States, and Treaties made, or which shall be made, under their Authority;–to all Cases affecting Ambassadors, other public Ministers and Consuls;–to all Cases of admiralty and maritime Jurisdiction;–to Controversies to which the United States shall be a Party;–to Controversies between two or more States;–between a State and Citizens of another State; (Note: changed by the Eleventh Amendment.)–between Citizens of different States,–between Citizens of the same State claiming Lands under Grants of different States, and between a State, or the Citizens thereof, and foreign States, Citizens or Subjects. (Note: changed by the Eleventh Amendment.) In all Cases affecting Ambassadors, other public Ministers and Consuls, and those in which a State shall be Party, the Supreme Court shall have original Jurisdiction. In all the other Cases before mentioned, the Supreme Court shall have appellate Jurisdiction, both as to Law and Fact, with such Exceptions, and under such Regulations as the Congress shall make. The Trial of all Crimes, except in Cases of Impeachment, shall be by Jury; and such Trial shall be held in the State where the said Crimes shall have been committed; but when not committed within any State, the Trial shall be at such Place or Places as the Congress may by Law have directed.

Section 3.

Treason against the United States, shall consist only in levying War against them, or in adhering to their Enemies, giving them Aid and Comfort. No Person shall be convicted of Treason unless on the Testimony of two Witnesses to the same overt Act, or on Confession in open Court. The Congress shall have Power to declare the Punishment of Treason, but no Attainder of Treason shall work Corruption of Blood, or Forfeiture except during the Life of the Person attainted.

Article IV

Section 1.

Full Faith and Credit shall be given in each State to the public Acts, Records, and judicial Proceedings of every other State. And the Congress may by general Laws prescribe the Manner in which such Acts, Records and Proceedings shall be proved, and the Effect thereof.

Section 2.

The Citizens of each State shall be entitled to all Privileges and Immunities of Citizens in the several States. A Person charged in any State with Treason, Felony, or other Crime, who shall flee from Justice, and be found in another State, shall on Demand of the executive Authority of the State from which he fled, be delivered up, to be removed to the State having Jurisdiction of the Crime. No Person held to Service or Labour in one State, under the Laws thereof, escaping into another, shall, in Consequence of any Law or Regulation therein, be discharged from such Service or Labour, but shall be delivered up on Claim of the Party to whom such Service or Labour may be due. (Note: changed by the Thirteenth Amendment.)

Section 3.

New States may be admitted by the Congress into this Union; but no new State shall be formed or erected within the Jurisdiction of any other State; nor any State be formed by the Junction of two or more States, or Parts of States, without the Consent of the Legislatures of the States concerned as well as of the Congress. The Congress shall have Power to dispose of and make all needful Rules and Regulations respecting the Territory or other Property belonging to the United States; and nothing in this Constitution shall be so construed as to Prejudice any Claims of the United States, or of any particular State.

Section 4.
The United States shall guarantee to every State in this Union a Republican Form of Government, and shall protect each of them against Invasion; and on Application of the Legislature, or of the Executive (when the Legislature cannot be convened) against domestic Violence.

Article V
The Congress, whenever two thirds of both Houses shall deem it necessary, shall propose Amendments to this Constitution, or, on the Application of the Legislatures of two thirds of the several States, shall call a Convention for proposing Amendments, which, in either Case, shall be valid to all Intents and Purposes, as Part of this Constitution, when ratified by the Legislatures of three fourths of the several States, or by Conventions in three fourths thereof, as the one or the other Mode of Ratification may be proposed by the Congress; Provided that no Amendment which may be made prior to the Year One thousand eight hundred and eight shall in any Manner affect the first and fourth Clauses in the Ninth Section of the first Article; and that no State, without its Consent, shall be deprived of its equal Suffrage in the Senate.

Article VI
All Debts contracted and Engagements entered into, before the Adoption of this Constitution, shall be as valid against the United States under this Constitution, as under the Confederation. This Constitution, and the Laws of the United States which shall be made in Pursuance thereof; and all Treaties made, or which shall be made,

under the Authority of the United States, shall be the supreme Law of the Land; and the Judges in every State shall be bound thereby, any thing in the Constitution or Laws of any State to the Contrary notwithstanding. The Senators and Representatives before mentioned, and the Members of the several State Legislatures, and all executive and judicial Officers, both of the United States and of the several States, shall be bound by Oath or Affirmation, to support this Constitution; but no religious Test shall ever be required as a Qualification to any Office or public Trust under the United States.

Article VII

The ratification of the conventions of nine states, shall be sufficient for the establishment of this Constitution between the states so ratifying the same.

Bill of Rights: Amendments I - X
(Ratified December 15, 1791)

Amendment I

Congress shall make no law respecting an establishment of religion, or prohibiting the free exercise thereof; or abridging the freedom of speech, or of the press; or the right of the people peaceably to assemble, and to petition the Government for a redress of grievances.

Amendment II

A well regulated Militia, being necessary to the security of a free State, the right of the people to keep and bear Arms, shall not be infringed.

Amendment III

No Soldier shall, in time of peace be quartered in any house, without the consent of the Owner, nor in time of war, but in a manner to be prescribed by law.

Amendment IV

The right of the people to be secure in their persons, houses, papers, and effects, against unreasonable searches and seizures, shall not be violated, and no Warrants shall issue, but upon probable cause, supported by Oath or affirmation, and particularly describing the place to be searched, and the persons or things to be seized.

Amendment V

No person shall be held to answer for a capital, or otherwise infamous crime, unless on a presentment or indictment of a Grand Jury, except in cases arising in the land or naval forces, or in the Militia, when in actual service in time of War or public danger; nor shall any person be subject for the same offense to be twice put in jeopardy of life or limb; nor shall be compelled in any criminal case to be a witness against himself, nor be deprived of life, liberty, or property, without due process of law; nor shall private property be taken for public use, without just compensation.

Amendment VI

In all criminal prosecutions, the accused shall enjoy the right to a speedy and public trial, by an impartial jury of the State and district wherein the crime shall have been committed, which district shall have been previously ascertained by law, and to be informed of the nature and cause of the accusation; to be confronted with the witnesses against him; to have compulsory process for obtaining witnesses in his favor, and to have the Assistance of Counsel for his defence.

Amendment VII

In Suits at common law, where the value in controversy shall exceed twenty dollars, the right of trial by jury shall be preserved, and no act tried by a jury, shall be otherwise re-examined in any Court of the United States, than according to the rules of the common law.

Amendment VIII

Excessive bail shall not be required, nor excessive fines imposed, nor cruel and unusual punishments inflicted.

Amendment IX

The enumeration in the Constitution, of certain rights, shall not be construed to deny or disparage others retained by the people.

Amendment X

The powers not delegated to the United States by the Constitution, nor prohibited by it to the States, are reserved to the States respectively, or to the people.

Amendment XI
(Ratified February 7, 1795)

The Judicial power of the United States shall not be construed to extend to any suit in law or equity, commenced or prosecuted against one of the United States by Citizens of another State, or by Citizens or Subjects of any Foreign State.

Amendment XII
(Ratified June 15, 1804)

The Electors shall meet in their respective states, and vote by ballot for President and Vice President, one of whom, at least, shall not be an inhabitant of the same state with themselves; they shall name in their ballots the person voted for as President, and in distinct ballots the person voted for as Vice-President, and they shall make distinct lists of all persons voted for as President, and of all persons voted for as Vice President and of the number of votes for each, which lists they shall sign and certify, and transmit sealed to the seat of the government of the United States, directed to the President of the Senate;—The President of the Senate shall, in the presence of the Senate and House of Representatives, open all the certificates and the votes shall then be counted;—The person having the greatest number of votes for President, shall be the President, if such number be a majority of the whole number of Electors appointed; and if no person have such majority, then from the persons having the highest numbers not exceeding three on the list of those voted for as President, the House of Representatives shall choose immediately, by ballot, the President. But in choosing the President, the votes shall be taken by states, the representation from each state having one vote; a quorum for this purpose shall consist of a member or members from two-thirds of the states, and a majority of all the states shall be necessary to a choice.

And if the House of Representatives shall not choose a President whenever the right of choice shall devolve upon them, before the fourth day of March next following, then the Vice President shall act as President, as in the case of the death or other constitutional disability of the President. (Note: superseded by section 3 of the Twentieth Amendment.)—The person having the greatest number of votes as Vice-President, shall be the Vice President, if such number be a majority of the whole number of Electors appointed, and if no person have a majority, then from the two highest numbers on the list, the Senate shall choose the Vice-President; a quorum for the purpose shall consist of two-thirds of the whole number of Senators, and a majority of the whole number shall be necessary to a choice. But no person constitutionally ineligible to the office of President shall be eligible to that of Vice President of the United States.

Amendment XIII
(Ratified December 6, 1865)

Section 1.
Neither slavery nor involuntary servitude, except as a punishment for crime whereof the party shall have been duly convicted, shall exist within the United States, or any place subject to their jurisdiction.

Section 2.
Congress shall have power to enforce this article by appropriate legislation.

Amendment XIV
(Ratified July 9, 1868)

Section 1.

All persons born or naturalized in the United States, and subject to the jurisdiction thereof, are citizens of the United States and of the State wherein they reside. No State shall make or enforce any law which shall abridge the privileges or immunities of citizens of the United States; nor shall any State deprive any person of life, liberty, or property, without due process of law; nor deny to any person within its jurisdiction the equal protection of the laws.

Section 2.

Representatives shall be apportioned among the several States according to their respective numbers, counting the whole number of persons in each State, excluding Indians not taxed. But when the right to vote at any election for the choice of electors for President and Vice-President of the United States, Representatives in Congress, the Executive and Judicial officers of a State, or the members of the Legislature thereof, is denied to any of the male inhabitants of such State, being twenty-one years of age, and citizens of the United States, or in any way abridged, except for participation in rebellion, or other crime, the basis of representation therein shall be reduced in the proportion which the number of such male citizens shall bear to the whole number of male citizens twenty-one years of age in such State.

Section 3.

No person shall be a Senator or Representative in Congress, or elector of President and Vice-President, or hold any office, civil or military, under the United States, or under any State, who, having previously taken an oath, as a member of Congress, or as an officer of the United States, or as a member of any State legislature, or as an executive or judicial officer of any State, to support the Constitution of the United States, shall have engaged in insurrection or rebellion against the same, or given aid or comfort to the enemies thereof. But Congress may by a vote of two-thirds of each House, remove such disability.

Section 4.

The validity of the public debt of the United States, authorized by law, including debts incurred for payment of pensions and bounties for services in suppressing insurrection or rebellion, shall not be questioned.

But neither the United States nor any State shall assume or pay any debt or obligation incurred in aid of insurrection or rebellion against the United States, or any claim for the loss or emancipation of any slave; but all such debts, obligations and claims shall be held illegal and void.

Section 5.

The Congress shall have power to enforce, by appropriate legislation, the provisions of this article.

Amendment XV
(Ratified February 3, 1870)

Section 1.

The right of citizens of the United States to vote shall not be denied or abridged by the United States or by any State on account of race, color, or previous condition of servitude.

Section 2.

The Congress shall have power to enforce this article by appropriate legislation.

Amendment XVI
(Ratified February 3, 1913)

The Congress shall have power to lay and collect taxes on incomes, from whatever source derived, without apportionment among the several States, and without regard to any census or enumeration.

Amendment XVII
(Ratified April 8, 1913)

The Senate of the United States shall be composed of two Senators from each State, elected by the people thereof, for six years; and each

Senator shall have one vote. The electors in each State shall have the qualifications requisite for electors of the most numerous branch of the State legislatures. When vacancies happen in the representation of any State in the Senate, the executive authority of such State shall issue writs of election to fill such vacancies: Provided, That the legislature of any State may empower the executive thereof to make temporary appointments until the people fill the vacancies by election as the legislature may direct. This amendment shall not be so construed as to affect the election or term of any Senator chosen before it becomes valid as part of the Constitution.

Amendment XVIII
(Ratified January 16, 1919)

Section 1.

After one year from the ratification of this article the manufacture, sale, or transportation of intoxicating liquors within, the importation thereof into, or the exportation thereof from the United States and all territory subject to the jurisdiction thereof for beverage purposes is hereby prohibited.

Section 2.

The Congress and the several States shall have concurrent power to enforce this article by appropriate legislation.

Section 3.

This article shall be inoperative unless it shall have been ratified as an amendment to the Constitution by the legislatures of the several States, as provided in the Constitution, within seven years from the date of the submission hereof to the States by the Congress. (Note: This amendment was repealed by the Twenty-First Amendment.)

Amendment XIX
(Ratified August 18, 1920)

The right of citizens of the United States to vote shall not be denied or abridged by the United States or by any State on account of sex.

Congress shall have power to enforce this article by appropriate legislation.

Amendment XX
(Ratified January 23, 1933)

Section 1.
The terms of the President and Vice President shall end at noon on the 20th day of January, and the terms of Senators and Representatives at noon on the 3d day of January, of the years in which such terms would have ended if this article had not been ratified; and the terms of their successors shall then begin.

Section 2.
The Congress shall assemble at least once in every year, and such meeting shall begin at noon on the 3d day of January, unless they shall by law appoint a different day.

Section 3.
If, at the time fixed for the beginning of the term of the President, the President elect shall have died, the Vice President elect shall become President.

If a President shall not have been chosen before the time fixed for the beginning of his term, or if the President elect shall have failed to qualify, then the Vice President elect shall act as President until a President shall have qualified; and the Congress may by law provide for the case wherein neither a President elect nor a Vice President elect shall have qualified, declaring who shall then act as President, or the manner in which one who is to act shall be selected, and such person shall act accordingly until a President or Vice President shall have qualified.

Section 4.
The Congress may by law provide for the case of the death of any of the persons from whom the House of Representatives may choose a President whenever the right of choice shall have devolved upon them, and for the case of the death of any of the persons from whom

the Senate may choose a Vice President whenever the right of choice shall have devolved upon them.

Section 5.
Sections 1 and 2 shall take effect on the 15th day of October following the ratification of this article.

Section 6.
This article shall be inoperative unless it shall have been ratified as an amendment to the Constitution by the legislatures of three-fourths of the several States within seven years from the date of its submission.

Amendment XXI
(Ratified December 5, 1933)
Section 1.
The eighteenth article of amendment to the Constitution of the United States is hereby repealed.

Section 2.
The transportation or importation into any State, Territory, or possession of the United States for delivery or use therein of intoxicating liquors, in violation of the laws thereof, is hereby prohibited.

Section 3.
This article shall be inoperative unless it shall have been ratified as an amendment to the Constitution by conventions in the several States, as provided in the Constitution, within seven years from the date of the submission hereof to the States by the Congress.

Amendment XXII
(Ratified February 27, 1951)
Section 1.
No person shall be elected to the office of the President more than twice, and no person who has held the office of President, or acted as President, for more than two years of a term to which some other person was elected President shall be elected to the office of the

President more than once. But this Article shall not apply to any person holding the office of President, when this Article was proposed by the Congress, and shall not prevent any person who may be holding the office of President, or acting as President, during the term within which this Article becomes operative from holding the office of President or acting as President during the remainder of such term.

Section 2.

This article shall be inoperative unless it shall have been ratified as an amendment to the Constitution by the legislatures of three-fourths of the several States within seven years from the date of its submission to the States by the Congress.

Amendment XXIII
(Ratified March 29, 1961)

Section 1.

The District constituting the seat of Government of the United States shall appoint in such manner as the Congress may direct: A number of electors of President and Vice President equal to the whole number of Senators and Representatives in Congress to which the District would be entitled if it were a State, but in no event more than the least populous State; they shall be in addition to those appointed by the States, but they shall be considered, for the purposes of the election of President and Vice President, to be electors appointed by a State; and they shall meet in the District and perform such duties as provided by the twelfth article of amendment.

Section 2.

The Congress shall have power to enforce this article by appropriate legislation.

Amendment XXIV
(Ratified January 23, 1964)

Section 1.

The right of citizens of the United States to vote in any primary or other election for President or Vice President, for electors for

President or Vice President, or for Senator or Representative in Congress, shall not be denied or abridged by the United States or any state by reason of failure to pay any poll tax or other tax.

Section 2.
The Congress shall have power to enforce this article by appropriate legislation.

Amendment XXV
(Ratified February 10, 1967)
Section 1.
In case of the removal of the President from office or of his death or resignation, the Vice President shall become President.

Section 2.
Whenever there is a vacancy in the office of the Vice President, the President shall nominate a Vice President who shall take office upon confirmation by a majority vote of both Houses of Congress.

Section 3.
Whenever the President transmits to the President pro tempore of the Senate and the Speaker of the House of Representatives his written declaration that he is unable to discharge the powers and duties of his office, and until he transmits to them a written declaration to the contrary, such powers and duties shall be discharged by the Vice President as Acting President.

Section 4.
Whenever the Vice President and a majority of either the principal officers of the executive departments or of such other body as Congress may by law provide, transmit to the President pro tempore of the Senate and the Speaker of the House of Representatives their written declaration that the President is unable to discharge the powers and duties of his office, the Vice President shall immediately assume the powers and duties of the office as Acting President. Thereafter, when the President transmits to the President pro

tempore of the Senate and the Speaker of the House of Representatives his written declaration that no inability exists, he shall resume the powers and duties of his office unless the Vice President and a majority of either the principal officers of the executive department or of such other body as Congress may by law provide, transmit within four days to the President pro tempore of the Senate and the Speaker of the House of Representatives their written declaration that the President is unable to discharge the powers and duties of his office. Thereupon Congress shall decide the issue, assembling within forty-eight hours for that purpose if not in session. If the Congress, within twenty-one days after receipt of the latter written declaration, or, if Congress is not in session, within twenty-one days after Congress is required to assemble, determines by two-thirds vote of both Houses that the President is unable to discharge the powers and duties of his office, the Vice President shall continue to discharge the same as Acting President; otherwise, the President shall resume the powers and duties of his office.

Amendment XXVI
(Ratified July 1, 1971)

Section 1.
The right of citizens of the United States, who are 18 years of age or older, to vote, shall not be denied or abridged by the United States or any state on account of age.

Section 2.
The Congress shall have the power to enforce this article by appropriate legislation.

Amendment XXVII
(Ratified May 7, 1992)

No Law, varying the compensation for the services of the Senators and Representatives shall take effect, until an election of Representatives shall have intervened.

Appendix C

Directory of the 111th Congress of the United States of America

House Membership
435 Members
5 Delegates
1 Resident
Commissioner

Party Divisions
256 Democrats
178 Republicans
0 Independents
1 Vacancy

Senate Membership
100 Senators
*(Vice President votes
in case of a tie)*

Party Divisions
58 Democrats
40 Republicans
2 Independents

The United States Senate

What is Senate Class?

Article I, section 3 of the Constitution requires the Senate to be divided into three classes for purposes of elections. Senators are elected to six-year terms, and every two years the members of one class—approximately one-third of the Senators—face election or reelection. Terms for Senators in Class I expire in 2013, Class II in 2009, and Class III in 2011.

*Order of Listing: Member Name / Party-State / Class /
Capital Address / Capital Phone Number / Email Address*

Murkowski, Lisa - (R - AK) Class III - 709 HART SENATE OFFICE
BUILDING WASHINGTON DC 20510 (202) 224-6665
Web Form: murkowski.senate.gov/contact./cfm

Begich, Mark - (D- AK) Class II - 825C HART SENATE OFFICE
BUILDING WASHINGTON DC 20510 (202) 224-3004
Web Form: begich.senate.gov/contact/contact.cfm

Sessions, Jeff - (R - AL) Class II - 335 RUSSELL SENATE OFFICE
BUILDING WASHINGTON DC 20510 (202) 224-4124
Web Form: sessions.senate.gov/email/contact.cfm

Shelby, Richard C. - (R - AL) Class III - 110 HART SENATE OFFICE
BUILDING WASHINGTON DC 20510 (202) 224-5744
E-mail: senator@shelby.senate.gov

Lincoln, Blanche L. - (D - AR) Class III - 355 DIRKSEN SENATE OFFICE
BUILDING WASHINGTON DC 20510 (202) 224-4843
Web Form: lincoln.senate.gov/webform.html

Pryor, Mark L. - (D - AR) Class II - 255 DIRKSEN SENATE OFFICE
BUILDING WASHINGTON DC 20510 (202) 224-2353
Web Form: pryor.senate.gov/contact/

Kyl, Jon - (R - AZ) Class I - 730 HART SENATE OFFICE BUILDING
WASHINGTON DC 20510 (202) 224-4521
Web Form: kyl.senate.gov/contact.cfm

McCain, John - (R - AZ) Class III - 241 RUSSELL SENATE OFFICE
BUILDING WASHINGTON DC 20510 (202) 224-2235
Web Form: mccain.senate.gov/public/index.cfm?FuseAction=Contact.Con...

Boxer, Barbara - (D - CA) Class III - 112 HART SENATE OFFICE
BUILDING WASHINGTON DC 20510 (202) 224-3553
Web Form: boxer.senate.gov/contact

Feinstein, Dianne - (D - CA) Class I - 331 HART SENATE OFFICE BUILDING WASHINGTON DC 20510 (202) 224-3841
Web Form: feinstein.senate.gov/public/index.cfm?FuseAction=ContactU...

Udall, Mark - (D - CO) Class II - 317 HART SENATE OFFICE BUILDING WASHINGTON DC 20510 (202) 224-5941
Web Form: markudall.senate.gov/contact/contact.cfm

Bennet, Michael F. - (D - CO) Class III - 702 HART SENATE OFFICE BUILDING WASHINGTON DC 20510 (202) 224-5852
Web Form: bennet.senate.gov/public/?p=TransitionalSiteEmailSenatorB...

Dodd, Christopher J. - (D - CT) Class III - 448 RUSSELL SENATE OFFICE BUILDING WASHINGTON DC 20510 (202) 224-2823
Web Form: dodd.senate.gov/index.php?q=node/3130

Lieberman, Joseph I. - (ID - CT) Class I - 706 HART SENATE OFFICE BUILDING WASHINGTON DC 20510 (202) 224-4041
Web Form: lieberman.senate.gov/contact/index.cfm?regarding=issue

Kaufman, Edward E. (D - DE) Class II - G11 DIRKSEN SENATE OFFICE BUILDING WASHINGTON DC 20510 (202) 224-5042
Web Form: kaufman.senate.gov/services/contact/

Carper, Thomas R. - (D - DE) Class I - 513 HART SENATE OFFICE BUILDING WASHINGTON DC 20510 (202) 224-2441
Web Form: carper.senate.gov/contact/

Martinez, Mel - (R - FL) Class III - 356 RUSSELL SENATE OFFICE BUILDING WASHINGTON DC 20510 (202) 224-3041
Web Form: martinez.senate.gov/public/index.cfm?FuseAction=ContactIn...

Nelson, Bill - (D - FL) Class I - 716 HART SENATE OFFICE BUILDING WASHINGTON DC 20510 (202) 224-5274
Web Form: billnelson.senate.gov/contact/email.cfm

Chambliss, Saxby - (R - GA) Class II - 416 RUSSELL SENATE OFFICE BUILDING WASHINGTON DC 20510 (202) 224-3521
Web Form: chambliss.senate.gov/public/index.cfm?FuseAction=ContactU...

Isakson, Johnny - (R - GA) Class III - 120 RUSSELL SENATE OFFICE BUILDING WASHINGTON DC 20510 (202) 224-3643
Web Form: isakson.senate.gov/contact.cfm

Akaka, Daniel K. - (D - HI) Class I - 141 HART SENATE OFFICE BUILDING WASHINGTON DC 20510 (202) 224-6361
Web Form: akaka.senate.gov/public/index.cfm?FuseAction=Contact.Home

Inouye, Daniel K. - (D - HI) Class III - 722 HART SENATE OFFICE BUILDING WASHINGTON DC 20510 (202) 224-3934
Web Form: inouye.senate.gov/abtform.html

Grassley, Chuck - (R - IA) Class III - 135 HART SENATE OFFICE BUILDING WASHINGTON DC 20510 (202) 224-3744
Web Form: grassley.senate.gov/public/index.cfm?FuseAction=Contact.H...

Harkin, Tom - (D - IA) Class II - 731 HART SENATE OFFICE BUILDING WASHINGTON DC 20510 (202) 224-3254
Web Form: harkin.senate.gov/c/

Risch, Jim - (R - ID) Class II - 483 RUSSELL SENATE OFFICE BUILDING WASHINGTON DC 20510 (202) 224-2752
Web Form: risch.senate.gov/webform.cfm

Crapo, Mike - (R - ID) Class III - 239 DIRKSEN SENATE OFFICE BUILDING WASHINGTON DC 20510 (202) 224-6142
Web Form: crapo.senate.gov/contact/email.cfm

Durbin, Richard - (D - IL) Class II - 309 HART SENATE OFFICE BUILDING WASHINGTON DC 20510 (202) 224-2152
Web Form: durbin.senate.gov/contact.cfm

Burris, Roland W. - (D - IL) Class III – 523 DIRKSEN SENATE OFFICE BUILDING WASHINGTON DC 20510 (202) 224-2854
Web Form: burris.senate.gov/contact/contact.cfm

Bayh, Evan - (D - IN) Class III - 131 RUSSELL SENATE OFFICE BUILDING WASHINGTON DC 20510 (202) 224-5623
Web Form: bayh.senate.gov/contact/email/

Lugar, Richard G. - (R - IN) Class I - 306 HART SENATE OFFICE
BUILDING WASHINGTON DC 20510 (202) 224-4814
E-mail: senator_lugar@lugar.senate.gov

Brownback, Sam - (R - KS) Class III - 303 HART SENATE OFFICE
BUILDING WASHINGTON DC 20510 (202) 224-6521
Web Form: brownback.senate.gov/CMEmailMe.cfm

Roberts, Pat - (R - KS) Class II - 109 HART SENATE OFFICE
BUILDING WASHINGTON DC 20510 (202) 224-4774
Web Form: roberts.senate.gov/public/index.cfm?FuseAction=ContactInf...

Bunning, Jim - (R - KY) Class III - 316 HART SENATE OFFICE
BUILDING WASHINGTON DC 20510 (202) 224-4343
Web Form: bunning.senate.gov/index.cfm?FuseAction=Contact.Email

McConnell, Mitch- (R - KY) Class II - 361-A RUSSELL SENATE OFFICE
BUILDING WASHINGTON DC 20510 (202) 224-2541
Web Form: mcconnell.senate.gov/contact_form.cfm

Landrieu, Mary L. - (D - LA) Class II - 724 HART SENATE OFFICE
BUILDING WASHINGTON DC 20510 (202) 224-5824
Web Form: landrieu.senate.gov/contact/index.cfm

Vitter, David - (R - LA) Class III - 516 HART SENATE OFFICE BUILDING
WASHINGTON DC 20510 (202) 224-4623
Web Form: vitter.senate.gov/?module=webformIQV1

Kennedy, Edward M. - (D - MA) Class I - 317 RUSSELL SENATE OFFICE
BUILDING WASHINGTON DC 20510 (202) 224-4543
Web Form: kennedy.senate.gov/senator/contact.cfm

Kerry, John F. - (D - MA) Class II - 304 RUSSELL SENATE OFFICE
BUILDING WASHINGTON DC 20510 (202) 224-2742
Web Form: kerry.senate.gov/v3/contact/email.html

Cardin, Benjamin L. - (D - MD) Class I - 509 HART SENATE OFFICE
BUILDING WASHINGTON DC 20510 (202) 224-4524
Web Form: cardin.senate.gov/contact/

Mikulski, Barbara A. - (D - MD) Class III - 503 HART SENATE OFFICE BUILDING WASHINGTON DC 20510 (202) 224-4654
Web Form: mikulski.senate.gov/mailform.html

Collins, Susan M. - (R - ME) Class II - 413 DIRKSEN SENATE OFFICE BUILDING WASHINGTON DC 20510 (202) 224-2523
Web Form: collins.senate.gov/public/continue.cfm?FuseAction=Contact...

Snowe, Olympia J. - (R - ME) Class I - 154 RUSSELL SENATE OFFICE BUILDING WASHINGTON DC 20510 (202) 224-5344
Web Form: snowe.senate.gov/contact.htm

Levin, Carl - (D - MI) Class II - 269 RUSSELL SENATE OFFICE BUILDING WASHINGTON DC 20510 (202) 224-6221
Web Form: levin.senate.gov/contact/index.cfm

Stabenow, Debbie - (D - MI) Class I - 133 HART SENATE OFFICE BUILDING WASHINGTON DC 20510 (202) 224-4822
Web Form: stabenow.senate.gov/email.htm

Franken, Al – (D - MN) Class II - 320 HART SENATE OFFICE BUILDING WASHINGTON DC 20510 (202) 224-5641
Web Form: franken.senate.gov/contact/contact.cfm

Klobuchar, Amy - (D - MN) Class I - 302 HART SENATE OFFICE BUILDING WASHINGTON DC 20510 (202) 224-3244
Web Form: klobuchar.senate.gov/emailamy.cfm

Bond, Christopher S. - (R - MO) Class III - 274 RUSSELL SENATE OFFICE BUILDING WASHINGTON DC 20510 (202) 224-5721
Web Form: bond.senate.gov/contact/contactme.cfm

McCaskill, Claire - (D - MO) Class I - 717 HART SENATE OFFICE BUILDING WASHINGTON DC 20510 (202) 224-6154
Web Form: mccaskill.senate.gov/contact.cfm

Cochran, Thad - (R - MS) Class II - 113 DIRKSEN SENATE OFFICE BUILDING WASHINGTON DC 20510 (202) 224-5054
Web Form: cochran.senate.gov/contact.htm

Wicker, Roger F. - (R - MS) Class I - 487 RUSSELL SENATE OFFICE BUILDING WASHINGTON DC 20510 (202) 224-6253
Web Form: wicker.senate.gov/public/index.cfm?FuseAction=ContactMe.E...

Baucus, Max - (D - MT) Class II - 511 HART SENATE OFFICE BUILDING WASHINGTON DC 20510 (202) 224-2651
Web Form: baucus.senate.gov/contact/emailForm.cfm?subj=issue

Tester, Jon - (D - MT) Class I - 204 RUSSELL SENATE OFFICE BUILDING WASHINGTON DC 20510 (202) 224-2644
Web Form: tester.senate.gov/Contact/

Burr, Richard - (R - NC) Class III - 217 RUSSELL SENATE OFFICE BUILDING WASHINGTON DC 20510 (202) 224-3154
Web Form: burr.senate.gov/public/index.cfm?FuseAction=Contact.Home

Hagan, Kay - (D - NC) Class II - B40A DIRKSEN SENATE OFFICE BUILDING WASHINGTON DC 20510 (202) 224-6342
Web Form: hagan.senate.gov/contact/contact.cfm

Conrad, Kent - (D - ND) Class I - 530 HART SENATE OFFICE BUILDING WASHINGTON DC 20510 (202) 224-2043
Web Form: conrad.senate.gov/contact/webform.cfm

Dorgan, Byron L. - (D - ND) Class III - 322 HART SENATE OFFICE BUILDING WASHINGTON DC 20510 (202) 224-2551
E-mail: senator@dorgan.senate.gov

Johanns, Mike - (R - NE) Class II - 404 RUSSELL SENATE OFFICE BUILDING WASHINGTON DC 20510 (202) 224-4224
Web Form: johanns.senate.gov/contact/public/?p=ContactSenatorJohanns

Nelson, E. Benjamin - (D - NE) Class I - 720 HART SENATE OFFICE BUILDING WASHINGTON DC 20510 (202) 224-6551
Web Form: bennelson.senate.gov/contact/email.cfm

Gregg, Judd - (R - NH) Class III - 393 RUSSELL SENATE OFFICE BUILDING WASHINGTON DC 20510 (202) 224-3324
Web Form: gregg.senate.gov/sitepages/contact.cfm

Shaheen, Jeanne - (D - NH) Class II - G55 DIRKSEN SENATE OFFICE BUILDING WASHINGTON DC 20510 (202) 224-2841
Web Form: shaheen.senate.gov/contact/contact.cfm

Lautenberg, Frank R. - (D - NJ) Class II - 324 HART SENATE OFFICE BUILDING WASHINGTON DC 20510 (202) 224-3224
Web Form: lautenberg.senate.gov/contact/

Menendez, Robert - (D - NJ) Class I - 317 HART SENATE OFFICE BUILDING WASHINGTON DC 20510 (202) 224-4744
Web Form: menendez.senate.gov/contact/contact.cfm

Bingaman, Jeff - (D - NM) Class I - 703 HART SENATE OFFICE BUILDING WASHINGTON DC 20510 (202) 224-5521
E-mail: senator_bingaman@bingaman.senate.gov

Udall, Tom - (D - NM) Class II - 110 HART SENATE OFFICE BUILDING WASHINGTON DC 20510 (202) 224-6621
Web Form: tomudall.senate.gov/contact/contact.cfm

Ensign, John - (R - NV) Class I - 119 RUSSELL SENATE OFFICE BUILDING WASHINGTON DC 20510 (202) 224-6244
Web Form: ensign.senate.gov/forms/email_form.cfm

Reid, Harry - (D - NV) Class III - 528 HART SENATE OFFICE BUILDING WASHINGTON DC 20510 (202) 224-3542
Web Form: reid.senate.gov/contact/index.cfm

Gillibrand Kristen E. - (D - NY) Class I - 531 DIRKSEN SENATE OFFICE BUILDING WASHINGTON DC 20510 (202) 224-4451
Web Form: kristengillibrand@gillibrand..senate.gov

Schumer, Charles E. - (D - NY) Class III - 313 HART SENATE OFFICE BUILDING WASHINGTON DC 20510 (202) 224-6542
Web Form: schumer.senate.gov/SchumerWebsite/contact/webform.cfm

Brown, Sherrod - (D - OH) Class I - 455 RUSSELL SENATE OFFICE BUILDING WASHINGTON DC 20510 (202) 224-2315
Web Form: brown.senate.gov/contact/

Voinovich, George V. - (R - OH) Class III - 524 HART SENATE OFFICE BUILDING WASHINGTON DC 20510 (202) 224-3353
Web Form: voinovich.senate.gov/public/index.cfm?FuseAction=Contact....

Coburn, Tom - (R - OK) Class III - 172 RUSSELL SENATE OFFICE BUILDING WASHINGTON DC 20510 (202) 224-5754
Web Form: coburn.senate.gov/public/index.cfm?FuseAction=ContactSena...

Inhofe, James M. - (R - OK) Class II - 453 RUSSELL SENATE OFFICE BUILDING WASHINGTON DC 20510 (202) 224-4721
Web Form: inhofe.senate.gov/contactus.htm

Merkley, Jeff - (D - OR) Class II - B40B DIRKSEN SENATE OFFICE BUILDING WASHINGTON DC 20510 (202) 224-3753
Web Form: merkley.senate.gov/contact/contact.cfm

Wyden, Ron - (D - OR) Class III - 230 DIRKSEN SENATE OFFICE BUILDING WASHINGTON DC 20510 (202) 224-5244
Web Form: wyden.senate.gov/contact/

Casey, Robert P., Jr. - (D - PA) Class I - 383 RUSSELL SENATE OFFICE BUILDING WASHINGTON DC 20510 (202) 224-6324
Web Form: casey.senate.gov/contact/

Specter, Arlen - (D - PA) Class III - 711 HART SENATE OFFICE BUILDING WASHINGTON DC 20510 (202) 224-4254
Web Form: specter.senate.gov/public/index.cfm?FuseAction=Contact.Co...

Reed, Jack - (D - RI) Class II - 728 HART SENATE OFFICE BUILDING WASHINGTON DC 20510 (202) 224-4642
Web Form: reed.senate.gov/contact/contact-share.cfm

Whitehouse, Sheldon - (D - RI) Class I - 502 HART SENATE OFFICE BUILDING WASHINGTON DC 20510 (202) 224-2921
Web Form: whitehouse.senate.gov/contact.cfm

DeMint, Jim - (R - SC) Class III - 340 RUSSELL SENATE OFFICE BUILDING WASHINGTON DC 20510 (202) 224-6121
Web Form: demint.senate.gov/public/index.cfm?FuseAction=Contact.Home

Graham, Lindsey - (R - SC) Class II - 290 RUSSELL SENATE OFFICE BUILDING WASHINGTON DC 20510 (202) 224-5972
Web Form: lgraham.senate.gov/index.cfm?mode=contact

Johnson, Tim - (D - SD) Class II - 136 HART SENATE OFFICE BUILDING WASHINGTON DC 20510 (202) 224-5842
Web Form: johnson.senate.gov/contact/

Thune, John - (R - SD) Class III - 493 RUSSELL SENATE OFFICE BUILDING WASHINGTON DC 20510 (202) 224-2321
Web Form: thune.senate.gov/public/index.cfm?FuseAction=Contact.Email

Alexander, Lamar - (R - TN) Class II - 455 DIRKSEN SENATE OFFICE BUILDING WASHINGTON DC 20510 (202) 224-4944
Web Form: alexander.senate.gov/public/index.cfm?FuseAction=Contact....

Corker, Bob - (R - TN) Class I - 185 DIRKSEN SENATE OFFICE BUILDING WASHINGTON DC 20510 (202) 224-3344
Web Form: corker.senate.gov/Contact/index.cfm

Cornyn, John - (R - TX) Class II - 517 HART SENATE OFFICE BUILDING WASHINGTON DC 20510 (202) 224-2934
Web Form: cornyn.senate.gov/public/index.cfm?FuseAction=Contact.Con...

Hutchison, Kay Bailey - (R - TX) Class I - 284 RUSSELL SENATE OFFICE BUILDING WASHINGTON DC 20510 (202) 224-5922
Web Form: hutchison.senate.gov/contact.html

Bennett, Robert F. - (R - UT) Class III - 431 DIRKSEN SENATE OFFICE BUILDING WASHINGTON DC 20510 (202) 224-5444
Web Form: bennett.senate.gov/contact/emailmain.html

Hatch, Orrin G. - (R - UT) Class I - 104 HART SENATE OFFICE BUILDING WASHINGTON DC 20510 (202) 224-5251
Web Form: hatch.senate.gov/public/index.cfm?FuseAction=Offices.Cont...

Warner, Mark R. - (D - VA) Class II - 459A RUSSELL SENATE OFFICE BUILDING WASHINGTON DC 20510 (202) 224-2023
Web Form: warner.senate.gov/public/index.cfm?p=contact

Webb, Jim - (D - VA) Class I - 144 RUSSELL SENATE OFFICE BUILDING WASHINGTON DC 20510 (202) 224-4024
Web Form: webb.senate.gov/contact/

Leahy, Patrick J. - (D - VT) Class III - 433 RUSSELL SENATE OFFICE BUILDING WASHINGTON DC 20510 (202) 224-4242
E-mail: senator_leahy@leahy.senate.gov

Sanders, Bernard - (I - VT) Class I - 332 DIRKSEN SENATE OFFICE BUILDING WASHINGTON DC 20510 (202) 224-5141
Web Form: sanders.senate.gov/comments/

Cantwell, Maria - (D - WA) Class I - 511 DIRKSEN SENATE OFFICE BUILDING WASHINGTON DC 20510 (202) 224-3441
Web Form: cantwell.senate.gov/contact/index.html

Murray, Patty - (D - WA) Class III - 173 RUSSELL SENATE OFFICE BUILDING WASHINGTON DC 20510 (202) 224-2621
Web Form: murray.senate.gov/email/index.cfm

Feingold, Russell D. - (D - WI) Class III - 506 HART SENATE OFFICE BUILDING WASHINGTON DC 20510 (202) 224-5323
Web Form: feingold.senate.gov/contact_opinion.html

Kohl, Herb- (D - WI) Class I - 330 HART SENATE OFFICE BUILDING WASHINGTON DC 20510 (202) 224-5653
Web Form: kohl.senate.gov/gen_contact.html

Byrd, Robert C. - (D - WV) Class I - 311 HART SENATE OFFICE BUILDING WASHINGTON DC 20510 (202) 224-3954
Web Form: byrd.senate.gov/byrd_email.html

Rockefeller, John D., IV - (D - WV) Class II - 531 HART SENATE OFFICE BUILDING WASHINGTON DC 20510 (202) 224-6472
Web Form: rockefeller.senate.gov/services/email.cfm

Barrasso, John - (R - WY) Class I - 307 DIRKSEN SENATE OFFICE BUILDING WASHINGTON DC 20510 (202) 224-6441
Web Form: barrasso.senate.gov/public/index.cfm?FuseAction=ContactUs...

Enzi, Michael B. - (R - WY) Class II - 379A RUSSELL SENATE OFFICE BUILDING WASHINGTON DC 20510 (202) 224-3424
Web Form: enzi.senate.gov/public/index.cfm?FuseAction=ContactInform...

The United States House of Representatives

Alabama - 7 Representatives

Bonner, Jo (R - 01) - 202-225-4931
http://bonner.house.gov/HoR/AL01/Contact+Jo/Email+Jo/
Bright, Sr., Bobby N. (D - 02) - 202-225-2901
https://forms.house.gov/bright/contact-form.shtml
Rogers, Mike (R - 03) - 202-225-3261
http://www.house.gov/mike-rogers/contact/index.shtml
Aderholt, Robert B. (R - 04) - 202-225-4876
http://aderholt.house.gov/?sectionid=195§iontree=195
Griffith, Parker (D - 05) - 202-225-4801
https://forms.house.gov/griffith/contact-form.shtml
Bachus, Spencer (R - 06) - 202-225-4921
http://www.house.gov/writerep/
Davis, Artur (D - 07) - 202-225-2665
http://www.house.gov/arturdavis/zipauth.shtml

Alaska - 1 Representative

Young, Don (R - At Large) - 202-225-5765
http://donyoung.house.gov/IMA/issue_subscribe.htm

American Samoa - 1 Delegate

Faleomavaega, Eni F. H. (D - At Large) - 202-225-8577
faleomavaega@mail.house.gov

Arizona - 8 Representatives

Kirkpatrick, Ann (D - 01) - 202-225-2315
https://forms.house.gov/kirkpatrick/contact-form.shtml
Franks, Trent (R - 02) - 202-225-4576
http://www.house.gov/franks/IMA/email.shtml
Shadegg, John B. (R - 03) - 202-225-3361
http://www.house.gov/formshadegg/emailtemplate.htm
Pastor, Ed (D - 04) - 202-225-4065
http://www.house.gov/writerep/
Mitchell, Harry E. (D - 05) - 202-225-2190
http://mitchell.house.gov/contact/
Flake, Jeff (R - 06) - 202-225-2635
http://www.house.gov/writerep/
Grijalva, Raul (D - 07) - 202-225-2435
http://grijalva.house.gov/?sectionid=49§iontree=249
Giffords, Gabrielle (D - 08) - 202-225-2542
http://giffords.house.gov/contact/email/

Arkansas - 4 Representatives

Berry, Marion (D - 01) - 202-225-4076
http://www.house.gov/berry/zipauth.shtml
Snyder, Vic (D - 02) - 202-225-2506
http://www.house.gov/snyder/contact/email.htm
Boozman, John (R - 03) - 202-225-4301
http://www.house.gov/writerep/
Ross, Michael A. (D - 04) - 202-225-3772
http://ross.house.gov/?sectionid=77§iontree=7677

California - 53 Representatives

Thompson, Mike (D - 01) - 202-225-3311
http://mikethompson.house.gov/contact/email.shtml

Herger, Wally (R - 02) - 202-225-3076
http://www.house.gov/herger/contact.shtml
Lungren, Daniel E. (R - 03) - 202-225-5716
http://lungren.house.gov/index.php?option=com_content&
task=view&id=146&
McClintock, Tom (R - 04) - 202-225-2511
http://doolittle.house.gov/email/
Matsui, Doris O. (D - 05) - 202-225-7163
http://matsui.house.gov/email.asp
Woolsey, Lynn C. (D - 06) - 202-225-5161
http://woolsey.house.gov/contactemailform.asp
Miller, George (D - 07) - 202-225-2095
http://georgemiller.house.gov/contactus/
Pelosi, Nancy (D - 08) - 202-225-4965
sf.nancy@mail.house.gov
Lee, Barbara (D - 09) - 202-225-2661
http://www.house.gov/writerep/
Vacant (- 10) - 202-225-1880
(Email information unavailable during vacancy)
McNerney, Jerry (D - 11) - 202-225-1947
http://mcnerney.house.gov/contact.shtml
Speier, Jackie (D - 12) - 202-225-3531
https://forms.house.gov/speier/contact-form.shtml
Stark, Fortney "Pete" (D - 13) - 202-225-5065
http://www.house.gov/stark/contact/index.htm
Eshoo, Anna G. (D - 14) - 202-225-8104
http://eshoo.house.gov/index.php?option=com_
content&task=view&id=68&Itemid=96
Honda, Mike (D - 15) - 202-225-2631
http://www.honda.house.gov/contactmike.shtml
Lofgren, Zoe (D - 16) - 202-225-3072
http://lofgren.house.gov/emailform.shtml
Farr, Sam (D - 17) - 202-225-2861
http://www.farr.house.gov/index.php?
option=com_content&task=view&id=202

Cardoza, Dennis (D - 18) - 202-225-6131
http://www.house.gov/writerep/
Radanovich, George P. (R - 19) - 202-225-4540
http://www.house.gov/radanovich/IMA/issue.htm
Costa, Jim (D - 20) - 202-225-3341
http://www.house.gov/formcosta/issue.htm
Nunes, Devin (R - 21) - 202-225-2523
http://www.nunes.house.gov/index.cfm?FuseAction=
ContactUs.ContactForm
McCarthy, Kevin (R - 22) - 202-225-2915
http://kevinmccarthy.house.gov/showpage.asp?ID=69
Capps, Lois (D - 23) - 202-225-3601
http://www.house.gov/capps/contact/send_an_email.shtml
Gallegly, Elton (R - 24) - 202-225-5811
http://www.house.gov/writerep/
McKeon, Howard P. "Buck" (R - 25) - 202-225-1956
http://mckeon.house.gov/contact.html
Dreier, David (R - 26) - 202-225-2305
http://dreier.house.gov/talkto.htm
Sherman, Brad (D - 27) - 202-225-5911
http://www.house.gov/sherman/contact/
Berman, Howard L. (D - 28) - 202-225-4695
http://www.house.gov/berman/contact/
Schiff, Adam (D - 29) - 202-225-4176
http://schiff.house.gov/HoR/CA29/Contact+Information/
Contact+Form.htm
Waxman, Henry A. (D - 30) - 202-225-3976
http://www.house.gov/waxman/contact.htm
Becerra, Xavier (D - 31) - 202-225-6235
http://becerra.house.gov/HoR/CA31/Hidden+Content/
Email+Signup+Form.htm
Chu, Judy (D - 32) - 202-225-5464
https://forms.house.gov/chu/contact-form.shtml
Watson, Diane E. (D - 33) - 202-225-7084
http://www.house.gov/watson/zipauth.shtml

Roybal-Allard, Lucille (D - 34) - 202-225-1766
http://www.house.gov/writerep/
Waters, Maxine (D - 35) - 202-225-2201
http://www.house.gov/waters/IMA/issue.htm
Harman, Jane (D - 36) - 202-225-8220
http://www.house.gov/harman/contact/email.shtml
Richardson, Laura (D - 37) - 202-225-7924
http://richardson.house.gov/IMA/issue_subscribe.htm
Napolitano, Grace (D - 38) - 202-225-5256
http://www.napolitano.house.gov/contact/feedback.htm
Sanchez, Linda T. (D - 39) - 202-225-6676
http://www.house.gov/writerep/
Royce, Edward R. (R - 40) - 202-225-4111
http://www.house.gov/writerep/
Lewis, Jerry (R - 41) - 202-225-5861
http://www.house.gov/jerrylewis/WritetoRepresentativeLewis.htm
Miller, Gary (R - 42) - 202-225-3201
http://garymiller.house.gov/Contact/
Baca, Joe (D - 43) - 202-225-6161
http://www.house.gov/writerep/
Calvert, Ken (R - 44) - 202-225-1986
http://www.house.gov/writerep/
Bono Mack, Mary (R - 45) - 202-225-5330
http://www.house.gov/formbono/issue.htm
Rohrabacher, Dana (R - 46) - 202-225-2415
http://www.house.gov/writerep/
Sanchez, Loretta (D - 47) - 202-225-2965
http://www.lorettasanchez.house.gov/forms/contact.html
Campbell, John (R - 48) - 202-225-5611
http://campbell.house.gov/Contact/
Issa, Darrell (R - 49) - 202-225-3906
http://issa.house.gov/index.cfm?FuseAction=Contact
Information.EmailDarrell
Bilbray, Brian P. (R - 50) - 202-225-0508
http://www.house.gov/bilbray/contact.shtml

Filner, Bob (D - 51) - 202-225-8045
http://www.house.gov/writerep/
Hunter, Duncan D. (R - 52) - 202-225-5672
https://forms.house.gov/hunter/contact-form.shtml
Davis, Susan A. (D - 53) - 202-225-2040
http://www.house.gov/susandavis/contact.shtml

Colorado - 7 Representatives

DeGette, Diana (D - 01) - 202-225-4431
http://www.house.gov/formdegette/zip_auth.htm
Polis, Jared (D - 02) - 202-225-2161
https://forms.house.gov/polis/contact-form.shtml
Salazar, John T. (D - 03) - 202-225-4761
http://www.house.gov/salazar/contact.shtml
Markey, Betsy (D - 04) - 202-225-4676
https://forms.house.gov/markey/contact-form.shtml
Lamborn, Doug (R - 05) - 202-225-4422
http://lamborn.house.gov/Contact/write.htm
Coffman, Mike (R - 06) - 202-225-7882
https://forms.house.gov/coffman/contact-form.shtml
Perlmutter, Ed (D - 07) - 202-225-2645
http://perlmutter.house.gov/IMA/issue_subscribe.htm

Connecticut - 5 Representatives

Larson, John B. (D - 01) - 202-225-2265
http://www.house.gov/writerep/
Courtney, Joe (D - 02) - 202-225-2076
http://www.house.gov/writerep/
DeLauro, Rosa L. (D - 03) - 202-225-3661
http://www.house.gov/delauro/IMA/issue.htm
Himes, James A. "Jim" (D - 04) - 202-225-5541
https://forms.house.gov/himes/contact-form.shtml

Murphy, Christopher S.(D - 05) - 202-225-4476
http://www.house.gov/formchrismurphy/ic_zip_auth.htm

Delaware - 1 Representative

Castle, Michael N. (R - At Large) - 202-225-4165
http://www.house.gov/formcastle/IMA/zipauth.html

District of Columbia - 1 Delegate

Norton, Eleanor Holmes (D - At Large) - 202-225-8050
http://www.norton.house.gov/forms/contact.html

Florida - 25 Representatives

Miller, Jeff (R - 01) - 202-225-4136
http://jeffmiller.house.gov/index.cfm?FuseAction=
Contact.Home
Boyd, Allen (D - 02) - 202-225-5235
http://www.house.gov/boyd/zip_authen.html
Brown, Corrine (D - 03) - 202-225-0123
http://www.house.gov/corrinebrown/IMA/issue.shtml
Crenshaw, Ander (R - 04) - 202-225-2501
http://www.house.gov/writerep/
Brown-Waite, Virginia (R - 05) - 202-225-1002
http://www.house.gov/formbrown-waite/IMA/issue_subscribe.htm
Stearns, Cliff (R - 06) - 202-225-5744
http://www.house.gov/writerep/
Mica, John L. (R - 07) - 202-225-4035
http://www.house.gov/mica/messageform.shtml
Grayson, Alan (D - 08) - 202-225-2176
https://forms.house.gov/grayson/contact-form.shtml
Bilirakis, Gus M. (R - 09) - 202-225-5755
http://www.house.gov/formbilirakis/issue_subscribe.htm

Young, C. W. (Bill) (R - 10) - 202-225-5961
Bill.Young@mail.house.gov
Castor, Kathy A. (D - 11) - 202-225-3376
http://www.house.gov/writerep/
Putnam, Adam (R - 12) - 202-225-1252
http://adamputnam.house.gov/contact.shtml
Buchanan, Vernon G. (R - 13) - 202-225-5015
http://buchanan.house.gov/contact.shtml
Mack, Connie (R - 14) - 202-225-2536
http://mack.house.gov/index.cfm?FuseAction=
ContactConnie.ContactForm
Posey, Bill (R - 15) - 202-225-3671
https://forms.house.gov/posey/contact-form.shtml
Rooney, Thomas J. (R - 16) - 202-225-5792
https://forms.house.gov/rooney/contact-form.shtml
Meek, Kendrick B. (D - 17) - 202-225-4506
http://kendrickmeek.house.gov/contact1.shtml
Ros-Lehtinen, Ileana (R - 18) - 202-225-3931
http://www.house.gov/writerep/
Wexler, Robert (D - 19) - 202-225-3001
http://www.wexler.house.gov/email.shtml
Wasserman Schultz, Debbie (D - 20) - 202-225-7931
http://wassermanschultz.house.gov/zipauth.htm
Diaz-Balart, Lincoln (R - 21) - 202-225-4211
http://diaz-balart.house.gov/index.cfm?FuseAction=
Offices.Contact
Klein, Ron J. (D - 22) - 202-225-3026
http://klein.house.gov/content/contact/
Hastings, Alcee L. (D - 23) - 202-225-1313
http://www.alceehastings.house.gov/index.php?option=
com_content&task=view&id=104&Itemid=
Kosmas, Suzanne M. (D - 24) - 202-225-2706
https://forms.house.gov/kosmas/contact-form.shtml
Diaz-Balart, Mario (R - 25) - 202-225-2778
http://www.house.gov/formmariodiaz-balart/ic_zip_auth.htm

Georgia - 13 Representatives

Kingston, Jack (R - 01) - 202-225-5831
http://kingston.house.gov/ContactForm/zipauth.htm
Bishop, Sanford D. Jr. (D - 02) - 202-225-3631
http://bishop.house.gov/display.cfm?content_id=229
Westmoreland, Lynn A. (R - 03) - 202-225-5901
http://www.house.gov/writerep/
Johnson, Jr., Henry C. "Hank" (D - 04) - 202-225-1605
http://hankjohnson.house.gov/contact.shtml
Lewis, John (D - 05) - 202-225-3801
http://www.house.gov/formjohnlewis/contact.html
Price, Tom (R - 06) - 202-225-4501
http://tomprice.house.gov/html/contact_form_email.cfm
Linder, John (R - 07) - 202-225-4272
http://linder.house.gov/index.cfm?FuseAction=
ContactJohn.ContactForm
Marshall, Jim (D - 08) - 202-225-6531
http://www.house.gov/writerep/
Deal, Nathan (R - 09) - 202-225-5211
http://www.house.gov/deal/contact.shtml
Broun, Paul C. (R - 10) - 202-225-4101
http://broun.house.gov/email.shtml
Gingrey, Phil (R - 11) - 202-225-2931
http://www.house.gov/formgingrey/IMA/issue.htm
Barrow, John (D - 12) - 202-225-2823
http://barrow.house.gov/contactemail.asp
Scott, David (D - 13) - 202-225-2939
http://www.house.gov/writerep/

Guam - 1 Delegate

Bordallo, Madeleine Z. (D - At Large) - 202-225-1188
http://www.house.gov/bordallo/IMA/issue.htm

Hawaii - 2 Representatives

Abercrombie, Neil (D - 01) - 202-225-2726
neil.abercrombie@mail.house.gov
Hirono, Mazie K. (D - 02) - 202-225-4906
http://hirono.house.gov/IMA/issue_subscribe.htm

Idaho - 2 Representatives

Minnick, Walt (D - 01) - 202-225-6611
https://forms.house.gov/minnick/contact-form.shtml
Simpson, Michael K. (R - 02) - 202-225-5531
http://www.house.gov/simpson/emailme.shtml

Illinois - 19 Representatives

Rush, Bobby L. (D - 01) - 202-225-4372
http://www.house.gov/rush/zipauth.shtml
Jackson, Jr., Jesse L. (D - 02) - 202-225-0773
http://www.jessejacksonjr.org/contact.htm
Lipinski, Daniel (D - 03) - 202-225-5701
http://www.house.gov/formlipinski/zipauth.html
Gutierrez, Luis V. (D - 04) - 202-225-8203
http://luisgutierrez.house.gov/singlepage.aspx?newsid=1262
Quigley, Mike (D- 05) - 202-225-4061
https://forms.house.gov/quigley/contact-form.shtml
Roskam, Peter J. (R - 06) - 202-225-4561
http://www.house.gov/writerep/
Davis, Danny K. (D - 07) - 202-225-5006
http://www.house.gov/davis/zipauth.htm
Bean, Melissa L. (D - 08) - 202-225-3711
http://www.house.gov/bean/issue_subscribe.htm
Schakowsky, Janice D. (D - 09) - 202-225-2111
http://www.house.gov/schakowsky/email.shtml

Kirk, Mark S. (R - 10) - 202-225-4835
http://www.house.gov/kirk/zipauth.shtml
Halvorson, Deborah L. "Debbie" (D - 11) - 202-225-3635
https://forms.house.gov/halvorson/contact-form.shtml
Costello, Jerry F. (D - 12) - 202-225-5661
http://www.house.gov/costello/IMA/issue_subscribe.htm
Biggert, Judy (R - 13) - 202-225-3515
http://judybiggert.house.gov/ContactJudy.aspx
Foster, Bill (D - 14) - 202-225-2976
http://foster.house.gov/Contact/
Johnson, Timothy V. (R - 15) - 202-225-2371
http://www.house.gov/writerep/
Manzullo, Donald A. (R - 16) - 202-225-5676
http://manzullo.house.gov/zipauth.aspx
Hare, Phil (D - 17) - 202-225-5905
http://hare.house.gov/Contact/zipauth.htm
Schock, Aaron (R - 18) - 202-225-6201
https://forms.house.gov/schock/contact-form.shtml
Shimkus, John (R - 19) - 202-225-5271
http://www.house.gov/shimkus/emailme.shtml

Indiana - 9 Representatives

Visclosky, Peter J. (D - 01) - 202-225-2461
http://www.house.gov/writerep/
Donnelly, Joe (D - 02) - 202-225-3915
http://donnelly.house.gov/issue_subscribe.shtml
Souder, Mark E. (R - 03) - 202-225-4436
http://souder.house.gov/index.cfm?FuseAction=
Contact.ContactForm
Buyer, Stephen E. (R - 04) - 202-225-5037
http://www.house.gov/writerep/
Burton, Dan (R - 05) - 202-225-2276
http://www.house.gov/burton/zipauth.htm

Pence, Mike (R - 06) - 202-225-3021
https://forms.house.gov/pence/IMA/contact_form.htm
Carson, André (D - 07) - 202-225-4011
http://carson.house.gov/contact.me.shtml
Ellsworth, Brad (D - 08) - 202-225-4636
http://www.ellsworth.house.gov/index.php?
option=com_content&task=view&id=126&Itemid=
Hill, Baron P. (D - 09) - 202-225-5315
http://baronhill.house.gov/IMA/issue_subscribe.shtml

Iowa - 5 Representatives

Braley, Bruce L. (D - 01) - 202-225-2911
http://braley.house.gov/contactform/
Loebsack, Dave (D - 02) - 202-225-6576
http://loebsack.house.gov/contactform/
Boswell, Leonard L. (D - 03) - 202-225-3806
http://boswell.house.gov/article.asp?id=279
Latham, Tom (R - 04) - 202-225-5476
tom.latham@mail.house.gov
King, Steve (R - 05) - 202-225-4426
http://www.house.gov/steveking/email.shtm

Kansas - 4 Representatives

Moran, Jerry (R - 01) - 202-225-2715
http://www.jerrymoran.house.gov/index.php?
option=com_content&task=view&id=117&Itemid=128
Jenkins, Lynn (R - 02) - 202-225-6601
https://forms.house.gov/jenkins/contact-form.shtml
Moore, Dennis (D - 03) - 202-225-2865
http://www.moore.house.gov/contact/index.shtml
Tiahrt, Todd (R - 04) - 202-225-6216
http://www.house.gov/tiahrt/IMA/issue_subscribe.htm

Kentucky - 6 Representatives

Whitfield, Edward (R - 01) - 202-225-3115
http://whitfield.house.gov/contact/index.shtml
Guthrie, S. Brett (R - 02) - 202-225-3501
https://forms.house.gov/guthrie/contact-form.shtml
Yarmuth, John A. (D - 03) - 202-225-5401
http://yarmuth.house.gov/?sectionid=
68§iontree=62968
Davis, Geoff (R - 04) - 202-225-3465
http://geoffdavis.house.gov/Contact.aspx
Rogers, Harold (R - 05) - 202-225-4601
http://halrogers.house.gov/Contact.aspx
Chandler, Ben (D - 06) - 202-225-4706
http://www.house.gov/writerep/

Louisiana - 7 Representatives

Scalise, Steve (R - 01) - 202-225-3015
https://forms.house.gov/scalise/contact-form.shtml
Cao, Anh "Joseph" (D - 02) - 202-225-6636
http://www.house.gov/writerep/
Melancon, Charlie (D - 03) - 202-225-4031
http://www.melancon.house.gov/index.php?
option=com_content&task=view&id=205
Fleming, John (R - 04) - 202-225-2777
https://forms.house.gov/fleming/contact-form.shtml
Alexander, Rodney (R - 05) - 202-225-8490
http://www.house.gov/writerep/
Cassidy, William "Bill" (R - 06) - 202-225-3901
https://forms.house.gov/cassidy/contact-form.shtml
Boustany, Jr., Charles W. (R - 07) - 202-225-
http://boustany.house.gov/ContactCharles.asp

Maine - 2 Representatives

Pingree, Chellie (D - 01) - 202-225-6116
https://forms.house.gov/pingree/contact-form.shtml
Michaud, Michael H. (D - 02) - 202-225-6306
http://www.michaud.house.gov/article.asp?id=389

Maryland - 8 Representatives

Kratovil, Jr., Frank M. (D - 01) - 202-225-5311
https://forms.house.gov/kratovil/contact-form.shtml
Ruppersberger, C. A. "Dutch" (D - 02) - 202-225-3061
http://dutch.house.gov/writedutch_za.shtml
Sarbanes, John P. (D - 03) - 202-225-4016
http://sarbanes.house.gov/issue_subscribe.html
Edwards, Donna F. (D - 04) - 202-225-8699
https://forms.house.gov/edwards/contact-form.shtml
Hoyer, Steny H. (D - 05) - 202-225-4131
http://hoyer.house.gov/contact/email.asp
Bartlett, Roscoe G. (R - 06) - 202-225-2721
http://bartlett.house.gov/Email_Roscoe/
Cummings, Elijah E. (D - 07) - 202-225-4741
http://www.house.gov/writerep/
Van Hollen, Jr., Christopher (D - 08) - 202-225-5341
http://vanhollen.house.gov/HoR/MD08/
Contact+Information/Web+Contact/Contact+Form.htm

Massachusetts - 10 Representatives

Olver, John W. (D - 01) - 202-225-5335
http://www.house.gov/olver/contact/index.html
Neal, Richard E. (D - 02) - 202-225-5601
http://www.house.gov/writerep/

McGovern, James P. (D - 03) - 202-225-6101
http://www.house.gov/writerep/
Frank, Barney (D - 04) - 202-225-5931
http://www.house.gov/writerep/
Tsongas, Niki (D - 05) - 202-225-3411
http://tsongas.house.gov/IMA/issue_subscribe.htm
Tierney, John F. (D - 06) - 202-225-8020
http://www.house.gov/tierney/IMA/email.shtml
Markey, Edward J. (D - 07) - 202-225-2836
http://markey.house.gov/index.php?option=
com_email_form&Itemid=124
Capuano, Michael E. (D - 08) - 202-225-5111
http://www.house.gov/capuano/contact/email.shtml
Lynch, Stephen F. (D - 09) - 202-225-8273
http://www.house.gov/writerep/
Delahunt, William D. "Bill" (D - 10) - 202-225-3111
william.delahunt@mail.house.gov

Michigan - 15 Representatives

Stupak, Bart (D - 01) - 202-225-4735
http://www.house.gov/stupak/IMA/issue2.htm
Hoekstra, Peter (R - 02) - 202-225-4401
http://www.house.gov/formhoekstra/IMA/email.htm
Ehlers, Vernon J. (R - 03) - 202-225-3831
http://www.house.gov/writerep/
Camp, Dave (R - 04) - 202-225-3561
http://camp.house.gov/WriteRep.aspx
Kildee, Dale E. (D - 05) - 202-225-3611
http://www.house.gov/writerep/
Upton, Fred (R - 06) - 202-225-3761
http://www.house.gov/writerep/
Schauer, Mark H. (D - 07) - 202-225-6276
https://forms.house.gov/schauer/contact-form.shtml

Rogers, Mike (R - 08) - 202-225-4872
http://www.mikerogers.house.gov/Contact.aspx
Peters, Gray C. (D - 09) - 202-225-5802
https://forms.house.gov/peters/contact-form.shtml
Miller, Candice S. (R - 10) - 202-225-2106
http://candicemiller.house.gov/Contact.aspx
McCotter, Thaddeus G. (R - 11) - 202-225-8171
http://mccotter.house.gov/HoR/MI11/Contact/Office+
Contact +Information/Zipcode+Authentication+Page.htm
Levin, Sander M. (D - 12) - 202-225-4961
http://www.house.gov/levin/levin_contact.shtml
Kilpatrick, Carolyn C. (D - 13) - 202-225-2261
http://www.house.gov/writerep/
Conyers, Jr., John (D - 14) - 202-225-5126
http://www.house.gov/writerep/
Dingell, John D. (D - 15) - 202-225-4071
http://www.house.gov/writerep/

Minnesota - 8 Representatives

Walz, Timothy J. (D - 01) - 202-225-2472
http://walz.house.gov/ContactForm/ZipAuth.htm
Kline, John (R - 02) - 202-225-2271
http://kline.house.gov/index.cfm?FuseAction=Contact
Information.ContactForm&To=mn02hwyr@housemail.
house.gov&CFID=19823850&CFTOKEN=41563932
Paulsen, Erik (R - 03) - 202-225-2871
https://forms.house.gov/paulsen/contact-form.shtml
McCollum, Betty (D - 04) - 202-225-6631
http://mccollum.house.gov/custom/mccollum-contactme.asp
Ellison, Keith (D - 05) - 202-225-4755
http://www.house.gov/writerep/
Bachmann, Michele (R - 06) - 202-225-2331
http://bachmann.house.gov/Email/

Peterson, Collin C. (D - 07) - 202-225-2165
http://collinpeterson.house.gov/email.html
Oberstar, James L. (D - 08) - 202-225-6211
http://wwwc.house.gov/oberstar/zipauth.htm

Mississippi - 4 Representatives

Childers, Travis W. (D - 01) - 202-225-4306
https://forms.house.gov/childers/contact-form.shtml
Thompson, Bennie G. (D - 02) - 202-225-5876
http://benniethompson.house.gov/HoR/MS02/
Contact+Bennie/Contact+Bennie.htm
Harper, Gregg (R - 03) - 202-225-5031
https://forms.house.gov/harper/contact-form.shtml
Taylor, Gene (D - 04) - 202-225-5772
http://www.house.gov/genetaylor/contactgene.htm

Missouri - 9 Representatives

Clay, Jr., William "Lacy" (D - 01) - 202-225-2406
http://lacyclay.house.gov/contact.htm
Akin, W. Todd (R - 02) - 202-225-2561
http://www.house.gov/akin/email.shtml
Carnahan, Russ (D - 03) - 202-225-2671
http://carnahan.house.gov/contact.shtml
Skelton, Ike (D - 04) - 202-225-2876
http://www.house.gov/skelton/zipauth.htm
Cleaver, II, Emanuel (D - 05) - 202-225-4535
http://www.house.gov/cleaver/IMA/issue.htm
Graves, Samuel B. (R - 06) - 202-225-7041
http://www.house.gov/graves/contact.shtml
Blunt, Roy (R - 07) - 202-225-6536
http://www.blunt.house.gov/Contact.aspx
Emerson, Jo Ann (R - 08) - 202-225-4404
http://www.house.gov/emerson/contact/

Luetkemeyer, Blaine (R - 09) - 202-225-2956
https://forms.house.gov/luetkemeyer/contact-form.shtml

Montana - 1 Representative

Rehberg, Dennis (R - At Large) - 202-225-3211
http://www.house.gov/writerep/

Nebraska - 3 Representatives

Fortenberry, Jeff (R - 01) - 202-225-4806
http://fortenberry.house.gov/contactform_zipcheck.shtml
Terry, Lee (R - 02) - 202-225-4155
http://www.house.gov/formleeterry/IMA/issue.htm
Smith, Adrian (R - 03) - 202-225-6435
http://www.house.gov/formadriansmith/issues_subscribe.htm

Nevada - 3 Representatives

Berkley, Shelley (D - 01) - 202-225-5965
http://berkley.house.gov/contact/email.html
Heller, Dean (R - 02) - 202-225-6155
http://www.house.gov/writerep/
Titus, Dina (D - 03) - 202-225-3252
https://forms.house.gov/titus/contact-form.shtml

New Hampshire - 2 Representatives

Shea-Porter, Carol (D - 01) - 202-225-5456
http://shea-porter.house.gov/?sectionid=84§iontree=84
Hodes, II, Paul W. (D - 02) - 202-225-5206
http://hodes.house.gov/contact.aspx

New Jersey - 13 Representatives

Andrews, Robert E. (D - 01) - 202-225-6501
http://www.house.gov/andrews/contact_form_za.shtml
LoBiondo, Frank A. (R - 02) - 202-225-6572
http://www.house.gov/lobiondo/IMA/issue.htm
Adler, John H. (D - 03) - 202-225-4765
https://forms.house.gov/adler/contact-form.shtml
Smith, Christopher H. (R - 04) - 202-225-3765
http://chrissmith.house.gov/zipauth.html
Garrett, E. Scott (R - 05) - 202-225-4465
http://www.house.gov/formgarrett/contact.shtml
Pallone, Jr., Frank (D - 06) - 202-225-4671
http://www.house.gov/pallone/contact.shtml
Lance, Leonard (R - 07) - 202-225-5361
https://forms.house.gov/lance/contact-form.shtml
Pascrell, Jr., Bill (D - 08) - 202-225-5751
http://www.pascrell.house.gov/feedback.cfm?
campaign=pascrell&type=Contact%20Bill
Rothman, Steven R. (D - 09) - 202-225-5061
http://rothman.house.gov/contact_steve.htm
Payne, Donald M. (D - 10) - 202-225-3436
http://www.house.gov/payne/IMA/email.shtml
Frelinghuysen, Rodney P. (R - 11) - 202-225-5034
http://frelinghuysen.house.gov/contactus/form.cfm
Holt, Rush D. (D - 12) - 202-225-5801
http://holt.house.gov/contact.shtml
Sires, Albio (D - 13) - 202-225-7919
http://www.house.gov/sires/IMA/issue_subscribe.shtml

New Mexico - 3 Representatives

Heinrich, Martin T. (D - 01) - 202-225-6316
https://forms.house.gov/heinrich/contact-form.shtml

Teague, Harry (R - 02) - 202-225-2365
http://pearce.house.gov/contact/issue_subscribe.htm
Luján, Ben R. (D - 03) - 202-225-6190
https://forms.house.gov/lujan/contact-form.shtml

New York - 29 **Representatives**

Bishop, Timothy H. (D - 01) - 202-225-3826
http://timbishop.house.gov/?sectionid=96§iontree=796
Israel, Steve J. (D - 02) - 202-225-3335
http://israel.house.gov/?sectionid=89§iontree=89
King, Peter T. (R - 03) - 202-225-7896
pete.king@mail.house.gov
McCarthy, Carolyn (D - 04) - 202-225-5516
http://www.house.gov/writerep/
Ackerman, Gary L. (D - 05) - 202-225-2601
http://www.house.gov/ackerman/pages/contact.html
Meeks, Gregory W. (D - 06) - 202-225-3461
congmeeks@mail.house.gov
Crowley, Joseph (D - 07) - 202-225-3965
http://crowley.house.gov/contact/index.asp
Nadler, Jerrold (D - 08) - 202-225-5635
http://www.house.gov/nadler/emailform.shtml
Weiner, Anthony D. (D - 09) - 202-225-6616
weiner@mail.house.gov
Towns, Edolphus (D - 10) - 202-225-5936
http://www.house.gov/towns/contact_form.shtml
Clarke, Yvette D. (D - 11) - 202-225-6231
http://clarke.house.gov/contactform_zipcheck.shtml
Velázquez, Nydia M. (D - 12) - 202-225-2361
http://www.house.gov/velazquez/IMA/issue_subscribe.htm
McMahon, Michael E. (D - 13) - 202-225-3371
https://forms.house.gov/mcmahon/contact-form.shtml

Maloney, Carolyn B. (D - 14) - 202-225-7944
http://maloney.house.gov/index.php?option=
com_email_form&Itemid=73
Rangel, Charles B. (D - 15) - 202-225-4365
http://www.house.gov/writerep/
Serrano, José E. (D - 16) - 202-225-4361
jserrano@mail.house.gov
Engel, Eliot L. (D - 17) - 202-225-2464
http://www.house.gov/writerep/
Lowey, Nita M. (D - 18) - 202-225-6506
http://lowey.house.gov/?sectionid=56§iontree=56
Hall, John J. (D - 19) - 202-225-5441
http://johnhall.house.gov/emailjohn.asp
Murphy, Scott (D - 20) - 202-225-5614
https://forms.house.gov/murphy/contact-form.shtml
Tonko, Paul D. (D - 21) - 202-225-5076
https://forms.house.gov/tonko/contact-form.shtml
Hinchey, Maurice D. (D - 22) - 202-225-6335
http://www.house.gov/hinchey/contact/zipauth.shtml
McHugh, John M. (R - 23) - 202-225-4611
http://mchugh.house.gov/zipauth.aspx
Arcuri, Michael A. (D - 24) - 202-225-3665
http://arcuri.house.gov/IMA/issue_subscribe.htm
Maffei, Daniel B. (D - 25) - 202-225-3701
https://forms.house.gov/maffei/contact-form.shtml
Lee, Christopher J. (R - 26) - 202-225-5265
https://forms.house.gov/lee/contact-form.shtml
Higgins, Brian M. (D - 27) - 202-225-3306
http://higgins.house.gov/email.asp
Slaughter, Louise McIntosh (D - 28) - 202-225-3615
http://www.louise.house.gov/index.php?
option=com_content&task=view&id=506&Itemid=153
Massa, Eric J. J. (D - 29) - 202-225-3161
https://forms.house.gov/massa/contact-form.shtml

North Carolina - 13 Representatives

Butterfield, Jr., G. K. (D - 01) - 202-225-3101
http://butterfield.house.gov/contactinfo.asp
Etheridge, Bobby (D - 02) - 202-225-4531
http://www.house.gov/etheridge/contactbob.htm
Jones, Jr., Walter B. (R - 03) - 202-225-3415
http://jones.house.gov/contact_form_email.cfm
Price, David E. (D - 04) - 202-225-1784
http://price.house.gov/contact/contact_form.shtml
Foxx, Virginia (R - 05) - 202-225-2071
http://www.house.gov/formfoxx/IMA/issue_subscribe.htm
Coble, Howard (R - 06) - 202-225-3065
howard.coble@mail.house.gov
McIntyre, Mike (D - 07) - 202-225-2731
http://www.house.gov/mcintyre/issue.shtml
Kissell, Larry (D - 08) - 202-225-3715
https://forms.house.gov/kissell/contact-form.shtml
Wilkins Myrick, Sue (R - 09) - 202-225-1976
http://myrick.house.gov/zipauth.shtml
McHenry, Patrick T. (R - 10) - 202-225-2576
http://mchenry.house.gov/zipauth.htm
Shuler, Heath (D - 11) - 202-225-6401
http://www.house.gov/writerep/
Watt, Melvin L. (D - 12) - 202-225-1510
http://watt.house.gov/IQform.asp
Miller, Brad (D - 13) - 202-225-3032
http://bradmiller.house.gov/?sectionid=17§iontree=917

North Dakota - 1 Representative

Pomeroy, Earl (D - At Large) - 202-225-2611
http://www.house.gov/formpomeroy/zipauth.htm

Northern Mariana Islands- 1 Representative

Sablan, Gregorio K. C. (D - At Large) 202-225-2646
https://forms.house.gov/sablan/contact-form.shtml

Ohio - 18 Representatives

Driehaus, Steve (D - 01) - 202-225-2216
https://forms.house.gov/driehaus/contact-form.shtml
Schmidt, Jean (R - 02) - 202-225-3164
http://www.house.gov/schmidt/contact.shtml
Turner, Michael R. (R - 03) - 202-225-6465
http://www.house.gov/miketurner/IMA/contact.shtml
Jordan, Jim (R - 04) - 202-225-2676
http://jordan.house.gov/IMA/issue_subscribe.htm
Latta, Robert E. (R - 05) - 202-225-6405
http://latta.house.gov/contactform_zipcheck.shtml
Wilson, Charles A. (D - 06) - 202-225-5705
http://www.charliewilson.house.gov/index.php?
option=com_content&task=view&id=139
Austria, Steve (R - 07) - 202-225-4324
https://forms.house.gov/austria/contact-form.shtml
Boehner, John A. (R - 08) - 202-225-6205
http://www.house.gov/writerep/
Kaptur, Marcy (D - 09) - 202-225-4146
http://www.kaptur.house.gov/index.php?
option=com_content&task=view&id=152
Kucinich, Dennis J. (D - 10) - 202-225-5871
http://www.house.gov/writerep/
Fudge, Marcia L. (D - 11) - 202-225-7032
https://forms.house.gov/fudge/contact-form.shtml
Tiberi, Patrick J. (R - 12) - 202-225-5355
http://www.house.gov/writerep/
Sutton, Betty (D - 13) - 202-225-3401
http://sutton.house.gov/about/emailform.cfm

LaTourette, Steven C. (R - 14) - 202-225-5731
http://latourette.house.gov/ContactSteve.aspx
Kilroy, Mary Jo (D - 15) - 202-225-2015
https://forms.house.gov/kilroy/contact-form.shtml
Boccieri, John A. (D - 16) - 202-225-3876
https://forms.house.govboccieri/contact-form.shtml
Ryan, Tim (D - 17) - 202-225-5261
http://timryan.house.gov/index.php?option=com_content&
task=view&id=129&Itemid=42
Space, Zachary T. (D - 18) - 202-225-6265
http://space.house.gov/?sectionid=61§iontree=2661

Oklahoma - 5 Representatives

Sullivan, John (R - 01) - 202-225-2211
http://sullivan.house.gov/contact/write.htm
Boren, Dan (D - 02) - 202-225-2701
http://www.house.gov/boren/emailsignup.shtml
Lucas, Frank D. (R - 03) - 202-225-5565
http://www.house.gov/lucas/zipauth.htm
Cole, Tom (R - 04) - 202-225-6165
http://www.cole.house.gov/contact-tom.html
Fallin, Mary (R - 05) - 202-225-2132
http://fallin.house.gov/send_email_zip_authentication.shtml

Oregon - 5 Representatives

Wu, David (D - 01) - 202-225-0855
http://www.house.gov/wu/email.shtml
Walden, Greg (R - 02) - 202-225-6730
http://walden.house.gov/index.cfm?FuseAction=
ContactGreg.Home
Blumenauer, Earl (D - 03) - 202-225-4811
http://blumenauer.house.gov/about/Contact.shtml

DeFazio, Peter A. (D - 04) - 202-225-6416
http://www.house.gov/formdefazio/contact.html
Schrader, Kurt (D - 05) - 202-225-5711
https://forms.house.gov/schrader/contact-form.shtml

Pennsylvania - 19 Representatives

Brady, Robert A. (D - 01) - 202-225-4731
http://www.house.gov/formrobertbrady/issue.htm
Fattah, Chaka (D - 02) - 202-225-4001
http://www.house.gov/writerep/
Dahlkemper, Kathleen A. (D - 03) - 202-225-5406
https://forms.house.gov/dahlkemper/contact-form.shtml
Altmire, Jason (D - 04) - 202-225-2565
http://altmire.house.gov/IMA/issue_subscribe.htm
Thompson, Glenn W. (R - 05) - 202-225-5121
https://forms.house.gov/glennthompson/contact-form.shtml
Gerlach, Jim (R - 06) - 202-225-4315
http://www.house.gov/writerep/
Sestak, Joe (D - 07) - 202-225-2011
http://sestak.house.gov/IMA/issue_subscribe.htm
Murphy, Patrick J. (D - 08) - 202-225-4276
http://www.patrickmurphy.house.gov/index.php?
option=com_content&task=view&id=55&Itemid=86
Shuster, Bill (R - 09) - 202-225-2431
http://www.house.gov/shuster/zipauth.htm
Carney, Christopher P. (D - 10) - 202-225-3731
http://carney.house.gov/contact.shtml
Kanjorski, Paul E. (D - 11) - 202-225-6511
http://kanjorski.house.gov/?option=com_content
&task=view&id=2&Itemid=
Murtha, John P. (D - 12) - 202-225-2065
https://forms.house.gov/murtha/IMA/issue_subscribe.htm

Schwartz, Allyson Y. (D - 13) - 202-225-6111
http://schwartz.house.gov/issue_subscribe.shtml
Doyle, Michael F. (D - 14) - 202-225-2135
http://www.house.gov/doyle/email_mike.shtml
Dent, Charles W. (R - 15) - 202-225-6411
http://dent.house.gov/contact.aspx
Pitts, Joseph R. (R - 16) - 202-225-2411
http://www.house.gov/pitts/contact.shtml
Holden, Tim (D - 17) - 202-225-5546
http://www.holden.house.gov/feedback.cfm?
campaign=Holden&type=Let's%20Talk
Murphy, Tim (R - 18) - 202-225-2301
http://www.house.gov/writerep/
Platts, Todd R. (R - 19) - 202-225-5836
http://www.house.gov/platts/email.shtml

Puerto Rico - 1 Delegate

Pierluisi, Pedro R. (D - At Large) - Resident Commissioner
202-225-2615
https://forms.house.gov/pierluisi/contact-form.shtml

Rhode Island - 2 Representatives

Kennedy, Patrick J. (D - 01) - 202-225-4911
http://www.house.gov/formpatrickkennedy/IMA/issue.htm
Langevin, James R. (D - 02) - 202-225-2735
http://langevin.house.gov/comments.shtml

South Carolina - 6 Representatives

Brown, Jr., Henry E. (R - 01) - 202-225-3176
http://brown.house.gov/writebrown/
Wilson, Joe (R - 02) - 202-225-2452
http://www.house.gov/formwilson/IMA/issue.htm

Barrett, J. Gresham (R - 03) - 202-225-5301
http://www.house.gov/formbarrett/writebarrett.htm
Inglis, Bob (R - 04) - 202-225-6030
http://inglis.house.gov/contact.asp?content=
sections/contact/write_inglis
Spratt, Jr., John M. (D - 05) - 202-225-5501
http://www.house.gov/spratt/email_john.shtml
Clyburn, James E. (D - 06) - 202-225-3315
http://clyburn.house.gov/zip_code_verify.cfm

South Dakota - 1 Representative

Herseth Sandlin, Stephanie (D - At Large) - 202-225-2801
stephanie.herseth@mail.house.gov

Tennessee - 9 Representatives

Roe, David Phil (R - 01) - 202-225-6356
https://forms.house.gov/roe/contact-form.shtml
Duncan, Jr., John J. (R - 02) - 202-225-5435
http://www.house.gov/duncan/contactform_zipcheck.shtml
Wamp, Zach (R - 03) - 202-225-3271
http://www.house.gov/wamp/contact_email.shtm
Davis, Lincoln (D - 04) - 202-225-6831
http://www.house.gov/writerep/
Cooper, Jim (D - 05) - 202-225-4311
http://www.cooper.house.gov/index.php?
option=com_content&task=view&id=117
Gordon, Bart (D - 06) - 202-225-4231
http://gordon.house.gov/contact/index.shtml
Blackburn, Marsha (R - 07) - 202-225-2811
http://www.house.gov/writerep/
Tanner, John S. (D - 08) - 202-225-4714
http://www.house.gov/writerep/

Cohen, Steve Ira (D - 09) - 202-225-3265
http://cohen.house.gov/index.php?option=
com_email_form&Itemid=111

Texas - **32 Representatives**

Gohmert, Louie (R - 01) - 202-225-3035
http://gohmert.house.gov/contact_louie.htm
Poe, Ted (R - 02) - 202-225-6565
http://poe.house.gov/email/
Johnson, Sam (R - 03) - 202-225-4201
http://www.house.gov/formsamjohnson/IMA/issue.htm
Hall, Ralph M. (R - 04) - 202-225-6673
http://www.house.gov/ralphhall/IMA/zipauth.htm
Hensarling, Jeb (R - 05) - 202-225-3484
http://www.house.gov/hensarling/contact_web.shtml
Barton, Joe (R - 06) - 202-225-2002
http://joebarton.house.gov/ContactJoe.aspx?Type=Contact
Culberson, John A. (R - 07) - 202-225-2571
http://www.culberson.house.gov/contactinfo.aspx
Brady, Kevin (R - 08) - 202-225-4901
rep.brady@mail.house.gov
Green, Al (D - 09) - 202-225-7508
http://www.house.gov/writerep/
McCaul, Michael T. (R - 10) - 202-225-2401
http://www.house.gov/writerep/
Conaway, K. Michael (R - 11) - 202-225-3605
http://conaway.house.gov/Contact/default.aspx#email
Granger, Kay (R - 12) - 202-225-5071
http://kaygranger.house.gov/?sectionid=46§iontree=46
Thornberry, Mac (R - 13) - 202-225-3706
http://www.house.gov/writerep/
Paul, Ron (R - 14) - 202-225-2831
http://www.house.gov/paul/contact.shtml

Hinojosa, Rubén (D - 15) - 202-225-2531
http://www.house.gov/writerep/
Reyes, Silvestre (D - 16) - 202-225-4831
http://wwwc.house.gov/reyes/voice_your_opinion.asp
Edwards, Chet (D - 17) - 202-225-6105
http://edwards.house.gov/html/contact_form_email.cfm
Jackson-Lee, Sheila (D - 18) - 202-225-3816
http://www.jacksonlee.house.gov/contact.shtml
Neugebauer, Randy (R - 19) - 202-225-4005
http://www.randy.house.gov/contact/
Gonzalez, Charles A. (D - 20) - 202-225-3236
http://www.gonzalez.house.gov/index.php?
option=com_content&task=view&id=170
Smith, Lamar (R - 21) - 202-225-4236
http://lamarsmith.house.gov/contact.aspx?section=Mail
Olson, Pete (R - 22) - 202-225-5951
https://forms.house.gov/olson/contact-form.shtml
Rodriguez, Ciro D. (D - 23) - 202-225-4511
http://www.rodriguez.house.gov/index.php?
option=com_content&task=view&id=70&Itemid=46
Marchant, Kenny (R - 24) - 202-225-6605
http://marchant.house.gov/emailkenny.shtml
Doggett, Lloyd (D - 25) - 202-225-4865
http://www.house.gov/doggett/doggett_ima/
doggett_get_address.htm
Burgess, Michael C. (R - 26) - 202-225-7772
http://www.house.gov/writerep/
Ortiz, Solomon P. (D - 27) - 202-225-7742
http://www.house.gov/formortiz/issue.htm
Cuellar, Henry (D - 28) - 202-225-1640
http://cuellar.house.gov/Contact/SendMeAnEmail.htm
Green, Gene (D - 29) - 202-225-1688
http://www.house.gov/green/contact/
Johnson, Eddie B. (D - 30) - 202-225-8885
http://www.house.gov/ebjohnson/IMA/issue_subscribe.shtml

Carter, John R. (R - 31) - 202-225-3864
http://www.house.gov/writerep/
Sessions, Pete (R - 32) - 202-225-2231
http://www.house.gov/sessionsform/emailform.htm

Utah - 3 Representatives

Bishop, Rob (R - 01) - 202-225-0453
http://robbishop.house.gov/ZipAuth.aspx
Matheson, James D. "Jim" (D - 02) - 202-225-3011
http://www.house.gov/matheson/contact.shtml
Chaffetz, Jason (R - 03) - 202-225-7751
https://forms.house.gov/chaffetz/contact-form.shtml

Vermont - 1 Representative

Welch, Peter (D - At Large) - 202-225-4115
http://www.house.gov/formwelch/issue_subscribe.htm

Virginia - 11 Representatives

Wittman, Robert J. (R - 01) - 202-225-4261
https://forms.house.gov/wittman/IMA/webforms/
issue_subscribe.htm
Nye, III, Glenn C. (D - 02) - 202-225-4215
https://forms.house.gov/nye/contact-form.shtml
Scott, Robert C. "Bobby" (D - 03) - 202-225-8351
http://www.house.gov/writerep/?Submit=Email+Bobby+Scott
Forbes, J. Randy (R - 04) - 202-225-6365
http://randyforbes.house.gov/zipauth.html
Perriello, Thomas S. P. (D - 05) - 202-225-4711
https://forms.house.gov/perriello/contact-form.shtml
Goodlatte, Bob (R - 06) - 202-225-5431
http://www.house.gov/goodlatte/emailbob.htm
Cantor, Eric I. (R - 07) - 202-225-2815
http://www.house.gov/writerep/

Moran, James P. "Jim" (D - 08) - 202-225-4376
http://moran.house.gov/zipauth.shtml
Boucher, Rick (D - 09) - 202-225-3861
http://www.boucher.house.gov/index.php?option=com_
content&task=view&id=645&Itemid=
Wolf, Frank R. (R - 10) - 202-225-5136
http://www.house.gov/formwolf/contact_email/emailzip.shtml
Connolly, Gerald E. "Gerry" (D - 11) - 202-225-1492
https://forms.house.gov/connolly/contact-form.shtml

Virgin Islands - 1 Delegate

Christian-Christensen, Donna M. (D - At Large) - 202-225-1790
http://www.house.gov/writerep/

Washington - 9 Representatives

Inslee, Jay (D - 01) - 202-225-6311
http://www.house.gov/inslee/contact/email.html
Larsen, Rick R. (D - 02) - 202-225-2605
http://www.house.gov/larsen/IMA/issue_subscribe.shtml
Baird, Brian (D - 03) - 202-225-3536
http://www.house.gov/baird/IMA/email.shtml
Hastings, Richard "Doc" (R - 04) - 202-225-5816
http://hastings.house.gov/ContactForm.aspx
McMorris Rodgers, Cathy (R - 05) - 202-225-2006
http://www.mcmorris.house.gov/IMA/issue_subscribe.htm
Dicks, Norman D. (D - 06) - 202-225-5916
http://www.house.gov/dicks/email.html
McDermott, Jim (D - 07) - 202-225-3106
http://www.house.gov/mcdermott/contact.shtml
Reichert, David G. "Dave" (R - 08) - 202-225-7761
http://www.house.gov/reichert/IMA/issue_subscribe.htm
Smith, Adam (D - 09) - 202-225-8901
http://www.house.gov/adamsmith/IMA/email.shtml

West Virginia - 3 Representatives

Mollohan, Alan B. (D - 01) - 202-225-4172
CongressmanMollohan@mail.house.gov
Capito, Shelley Moore (R - 02) - 202-225-2711
http://www.house.gov/writerep/
Rahall, II, Nick J. (D - 03) - 202-225-3452
http://www.rahall.house.gov/index.php?
option=com_content&task=view&id=521&Itemid=162

Wisconsin - 8 Representatives

Ryan, Paul (R - 01) - 202-225-3031
http://www.house.gov/ryan/email.htm
Baldwin, Tammy (D - 02) - 202-225-2906
http://www.house.gov/formbaldwin/IMA/get_address.htm
Kind, Ron (D - 03) - 202-225-5506
http://www.house.gov/kind/contact.shtml
Moore, Gwen (D - 04) - 202-225-4572
http://www.house.gov/gwenmoore/contact.shtml
Sensenbrenner, Jr., F. James (R - 05) - 202-225-5101
http://sensenbrenner.house.gov/email_zip.htm
Petri, Thomas E. (R - 06) - 202-225-2476
http://www.obey.house.gov/index.php?option=com_content&
task=view&id=364&Itemid=1
Obey, David R. (D - 07) - 202-225-3365
http://www.obey.house.gov/index.php?option=com_content&
task=view&id=364&Itemid=1
Kagen, Steve (D - 08) - 202-225-5665
http://kagen.house.gov/IMA/issue_subscribe.htm

Wyoming - 1 Representative

Lummis, Cynthia M. (R - At Large) - 202-225-2311
https://forms.house.gov/lummis/contact-form.shtml

Politics of Life Seminar

Register for a *Politics of Life Seminar* today. Enhance your socioeconomic sphere of influence by applying strategies that elevate your social standing and generate wealth. Join a "Politics of Life" team to stay updated on constitutional breaches that exist today and to foster support for repealing or modifying laws and policies which have decreased the scope of our freedoms and diminished our well-being. Receive your team assignment, and begin the work of the next eight years to restore integrity to our national government. Begin now to develop and coordinate grassroots movements to establish democratic governments like ours in other countries through pacts of peace, cooperation, education, and commerce.

To book the author for a speaking engagement; go to: www.healthylivingusa.com; click **Speakers** on the navigation bar and follow the prompts or email author@healthylivingusa.com

To register for a Politics of Life Seminar, go to: www. healthylivingusa.com; click **Seminars** on the navigation bar and follow the prompts.

To order additional copies of The 2008 Presidential Election Handbook and Commentary: The Connection to Hope, go to: www. healthylivingusa.com; click **Books** on the navigation bar and follow the prompts.

To place an order for a framed title from the Poetry of the Heart Collection, go to: www. healthylivingusa.com; click **Poetry** on the navigation bar and follow the prompts.

To register for a Personalized Training and Fitness Boot Camp, go to: www. healthylivingusa.com; click **Fitness Boot Camp** on the navigation bar and follow the prompts.

www.ingramcontent.com/pod-product-compliance
Lightning Source LLC
Chambersburg PA
CBHW050507270326
41927CB00009B/1932